Learning Through Woodwork

This essential guide provides clear and comprehensive support for those looking to introduce creative woodwork into early years settings. With theory, practical advice, stunning colour images and case studies, the book will inspire practitioners to embrace woodwork and encourage children's independent creative learning.

Focusing on the numerous benefits that working with wood offers young children, from boosting their self-esteem and problem-solving skills, to enhancing their communication and social development, the author draws on over 25 years of experience to discuss each and every aspect of establishing woodwork in the early years curriculum. Including practical information on materials and tools, staff training, and health and safety advice, this go-to guide provides a treasure trove of ideas to engage children at various stages of development, drawing the maximum benefit from working with wood and tools.

Both inspiring and informative, *Learning Through Woodwork* will become an essential tool for early years practitioners and teachers wishing to explore and develop woodwork provision.

Pete Moorhouse is a professional sculptor and artist educator, with over 25 years' experience of working in schools and early years settings. He is currently resident artist educator at St Werburgh's Park Nursery School, Bristol, UK. He is an Honorary Research Fellow at the University of Bristol and an associate trainer for Early Education.

Learning Through Woodwork

Introducing Creative Woodwork in the Early Years

Pete Moorhouse

Routledge
Taylor & Francis Group
LONDON AND NEW YORK

First published 2018
by Routledge
2 Park Square, Milton Park, Abingdon, Oxon OX14 4RN

and by Routledge
711 Third Avenue, New York, NY 10017

Routledge is an imprint of the Taylor & Francis Group, an informa business

© 2018 Pete Moorhouse

The right of Pete Moorhouse to be identified as author of this work has been asserted by him in accordance with sections 77 and 78 of the Copyright, Designs and Patents Act 1988.

All rights reserved. No part of this book may be reprinted or reproduced or utilised in any form or by any electronic, mechanical, or other means, now known or hereafter invented, including photocopying and recording, or in any information storage or retrieval system, without permission in writing from the publishers.

Trademark notice: Product or corporate names may be trademarks or registered trademarks, and are used only for identification and explanation without intent to infringe.

All images © Pete Moorhouse unless otherwise stated.

Kind permission for use of images has been granted by: © Community Playthings; © Early Education (www.early-education.org.uk) Early Education work to ensure that early childhood teachers and practitioners have the support so that all children can fulfil their potential by providing training and resources and campaigning; © Imperial War Museum

British Library Cataloguing-in-Publication Data
A catalogue record for this book is available from the British Library

Library of Congress Cataloging-in-Publication Data
Names: Moorhouse, Pete, author.
Title: Learning through woodwork : introducing creative woodwork in the
    early years.
Description: Abingdon, Oxon ; New York : Routledge, 2017. |
    Includes bibliographical references.
Identifiers: LCCN 2017036311 (print) | LCCN 2017037378 (ebook) |
    ISBN 9781315114811 (ebook) | ISBN 9781138071087 (hardback) |
    ISBN 9781138071100 (pbk.) | ISBN 9781315114811 (ebk.)
Subjects: LCSH: Woodwork—Study and teaching (Elementary)
Classification: LCC TT180 (ebook) | LCC TT180 .M644 2017 (print) |
    DDC 684/.08—dc23
LC record available at https://lccn.loc.gov/2017036311

ISBN: 978-1-138-07108-7 (hbk)
ISBN: 978-1-138-07110-0 (pbk)
ISBN: 978-1-315-11481-1 (ebk)

Typeset in Univers LT Std
by Swales & Willis Ltd, Exeter, Devon, UK
Printed by CPI Group (UK) Ltd, Croydon, CR0 4YY

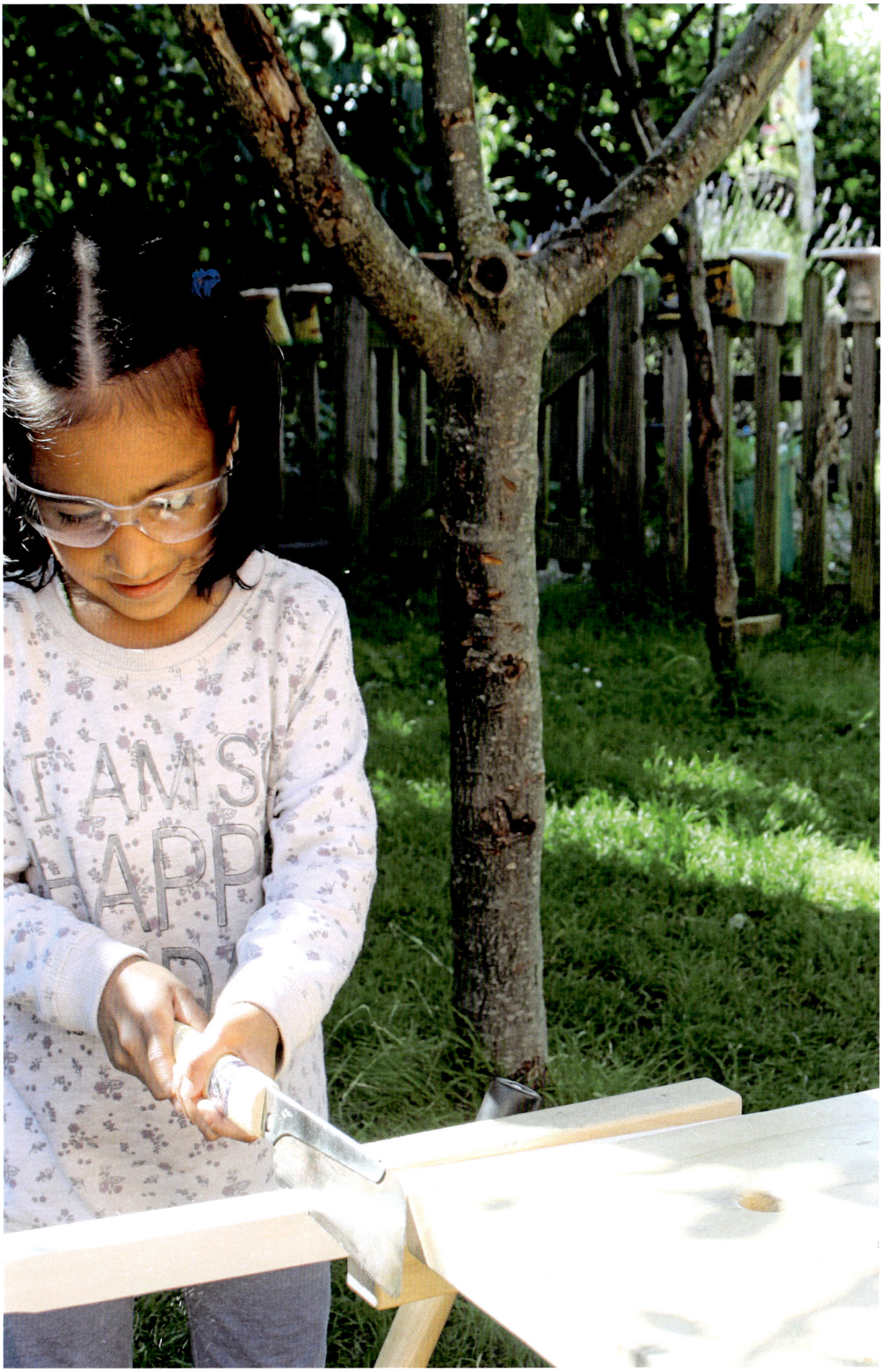

This book is dedicated to all the young children who have not yet experienced woodwork. My gratitude goes to all the children I have learnt from. My thanks also go to the pioneering early advocates of woodwork for their inspiration and vision, to the supportive nursery and primary schools I have worked in, especially everyone at St Werburgh's Park Nursery School in Bristol. Thank you to the wider early years community for your encouragement, support and enthusiasm and to those who have contributed or helped make this book possible. Finally, thanks to my family, for their love and humour and particularly their patience.

Woodwork is active learning at its best.
Tina Bruce, CBE

Contents

List of case studies	*xii*
Author's note	*xiii*
Disclaimer	*xiv*
Foreword by Tina Bruce	*xv*
Foreword by Rachel Edwards	*xvi*
About the author	*xvii*

1 Introduction: why woodwork?   **1**
   A unique experience   2
   Engaging hands, minds and hearts   2
   Building self-esteem and confidence   3
   Encompassing all areas of learning and development   3
   The experience of making   5
   Long tradition of woodwork in early childhood education   6
   Introducing woodwork   8

2 Historical and pedagogical context   **11**
   International perspectives   12
   Active learning encouraged by pioneering theorists   12
   The influence of Friedrich Froebel   12
   Sloyd education in Scandinavia   13
   Introduction of woodwork in the UK   14
   Margaret McMillan and Susan Isaacs   15
   Steiner Waldorf   15
   Later advocates   16
   The decline of woodwork   16
   The current situation and the changing tide   16

3 Learning and development   **19**
   Characteristics of effective learning   20
     Curiosity   21
     Playing and exploring   22
     Active learning   22
     Creative and critical thinking   24
   EYFS prime curriculum areas   27
     Personal, social and emotional development   27
     Physical development   38
     Communication and language   42
   EYFS specific curriculum areas   44
     Mathematics   44
     Understanding the world   49
     Expressive arts and design   53
     Literacy   59

	Skills for life: beyond the curriculum	60
	Sustainability	60
	Observation and assessment	62
	Observing and monitoring progress	63
	Schema	63
	Skills checklist	64

4 Equal opportunities — 67
Disadvantaged children: diminishing differences – closing the gap — 68
Gender — 69
Special educational needs and disabilities (SEND) — 70
English as an additional language (EAL) — 72
Left-handed children — 72

5 Adult support — 75
Staffing of activity 'sessions' and continuous provision — 76
Adult role in supporting learning — 78
Involving parents and carers — 83

6 Getting started — 87
What age to start? — 88
Stages of development — 89
Investigating wood — 94
Establishing a woodworking area — 97
Workbench — 100
Types of wood and other materials — 104
How to introduce tools — 112
Tools and equipment — 115
How to use tools — 116
Consumables — 135

7 Extended learning projects — 141
Sculpture — 142
Sound garden — 145
Wooden frieze — 148
House — 149
Deconstruction — 153
Mud kitchen — 155

8 Health and safety — 159
Understanding risk — 160
Risk assessment — 164
Health and safety checklist — 168
First aid — 170
Staff training — 171

9 Final words — 177

Bibliography — *180*
Resources and suppliers — *184*
Index — *188*

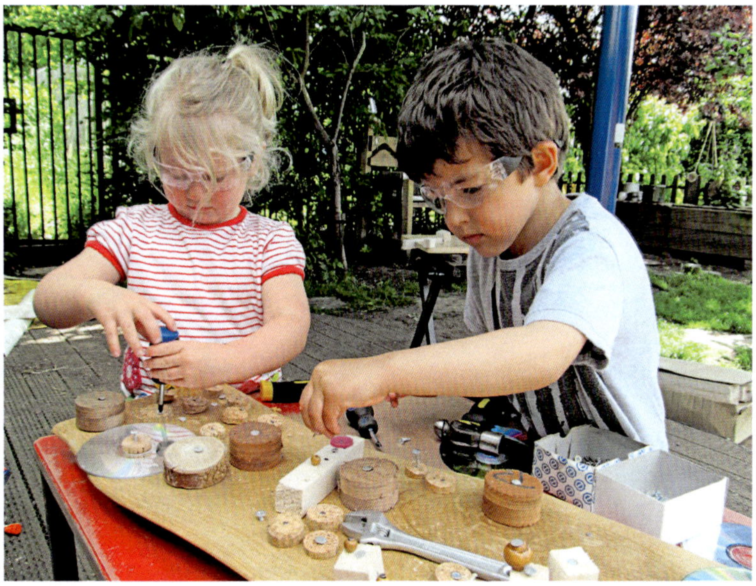

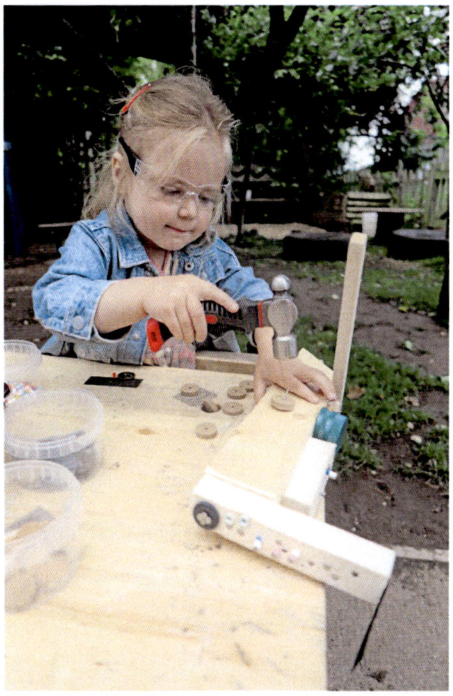

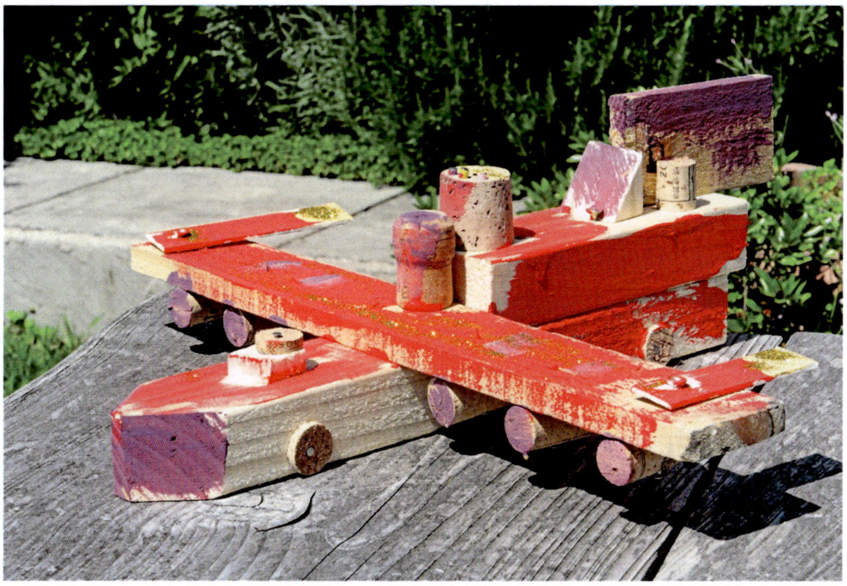

Case studies

3.1	Max and the *Titanic*	56
3.2	Sustained concentration and engagement	64
4.1	Engaging and capturing interest	71
4.2	The challenge of woodwork for everyone	71
5.1	Interaction	82
7.1	Extended thinking during the sound garden project	146
7.2	Problem-solving during the house project	151

Author's note

I have been introducing children to the delights of woodwork for many years and have seen first-hand the immense enjoyment and rich cross-curricular learning that flows from working with tools and wood.

In the last decade I have been on a mission to promote creative woodworking with young children. I passionately believe that all children should have the opportunity to work with wood and benefit from the rich associated learning. To get the message out I have written many articles in educational journals, presented at conferences throughout the UK and overseas and regularly delivered training in schools. This book forms part of this message and to this end I commend Routledge for their support. There has been much encouragement from many prominent educationalists; EYs consultants and advisers, head teachers and inspectors, and woodwork is now once again widely seen as contributing to outstanding practice.

Disclaimer

All information and guidance is offered with the best intention for positive outcomes for young children's learning and development. It is important that woodwork is introduced with the correct instruction and is closely monitored and that safety guidelines are strictly adhered to. No legal responsibility can be taken by the author or publishers for any accidents, injury or prosecution of any kind. It is your responsibility to introduce woodwork appropriately to your particular setting and respond accordingly to the individual children taking part. The guidance in the book is intended to be supported by training, including hands-on practical experience of working with tools.

Terminology

I use the word 'teacher' throughout the book to refer to the teacher, teaching assistant, practitioner or any adult who works with children, and 'setting' to refer to the classroom, nursery, children's centre, or place where children meet. 'Early years' is used to refer to early childhood education, and in the context of woodwork I am referring to children aged 3 to 5.

Foreword by Tina Bruce

Every so often a book is written that helps practitioners to develop their work in deep and far-reaching ways. This is that sort of book.

Woodwork has always been included in early childhood practice over the last hundred years. It is a tried and tested experience, with an honourable tradition, emerging from the pioneer nursery schools in the late nineteenth century. But good practice is easier to lose than to sustain.

Because of an over-emphasis on health and safety in the 1980s and 1990s, and lack of training in the safe provision of woodwork experiences for practitioners, most of the excellent practice has vanished. But it can and is being recaptured, and this book has arrived at a timely moment for doing just that. It is written by a well-respected artist who regularly works with young children, and his expertise shines through the book.

It sets out very clearly and practically why woodwork is important, how to make a woodwork area, what tools to provide, how to use them and how to encourage children to be safe, skilled and creative. This book should be in every early childhood setting, and parents and grandparents will also find it helpful.

Tina Bruce CBE
Professor, University of Roehampton

Foreword by Rachel Edwards

This book covers in considerable depth the impact woodworking can have in early years education. It looks in detail at the many learning and development outcomes and gives a comprehensive account of what you need to get started.

Pete's enthusiasm is clearly apparent as is his commitment to encouraging children's creative thinking. It is clear that using wood as a creative material can help develop children's imagination and creativity as well as develop many other skills. Working alongside Pete, I have seen children learning at the deepest level. For some children, working with wood was the key that unlocked the barriers to learning. The impact has been long term.

Woodwork has demonstrated that it is a very popular activity with children, and provides a rich source of enjoyment as well as learning. I have seen at first hand how young children, their parents and carers, and the adults who work with them, have been inspired by being involved in it.

I very much encourage you to introduce woodwork in your setting and I am sure that you will find this book an invaluable resource.

Rachel Edwards
Head Teacher, Park School and Children's Centre, Gloucestershire

About the author

Pete Moorhouse has been successfully introducing woodwork to children in early years education for many years. He is a professional sculptor, public artist and artist educator, with over 25 years' experience of working in schools and early years settings.

Pete has undertaken many artist residences in early years settings and is currently Artist Educator at St Werburgh's Park Nursery School, Bristol, where he works together with children on various activities and provocations to promote creativity and creative thinking. His practice is particularly influenced by Froebellian ideas and the Reggio Emilia *atelieristas*. Pete is an associate trainer for Early Education and delivers continuous professional development (CPD) training and conference presentations. Pete is also part of the International Creative Education Network and the International Art in Early Childhood Association.

When most settings were deterred by widespread fears around safety and litigation, Pete continued almost singlehandedly to promote and advocate for the inclusion of woodwork in early years provision. For the last decade Pete has been on a mission, extolling the virtues of woodwork up and down the country. He has spread the message by presenting at conferences, delivering training, writing journal articles, supporting educational suppliers and taking the message overseas from mainland Europe to the Middle East and from Japan to Bhutan

Pete is an honorary research fellow at the Graduate School of Education, University of Bristol, and is conducting ongoing research into the impact of woodwork and creative and critical thinking in early years education. Pete also collaborates on an international research project to promote woodworking in early years education (The Big Bang, Small Hands project) and has had books and journal articles published about creative woodwork. He is chair of the Early Years Woodwork Association.

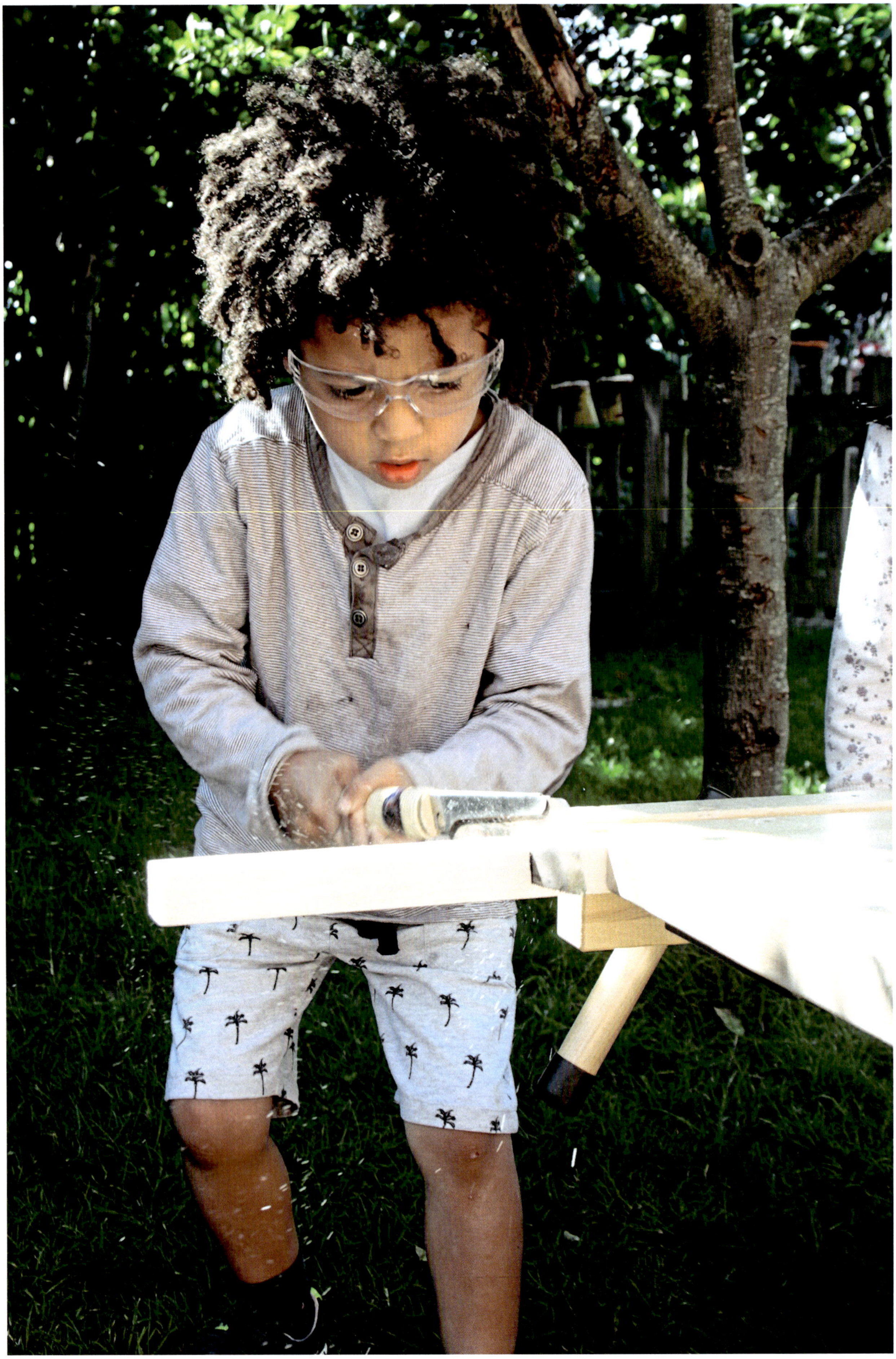

CHAPTER 1

Introduction

Why woodwork?

Woodwork is a bit like a magic carpet of skills which last a lifetime. It involves curiosity, creativity and a rich opportunity to engage with process based learning leading to deep involvement and satisfaction.

Kathryn Solly, former head teacher,
Chelsea Open Air Nursery; early years consultant

Chapter overview

In this chapter I provide an overview of the value of woodwork in early childhood education. I explain how woodwork provides a truly unique experience through children tinkering and making creations with real tools and look at how this impacts on children's self-esteem and confidence. I emphasise the rich associated learning and development and highlight the long tradition woodwork has had in early education.

- A unique experience ▶ 2
- Engaging hands, minds and hearts ▶ 2
- Building self-esteem and confidence ▶ 3
- Encompassing all areas of learning and development ▶ 3
- The experience of making ▶ 5
- Long tradition of woodwork in early childhood education ▶ 6
- Introducing woodwork ▶ 8

Introduction

A unique experience

There is something really special about woodwork. It is so different from other activities. The smell and feel of wood, using real tools, working with a natural material, the sounds of hammering and sawing, hands and minds working together to express their imagination and to solve problems, the use of strength and coordination: all go together to captivate young children's interest. It provides a truly unique experience. There are many aspects that contribute to the profound impact of woodworking with children.

Engaging hands, minds and hearts

As an artist educator working in early years settings I have introduced children to many creative provocations. Woodwork has really stood out from the others because of the high and sustained levels of engagement and the sheer enjoyment it provides. It is hugely popular with children and provides a profound learning experience. To come into a setting and hear the sounds of children happily hammering and sawing away, and to see them deeply engaged, is a real delight. Visiting teachers always comment on the children's deep levels of concentration and engagement, and are further surprised to find the same children still deeply focused working on their creations an hour or two later. It is not unusual for children to spend all morning at the woodwork bench. Woodwork really engages hands, minds and hearts.

Having the opportunity to learn with their hands and mind together makes the world seem less distant and abstract, making learning more relevant. Working efficiently with hand tools and implements is an important area of development both in the acquisition of technique and in the mastery of movement and is beneficial in many other applications.

Initially we observe children working with their hands, constructing models and working on projects, but in fact the real transformation is inside the child – personal development is at the heart of woodwork.

Building self-esteem and confidence

Woodwork is a powerful medium for building self-esteem and confidence. This is for a combination of reasons. Children feel empowered and valued by being trusted and given responsibility to work with real tools. They accomplish tasks that they initially perceive to be difficult and they persist at challenging tasks. They show satisfaction in their mastery of new skills and take immense pride in their creations. This sense of empowerment and achievement provides a visible boost to their self-esteem and self-confidence. Children have a natural desire to construct and build. They learn how things work and discover that they can shape the world around them by making. This imparts a can-do attitude and imbues children with a strong sense of agency – having a proactive disposition towards the world – a belief they can shape their world.

Encompassing all areas of learning and development

When we analyse a woodworking session it is extraordinary to see just how much learning is involved. It encompasses all areas of learning and development and invites connections between different aspects of learning. It supports current thinking on how children learn best, embracing all the characteristics of effective learning and thus fostering confident, creative children with passion for life-long learning. Woodwork really can be central to curriculum. It incorporates mathematical thinking, scientific investigation, developing knowledge of technology, a deepening

Introduction

understanding of the world, as well as physical development and coordination, communication and language, and personal and social development.

Woodwork provides another medium through which children can express themselves. Creative and critical thinking skills are central both in terms of imagination and problem-solving as children make choices, find solutions, learn through trial and error and reflect on their work.

Children are drawn in as they explore possibilities, rise to challenges and find solutions. Woodwork is really unrivalled in terms of providing children with problem-solving opportunities and challenge.

Some children particularly flourish when working with wood, enjoying working three-dimensionally and working with their hands. It is hard to predict who will respond particularly positively as the skills are so different from those usually used in early years. The experience of woodwork can really be the key that unlocks some children's learning.

Woodwork lends itself to incrementally building on previous learning and skills. There are multiple layers of learning and increasing challenge as new tools are introduced, as techniques are refined and built upon and as thinking skills are developed, and these all go to extend what children are able to do. Both Lev Vygotsky and Jerome Bruner wrote about how powerful woodwork is for extending what children are able to do unaided. I talk about this in more detail in Chapter 3.

Woodwork also provides an aesthetic experience as children experience the beauty of wood. They encounter its warm feel, its smell, textures, and how with simple actions they can change it. There is also a beauty in the way we can use simple tools to manipulate materials. It is certainly an activity that can transcend the everyday and elevate the soul.

Introduction

Essentially, woodwork is a 'win-win': children greatly enjoy it and remain engaged for extended periods *and* it provides a rich multitude of associated learning and development.

The experience of making

Woodwork is really about children *making*, embracing the processes of making and empowering children to become makers with a 'can-do' spirit. With woodwork we are in essence looking at making with simple technology. Resistant materials are the most suitable medium to work with, with wood being the most accessible and easily worked by young children. Wood is so versatile in the ways it can be manipulated. Of course other materials (such as acrylic, rubber, cork, etc.) can be incorporated to this making experience, which only furthers children's knowledge and understanding. Making with tools offers a multi-layered learning experience and children will encounter increasing levels of challenge and complexity.

Currently, there is a surge of interest in *making* in general – often referred to as the Maker Movement,[1] and encouraged through community initiatives such as 'hack spaces' that promote interdisciplinary making and through a proliferation of online video tutorials covering all sorts of making projects. This is enthusing and engaging young people all over the world. The value of hands-on making is once again being appreciated, countering the current consumerist culture with curiosity-driven experiential learning. In today's society there is an emphasis on continuously buying new products and disposing of them when broken. Woodwork provides children with a basic insight into the skills needed to make and repair rather than consume and dispose.

Introduction

Long tradition of woodwork in early childhood education

Wood, along with clay and stone, has been used throughout history by humans in a vast number of applications, and is deep-rooted in the heritage of all cultures. Working with wood also has a long tradition in education. Right from the beginnings of early education woodwork was embraced notably by Froebel. When formal elementary education was introduced in the UK in the 1870s, woodwork immediately formed part of the curriculum. The initial nursery schools included woodwork, being inspired by Froebel, and later by the Scandinavian sloyd movement that also advocated the value of woodwork in education. Woodwork was commonplace across the country; in fact, it would have been the exception to come across a setting not offering woodwork.

Woodwork remained very much embedded in the curriculum for many decades but was then nearly completely eradicated in the 1980s and 1990s. This was due to the rise of a litigation culture and overzealous health and safety measures combined with changing educational priorities.

Nowadays there is a resurgence of interest in woodworking in early years education and there are an increasing number of settings that have reintroduced woodwork, with some making it part of their core provision by having a woodwork station in every classroom or in the outdoor area. This increasing interest is evident in many countries, across all continents, and suggests that woodwork can once again play a significant role in education.

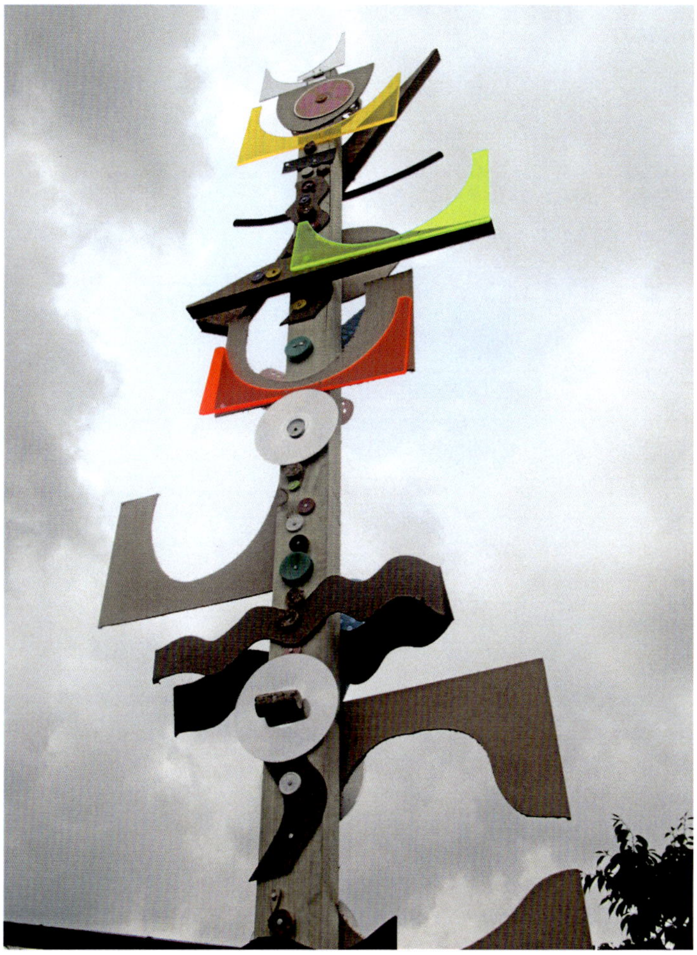

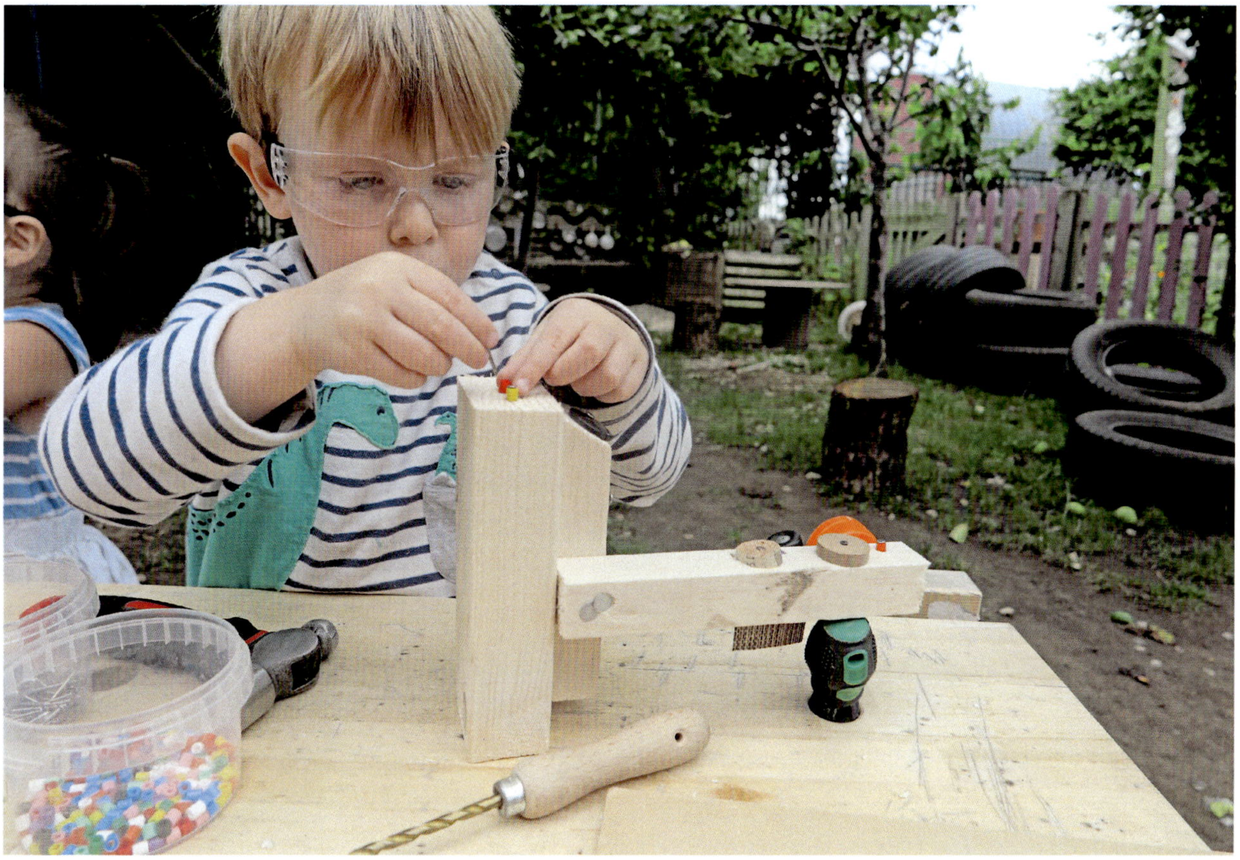

Introduction

Some teachers and parents are surprised that we introduce woodwork to children as young as three, but it must be emphasised that it is a low-risk activity when introduced and monitored correctly. We have been successfully woodworking with pre-school children for many years with no significant incidents. In Chapter 7, I discuss the health and safety measures we need to put in place to ensure woodwork is a safe and rewarding experience for all.

Children are surrounded by complex technology but this has limited their experience of basic technology, with fewer opportunities to watch and learn and to understand processes. Today many children may never use tools throughout their entire education and in recent years there has been a marked decline of woodwork in primary and secondary schools.

The confidence to work with tools provides a skill set for life. Many children will need practical skills for their future work and woodwork in the early years could well be children's only experience of working with tools. Fortunately, working with tools leaves a deep memory – so even if early childhood education is their only experience of working with wood it will leave a long-lasting impression. Many adults recount that experiencing woodwork as a child is one of the memories from early childhood that still really stands out.

Introducing woodwork

In Chapters 5 and 6, I look at the all practicalities of implementing woodwork, how to staff and monitor woodwork, how to set up a woodworking area, and how to introduce tools.

With woodwork, children can develop their learning at their own pace and find their own challenges. Once they have mastered basic skills, they move into open-ended exploration – tinkering, exploring possibilities and then making unique creations. Their imagination, creative thinking and problem-solving skills really flourish as they meet and conquer new challenges.

It is reassuring to know that woodwork is endorsed by many pioneering educationalists, eminent writers, early years consultants, inspectors and advisors – many of whom have contributed quotes for this book.

I very much hope this book will give you the encouragement, confidence and the practical know-how to introduce woodwork safely to your children. I have assumed no previous knowledge about woodwork to ensure the book is useful to a wide readership. This book focuses on woodwork with children aged 3 to 5 in early years educational settings, but the principles and methods are equally applicable to slightly older children.

Woodwork is one of the most popular activities and incorporates so much learning. Let's make the opportunity of woodwork available to all children!

> Next time I'm going to make a flying hedgehog with wings. I'm going to use lots of nails. I'm not going to hammer them in all the way so they stick up. I'm going to join thin wood for the wings, then paint them.
>
> Sam, age 3

Note

1 The term originated in the USA and is the umbrella term for independent inventors, designers and tinkerers.

Source: © Imperial War Museum (D 21854)

CHAPTER 2

Historical and pedagogical context

Woodwork should always be seen as part and parcel of the curriculum – not something that sits outside it. I think this is very important. It's a tremendously creative activity, which offers so many opportunities for enhancing children's cross-curricular learning and development. It's imperative to follow children's interests and that should be the philosophy with woodwork, as in every area of learning and teaching.

Jamie Wilson, deputy head teacher, Liverpool

Chapter overview

In this chapter I look at how woodwork with young children has been embraced around the world. I look at the rich history of woodwork in early childhood education dating back approximately 180 years to the pedagogy of Friedrich Froebel. I explain how the value of woodwork spread amongst the early pioneering educators, then look at how it developed over the years and discuss the resurgence of woodwork today.

International perspectives ▶ 12
Active learning encouraged by pioneering theorists ▶ 12
The influence of Friedrich Froebel ▶ 12
Sloyd education in Scandinavia ▶ 13
Introduction of woodwork in the UK ▶ 14
Margaret McMillan and Susan Isaacs ▶ 15
Steiner Waldorf ▶ 15
Later advocates ▶ 16
The decline of woodwork ▶ 16
The current situation and the changing tide ▶ 16

Historical and pedagogical context

International perspectives

Around the world there are many countries that embrace woodworking with young children. Working with wood is a universal language that crosses cultural boundaries. Different countries may have slightly differing tools but in essence it is a similar experience and one that deeply engages young children.

In Scandinavian countries woodwork has long been established in their early years curricula. In New Zealand the Ministry of Education names carpentry (Tarai rakau) as a valuable play activity that supports the principles and strands of Te Whāriki curriculum with many settings having a woodwork corner. In other countries woodwork is less established but there are many individual settings that have been successfully providing woodwork for many years, with examples from Japan to the United States. In the UK woodwork was once firmly established, then was practically eradicated during the 1980s and 1990s due to health and safety fears, but thankfully is now being re-established.

Active learning encouraged by pioneering theorists

Hands-on education has been advocated by educational theorists for centuries. Comenius (1592–1670), Rousseau (1712–1758) and Pestalozzi (1746–1827) all passionately advocated the importance of active learning, learning holistically through the senses and working with the hands. Active learning was seen to be beneficial to all areas of child development. Their forward thinking paved the way for subsequent developments in early education.

The influence of Friedrich Froebel

The earliest records of woodwork with young children come from the pioneering work of Friedrich Froebel (1782–1852), the founder of the kindergarten movement. His view was of children as holistic learners who learned most effectively by being active with their hands and minds. Froebel emphasised giving children hands-on involvement in practical learning. He believed in combining imagination and physical movement in exploring interests.

> To learn a thing in life and through doing is much more developing, cultivating and strengthening than to learn it merely through the verbal communication of ideas.
>
> (Froebel 1826)

Froebel initially introduced wooden 'gifts' to children: objects that would stimulate curiosity and could be manipulated and explored to encourage learning, especially three-dimensional thinking. Froebel then introduced 'occupations' that incorporated practical work and were in part seen as preparation for later manual training and future work. Occupations included working with paper, paint, clay and wood. Froebel's original kindergarten no longer exists, but the school he co-founded in Keilhau continues to embrace woodwork to this very day. Gustav Kalb, who was very much inspired by Froebel, wrote *The First Lessons in Hand and Eye Training* in 1895, which further developed and elaborated on Froebel's ideas for using wood in kindergarten and with older children.

Joseph Judd, a teacher trainer for the National Froebel Union in the UK, wrote in 1906:

> Of the many and varied schemes of practical work devised with the object of training the hand to deftness and the eye to accuracy in observation, none has met with so widespread acceptance as woodwork. The required material, being a direct and universal product of nature, is readily obtainable, cheap, and easily worked into forms of beauty, either in its natural or prepared state. Its ready adaptability to a course of handwork is a continuation of the gifts and occupations.
>
> Woodwork as an occupation is designed to cultivate the active and creative instincts; to give practice in failure and success; to test the ability to concentrate the mind whilst doing a definite thing; to provide means of communication between the teacher and the child, whereby the latter can render observant information, from which the teacher can impart more exact knowledge; to open up an avenue of research for the student of child life, and to give to the teacher full scope for individualism in the attainment of educational ideals.
>
> (Judd 1906)

Sloyd education in Scandinavia

Inspired by Froebel, woodwork then spread to Scandinavia through the sloyd education movement. The name sloyd (slöjd in Swedish) is derived from the term for creative handicraft. Due to the pioneering work of Uno Cygnaeus (1810–1888) it became mandatory to introduce craft into Finnish folk schools in 1866. Cygnaeus's intent was to develop children's practical knowledge and aesthetic sense and improve children's thinking. He saw his work as being a natural development of Froebel's kindergarten.

Sloyd aimed to develop practical knowledge, the ability to solve practical problems through knowledge of different working processes, and to learn how to evaluate work and refine work through experimentation. Woodwork was at the forefront but other crafts such as paper folding and work with fabrics were included. Working with the hands was thought to enhance cognitive development and give greater relevance to learning, and was seen to build confidence and instil a respect for the dignity of labour.

In 1872 sloyd was introduced to Sweden by Otto Salomon (1849–1907), who was a passionate advocate of woodwork and was strongly influenced by Cygnaeus and Froebel. In 1875 Otto Salomon started a School of Crafts at Nääs (Nääs, 1875–1966), near Gothenburg, where he worked to popularise the educational sloyd movement and trained teachers from all over the world. The Nääs School's special educational methods made sure all students who trained there gained a solid grounding in knowledge and theory of sloyd as well as learning practical skills.

Historical and pedagogical context

The Nääs School was extremely successful and it gained a far-reaching reputation, being attended by many hundreds of international teachers including a number of pioneering early British educators. At one time 19 different nationalities took part in one of the courses. It continued to deliver training right through until the late 1960s. Solomon's book *The Teacher's Handbook of Sloyd* was translated into English in 1891. The sloyd movement was embraced across all the Scandinavian countries: Finland, Sweden, Denmark, Norway and Iceland, where the pedagogy still plays an important part in education today.

In sloyd, woodworking projects were designed to build incrementally on the child's growing skills. This was accomplished by making the projects grow in degree of difficulty over a period of time, through the introduction of complexity and through the gradual introduction of more difficult woodworking tools. There was seen to be development from the known to the unknown, easy to difficult, simple to complex and concrete to abstract.

Salomon in his book *The Theory of Educational Sloyd* stated a number of principles:

1. To instil a taste for and an appreciation of work in general
2. To create a respect for hard, honest, physical labour
3. To develop independence and self-reliance
4. To provide training in the habits of order, accuracy, cleanliness and neatness
5. To train the eye to see accurately and to appreciate the sense of beauty in form
6. To develop the sense of touch and to give general dexterity to the hands
7. To inculcate the habits of attention, industry, perseverance and patience
8. To promote the development of the body's physical powers
9. To acquire dexterity in the use of tools
10. To execute precise work and to produce useful products.

(Salomon 1891)

Introduction of woodwork in the UK

Froebel's ideas and those of the sloyd movement both influenced the introduction of woodwork in the UK and many other countries. Ideas and practices were adapted, responding to the particular styles of tools available and established techniques. This resulted in slightly different approaches to woodwork from country to country whilst still retaining a strong common core.

In the UK, from the 1850s onwards there are examples of individual elementary and nursery settings including woodwork in their provision. Interest grew rapidly in the 1880s and 1890s. The Froebel Society (1874) The National Froebel Union (1887) and the Sloyd Association (1888), all based in London, played significant roles in disseminating information. Many UK teachers returning from the Nääs training college helped spread the word and teachers also participated in sloyd summer schools in the UK. For 20 years, between 1882 and 1902, *Hand and Eye Journal: Sloyd, kindergarten and all forms of manual training* was published to support hand and eye training with the ambition to promote sloyd within the Froebel movement. Teacher trainer and Froebellian Joseph Judd wrote:

> Tools have a strange fascination upon all children, they love to hammer, to cut, to make, and under trained guidance simple woodwork undoubtedly stimulates latent inventive talents more quickly than any other known medium.

(Judd 1906)

From the outset, when elementary schools were being formally established in the 1870s and 1880s woodwork formed part of the curriculum, although at the time it was often only available for boys, with girls often doing needlework. Emerging nursery schools also incorporated woodwork, again inspired by Froebel and sloyd and also in response to the need to prepare children for elementary school.

Source: © Early Education

Margaret McMillan and Susan Isaacs

Pioneering British educators Margaret McMillan (1860–1931) and Susan Isaacs (1885–1948) both realised the potential of woodwork and viewed children as intrinsically competent learners who learned best when being active. McMillan had children experience working with wood from a young age and Isaacs, who was influenced by Jean Piaget's work, saw the children's actions on materials as being fundamental for learning. Isaacs' Malting House School placed emphasis on allowing children to follow their curiosity in all areas of learning and found that in this way woodworking posed wonderful questions as children explored their designs and creations with high levels of persistence. The woodwork equipment at Malting House School incorporated a drill press and small lathe – both operated by nursery children! Both McMillan's and Isaacs' practice had a significant impact on encouraging other schools to embrace woodwork.

Steiner Waldorf

Steiner Waldorf education (first school founded in 1919) by Rudolf Steiner (1861–1925) also strongly advocated the use of woodwork, emphasising the education of head, heart and hands, especially to awaken creativity and for useful application later in life and in work. The majority of Steiner settings offer woodworking but introduce it when the children are approximately 6 or 7 years old. Again, emphasis is placed on just how enriching woodwork is for self-esteem and confidence.

Later advocates

Many educators within the progressive education movement also saw value in woodwork, emphasising the importance of learning through action. Dewey (1859–1952) and Kilpatrick (1871–1965) encouraged learning through experience, where children engage with real-life experiences using authentic materials and follow a child-centred curriculum.

Piaget (1896–1980) pioneered research into how children learn, writing extensively about the psychology of child development. In his book *To Understand Is to Invent* (1973) he emphasised active learning and the importance of cultivating the experimental mind. He viewed children as individual learners who add new concepts to prior knowledge to construct, or build, understanding for themselves, and this was best achieved through experience-based educational opportunities such as woodwork. Jerome Bruner (1915–2016) wrote about the 'play spiral', again citing woodwork as an ideal medium for young children's learning (Bruner 1960). According to Bruner, children initially engage at their current level, but when they revisit they are revisiting with increased knowledge. The children become more expert with every encounter with woodwork. This is very true, with children becoming so much more competent as the year unfolds with regular access to woodwork. Bruner was a firm believer that children's learning should be generated by interest in the material.

The decline of woodwork

Woodwork remained an integral part of early education throughout the UK right through until the 1960s. With the improving economy, culturally there was less emphasis on making and repairing with increasing opportunities to purchase new commercial products. Woodwork was seen by many as being old-fashioned and became less popular, with the result that some woodworking areas began to disappear. At the same time woodwork was seen by many as a subject that best suited 'non-academic' children, which also had an impact on its decline.

The real nail in the coffin was the demise that occurred in the 1980s and 1990s when there was an increasing focus on health and safety, largely due to concerns over an onerous litigation culture, which discouraged settings from doing any activities that were perceived as having an element of risk, including work with resistant materials such as woodwork. This was at the expense of the wonderful opportunities and benefits offered by woodwork and the low levels of risk when properly managed.

This all coincided with a decline of woodwork in primary and secondary schools. The majority of primary schools avoid work with resistant materials in Design and Technology (D&T). In 1986 the secondary education curriculum shifted away from woodwork and metalwork to D&T, which placed a greater emphasis on design as this was seen to be more intellectually rigorous and useful. In 2004 D&T was no longer compulsory, and now D&T is no longer available as a GCSE option in nearly half of all secondary schools (Turner 2017).

The current situation and the changing tide

This has left many children having no experience at all of working with tools in their entire education. This is clearly a disservice to children, with many being denied this opportunity unless they are fortunate to be able to learn these skills in the home environment. Many children will need practical skills to work as electricians, plumbers, technicians, carpenters, builders and mechanics. There are a vast number of jobs in which the ability to be competent with tools plays an important element, from creating prototypes in engineering and technology to using medical instruments in surgery. Recently, several universities have published reports about prospective students missing the practical skills set required, skills that are particularly relevant to subjects such as engineering, product design and science. Practical skills with tools are also immensely useful to us all in our daily lives, be it doing DIY projects, undertaking hobbies or making repairs.

Historical and pedagogical context

Fortunately, the tide is turning. Today there is a renewed interest in woodwork both in the UK and worldwide, following on from more balanced attitudes towards risk. The rise of the Forest School movement has had a positive impact in that it is encouraging children to experience working with basic tools, and currently the importance of woodwork for developing creative and critical thinking is increasingly being valued.

In recent years there have been several influential reports encouraging schools to embrace activities that do contain a certain element of risk. In the UK in 2010 Lord Young was commissioned to audit health and safety across industry and education. The resulting report entitled 'Common Sense, Common Safety' clearly stated that young people should not be denied opportunities just because activities contain an element of risk. Risk assessment should allow children to do the activity safely rather than to prohibit it. The resulting recommendations from the report were immediately accepted by the government. (This is discussed in depth in Chapter 8.)

Today, educationalists are starting to advocate greater emphasis on the importance of creativity. The early educational pioneers largely placed focus on developing skills for the workplace, which very much reflected the prevailing thinking and cultural norms of the time. Nowadays, it is clear that creativity should be one of the most valued aspects of education in our rapidly changing world with the need to be more responsive and innovative. Thinking skills that support creativity, creative and critical thinking, are very much developed through woodwork. There is also a strong argument that making-orientated learning in education in general will also be positive for the economy – encouraging the formation of new small enterprises embracing innovative thinking and an entrepreneurial mind set (Anderson 2012).

To summarise my pedagogy that runs throughout this book, I believe it is important to:

1. Empower children to be as independent as possible – fostering a confident 'can-do' spirit and building self-esteem.
2. Nurture curiosity and an interest in *making* through using real tools and materials (especially important in our increasingly digital world).
3. Encourage children to develop creative and critical thinking skills and with it the passion for life-long learning.

Of course this is a simplification; there are so many other important aspects to woodwork as we will see in Chapter 3.

Today, woodwork with young children is endorsed by many pioneering educationalists, eminent writers, early years consultants, inspectors and advisors. The influential Early Childhood Environment Rating Scale (ECERS) (Harms and Clifford 2004) refers to woodwork contributing to excellent provision, citing the importance of having a woodwork area with a workbench and embracing projects such as making wooden sculptures.

The renewed interest in making and emphasis on creativity, along with a more balanced approach to health and safety, has encouraged an ever-increasing number of settings reintroducing woodwork.

> Today we are seeing a resurgence of interest in woodwork. When I observe children woodworking I am always impressed by their deep focus and engagement and their high-level thinking. Woodwork really has a profound impact on children and I would encourage all settings to incorporate a woodwork area
>
> (Lucy Freeman, assistant head teacher, St Werburgh's Park Nursery School, Bristol)

I worked for a long time to make my caravan, all morning, now I need to take it on holiday.
Anna, age 4

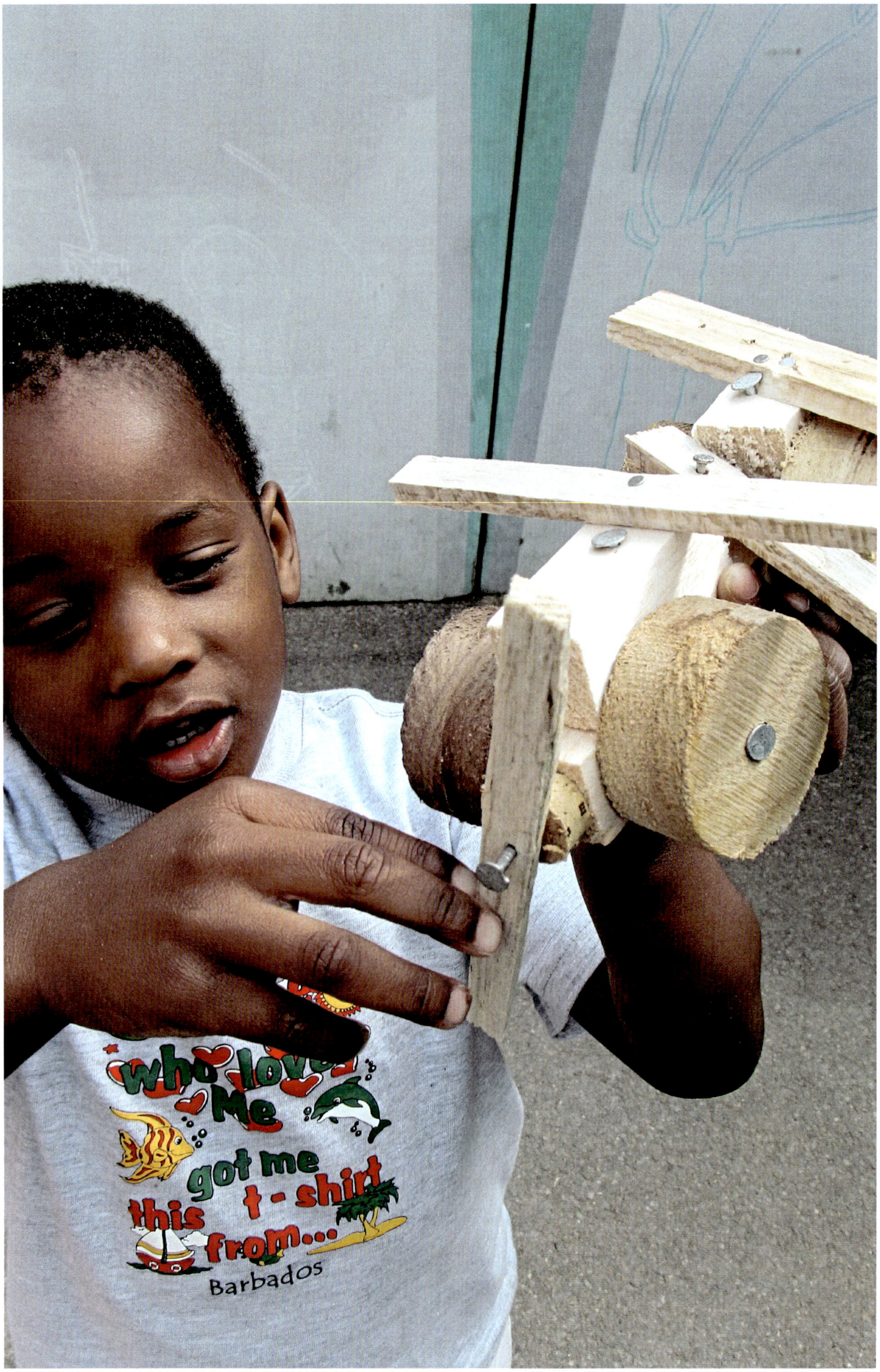
who loves
Me
got me
t-shirt
this
from...
Barbados

CHAPTER 3

Learning and development

> Woodwork is a powerful tool for developing children's creative and critical thinking. There are countless opportunities for children to solve complex problems and express their limitless imagination. Our experience at St Werburgh's Park Nursery School has been that woodwork is one of the children's favourite activities; the impact on children's learning and development is clearly evident.
> Liz Jenkins, Head Teacher, St Werburgh's Park Nursery School, Ofsted inspector

Chapter overview

This chapter looks in considerable depth at the rich learning and development that is associated with woodwork. I look at how woodwork supports children's learning dispositions and builds on how they learn best: through rich experiential learning. I explain how woodwork embraces all the specific areas of the curriculum with particular emphasis on personal development and thinking skills. The chapter also looks at how woodwork can develop children's thinking around sustainability and concludes with thoughts about monitoring progression in children's creative development.

Characteristics of effective learning ▶ 20
  Curiosity ▶ 21
  Playing and exploring ▶ 22
  Active learning ▶ 22
  Creative and critical thinking ▶ 24
EYFS prime curriculum areas ▶ 27
  Personal, social and emotional development ▶ 27
  Physical development ▶ 38
  Communication and language ▶ 42
EYFS specific curriculum areas ▶ 44
  Mathematics ▶ 44
  Understanding the world ▶ 49
  Expressive arts and design ▶ 53
  Literacy ▶ 59
Skills for life: beyond the curriculum ▶ 60
Sustainability ▶ 60
Observation and assessment ▶ 62
  Observing and monitoring progress ▶ 63
  Schema ▶ 63
  Skills checklist ▶ 64

Learning and development

Initially, it could perhaps be easy to see woodwork as a peripheral activity – something that is offered as a bit of an extra. But I believe it lies at the heart of the curriculum being rich in associated learning and development and encompassing core aspects of the Early Years Foundation Stage (EYFS) curriculum. As my practice is based in England I will focus on the EYFS curriculum, but it has much in common with other early childhood curricula, such as the International Baccalaureate Primary Years Program (PYP), and I have expanded some sections to encompass areas that are emphasised by other programs, such as Scotland's 'Curriculum for Excellence', Wales' Foundation Phase, and New Zealand's 'Te Whāriki'.

The aspects of curriculum can be a useful resource to refer back to when planning and evaluating sessions. They show how woodwork really embraces many aspects of learning and development, and as an activity can be central to curriculum planning. Woodwork is very much cross-curricular in that it involves all areas of learning and makes links and connections between them.

Characteristics of effective learning

Woodwork can be seen to embrace all the characteristics of effective learning. These are the essential elements that underlie how children learn. Through the investigation of wood, exploration of the properties of materials and learning through first-hand experience of manipulating tools and being creative, children develop a long-lasting style of effective learning.

EYFS characteristics of effective learning are:

Playing and exploring:	Finding out and exploring
	Playing with what they know
	Being willing to 'have a go'
Active learning:	Being involved and concentrating
	Keeping trying
	Enjoying what they set out to do

Creative and critical thinking: Having their own ideas
 Making links
 Choosing ways to do things

Curiosity

Curiosity lies at the heart of children's learning – the spirit of enquiry. This is a fundamental disposition that underpins all three of the characteristic areas above. It provides the intrinsic motivation to explore. Babies are born curious with a drive to discover the world around them. In early childhood this curiosity drives children's desire to explore and play. It is the catalyst for motivation and engagement and it encourages making connections, noticing and wondering and the posing of new questions as children express their imaginations. Curiosity is a way of being and of seeing the world as full of wonder and possibility. Curiosity leads to the joy of discovering new things, exploring new knowledge, skills and places. Most early years children bring this disposition of curiosity with them as they experience working with wood. Some children do not show these high levels of curiosity due to certain early childhood experiences or deprivation, so it is crucial that we do all we can to reignite and foster it to readdress disadvantage. Woodwork often proves to be a medium with the potential to do this. Many schools using their 'Pupil Premium' funding[1] for woodworking equipment see the value woodwork can bring to disadvantaged children. Curiosity is a fundamental disposition to woodwork, tinkering and making in general. Maintaining curiosity is crucial for life-long learning, but unfortunately as many children progress through school they do not have the conditions or opportunity to do this.

Learning and development

Playing and exploring

> Play is the highest expression of human development in childhood for it alone is the free expression of the child's soul.
>
> (Froebel 1826)

In woodwork, children explore what they can do with the tools, playing with possibilities. Curiosity is at the heart of their explorations as they test out, investigate and experiment. Initially, many children are a little apprehensive about woodwork when faced with the challenge of using equipment that is new to them, but with the correct support and encouragement they invariably find it very easy. Being willing to have a go and not being restricted by fears is an important attribute of embracing new experience. Regular woodwork sessions will embed and build upon existing skills, and as children expand their thinking and set themselves new challenges their skill set and knowledge really develops.

Active learning

Woodwork is learning by doing. When children are actively learning they show high concentration levels and are deeply engaged.

Learning and development

Ferre Laevers at Leuven University in Belgium designed an involvement scale as a way of monitoring children's engagement. The scale runs from 1 to 5. Level 5 is described as children showing sustained intense activity. Children should show some of the indicators of involvement such as concentration, creativity, energy and persistence (clearly all very present in woodwork) and the intensity should be continuous for an extended period (there are exceptional possibilities for this with woodwork). Children's involvement with woodwork is often consistently sustained at level 5 or above the scale!

In woodwork, children show extremely high levels of involvement with focused concentration and engagement. Using tools necessitates a certain level of concentration. With a strong desire to create something, children will further focus and concentrate as they solve problems and refine their work. Children often show concentration levels rarely seen elsewhere, but it is not just the depth of children's focus – they also remain engaged for extended periods of time. It is not unusual for children to work throughout a session at the woodwork table.

Children show great pride in their constructions as well as taking much satisfaction from the process. I remember one boy persisting with the challenge of making a car, trying to ensure that all the wheels rotated. He had to solve problems many times, refining his design and method until he finally succeeded. Then, once his work was complete, he carefully removed all the parts, put them back in the boxes to be used another day and moved on to another activity – with the swagger and confidence of one very satisfied child! He now has learning skills that can be built upon in making an even more complex design next time. Woodwork can be seen as an activity that promotes agency, developing children's sense of who they are and their ability to act in any given environment.

Both Vygotsky's *zones of proximal development* and Carol Dweck's work on *mindsets* are particularly relevant in relation to this active learning characteristic.

Proximal development – layers of learning

Woodwork is an excellent way of supporting children to expand their *zone of proximal development* (Vygotsky 1978 [1930]) as they increase what they are able to do without the need for adult help. Vygotsky (1896–1934) wrote about woodwork as being a wonderful activity for illustrating the developmental stages in children's learning. As children progressed from being supported to learn new skills and solve problems, they moved on to working unaided, extending and building on their knowledge and learning, extending what he called their *zone of proximal development*. What a child can do with adult support today they will be able to do safely for themselves tomorrow. This further motivates children to attempt more challenging tasks. Children get great pleasure from being able to master new skills and achieve what they could not do previously. The value of this scaffolded progression was also advocated by Jerome Bruner, who wrote about children learning through *the play spiral*.

Growth mindset

Carol Dweck, a psychology professor at Stanford University, has written extensively about mindsets (Dweck 2006, 2012) and how they underpin how children learn. She talks of 'fixed' and 'growth' mindsets. People with a fixed mindset tend to believe that their capabilities are set, and cannot be developed. People with a growth mindset tend to believe that their capabilities can be improved and expanded. A growth mindset tolerates challenge, risk and failure, while a fixed mindset avoids these. Fixed mindsets will hold children back from exploring new areas and developing unknown capabilities.

Dweck's growth mindset model fits with the type of development that occurs within woodwork and making in general. With the multiple layers of learning it encompasses, children are constantly expanding their capabilities and developing a proactive can-do attitude. Children discover what they can do with what they have previously learnt. Children look for new solutions

Learning and development

and ways to improve, and this helps to develop a growth mindset which in turn will set them up as life-long learners.

Creative and critical thinking

I know no other activity that promotes creativity and critical thinking in quite the same way that woodwork does, and I believe this is really at the heart of woodwork's appeal and success.

Opportunities to develop young children's creative and critical thinking skills should be readily embraced. We live in a world that is changing too rapidly for the education system to respond to and many children now in their early years will have future professions that do not currently exist. It is more important than ever before that the new generation is able to think creatively, adapt and innovate, and develop problem-solving skills to meet the challenges of our rapidly changing world.

Curiosity and imagination lay the foundations for children's powerful thinking. Children begin to express their imagination, develop their own original ideas, and make their own choices about how to do things. ('I'm going to make a dinosaur with teeth'; 'I'm going to make a ladder to get to the moon'.) They think of possible ways to adapt their work and will use their imagination as they search through a box of offcuts looking for what shape will be most useful to suit their need. They create designs and develop and refine their work through creative thinking and critical thinking processes. Woodwork is extraordinary in the way that it can incorporate so many creative and critical thinking skills.

Creative thinking	Critical thinking
Expanding options/including divergent thinking	Narrowing options/including convergent thinking
Generating multiple ideas	Analysing
Playing with possibilities	Synthesising
Deferring judgement	Thinking clearly: clarifying, processing
Enlarging perspectives	Reasoning
Seeking out the unusual	Selecting: based on observation/evidence
Combining/integrating elements	Making judgements, making decisions
Visualising	Categorising
Imagining options	Refining, distilling
Building on others' ideas	Hone in/focus
Using intuition/hunches	Predicting
Many right answers	Making connections
Playful	Connecting through recall/memory
Looking for possibilities	Assessing
Suspended judgement	Reflecting and evaluating
Lateral thinking	Hypostatising and hypothesis testing
Speculating	Justifying

Children use their imagination in many ways as they develop ideas, choosing how best to work with the resources available and then coming up with different potential solutions to problems and applying these. Woodwork is unrivalled in the way that it provides opportunities for problem-solving. Children will reason, analyse, choose options and reflect on their work. This deep cognitive involvement in their work is clearly apparent.

Their analytical reasoning skills are enhanced in many ways. There are many opportunities for strategising and choosing appropriate solutions to problems: 'How can I best join these pieces?', 'How could I make a . . .?', 'How can I use the tool to . . .?', 'How can I get a nail to stand up straight?'. This will often involve speculation, intuition, testing hunches, and using trial and error. Children reflect on the work, both on the process and product, reviewing what worked and what didn't and assessing if things could have been done differently. They can reflect on the process, tools, outcomes and safety aspects. Having children take photographs to document their work can aid this reflection. As children review they may also make links to other areas of learning.

Children will be using these creative and critical thinking skills almost simultaneously, fluctuating between the two. Mihaly Csikszentmihalyi (b.1932) alluded to this as being the 'state of flow'. He went on to suggest that the state of flow produced a feeling of happiness and inner fulfilment. Young children are highly complex thinkers who need the experience of 'flow'. This is a mental state in which 'in an activity that nothing else seems to matter; the experience is so enjoyable that people will continue to do it even at great cost, for the sheer sake of doing it' (Csikszentmihalyi 1990: 4). He also wrote that flow was most likely to occur in situations combining high skills with a high level of challenge.

Total involvement in an activity, resulting in a state of flow, can be described as:

- intense and focused concentration on present moment
- merging of action and awareness
- loss of reflective self-consciousness
- a sense of personal control over the situation
- distorted sense of time
- the activity feeling intrinsically rewarding.

Silvano Arieti in his book *Creativity: The Magic Synthesis* (1976) also highlighted that the synergy between creative and critical thinking leads the way towards creativity.

Imagination

As the children become familiar with the tools and their possibilities, their creative thinking and imagination really begin to emerge. When children develop their own ideas the resulting work is highly individual and shows enormous variety, incorporating many different ways of working. Some children

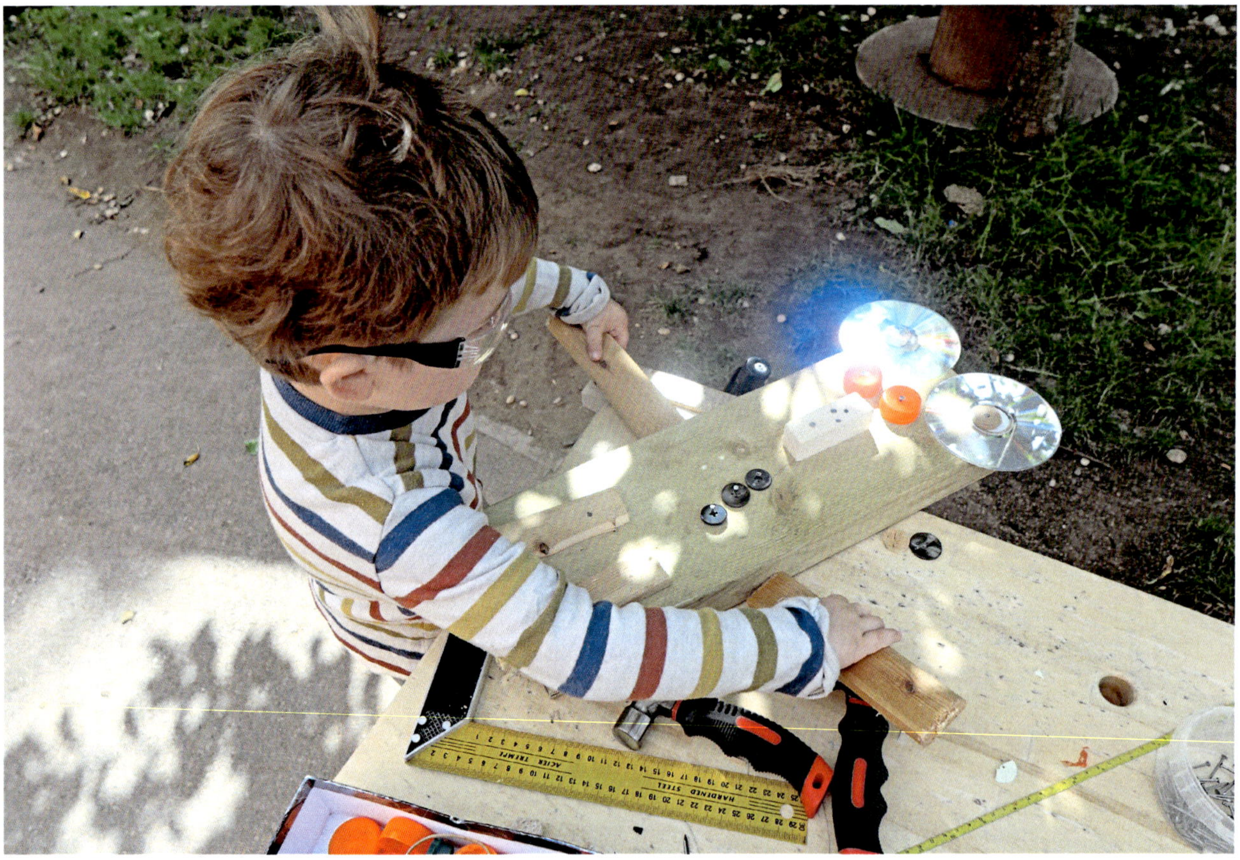

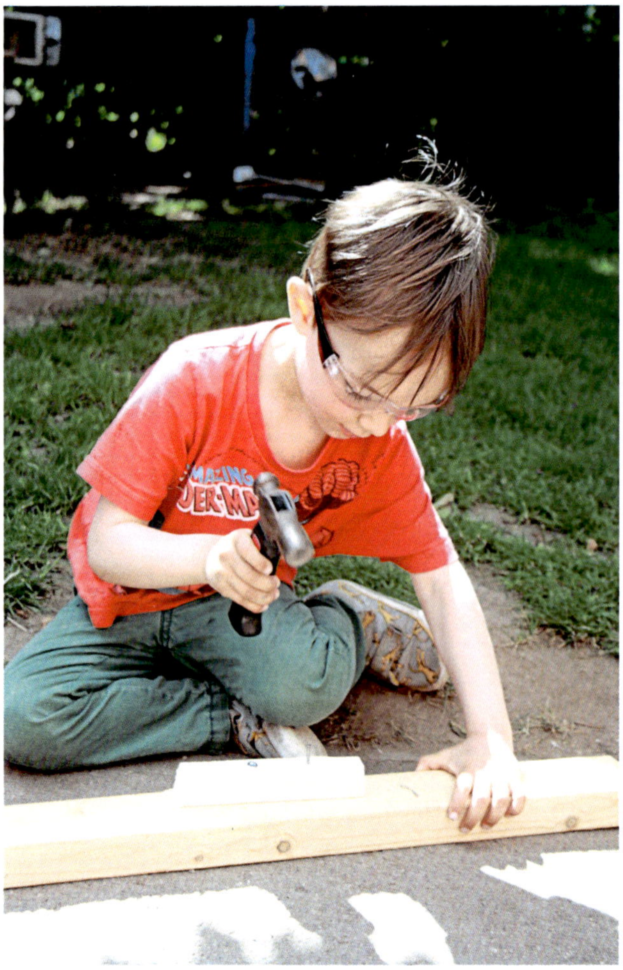

take delight purely in the process as they experiment with different tools, but some explore narratives and create scenes. Others will explore simple concepts such as making wheels that actually turn. Much of the work is representational, for example spiky hedgehogs, flying lamp posts, or superpower heliplanes, whilst others explore shape and form as they create abstract artworks.

Open-ended exploration

Allow children to follow their interests and develop inquiry-based learning. Children should follow their own interests rather than having teachers initiate set activities where children follow set instructions to complete a particular project such as making bird boxes. When children are following their own interests and solving their own problems, refining and developing their own ideas, reflecting on and evaluating their work, this provides intrinsic motivation and high levels of engagement and enjoyment.

Extending thinking

Encouraging children's creative critical thinking skills will enhance all areas of learning and develop their potential creativity. They will enhance life chances by helping with decision-making and responding to opportunity and adversity. They develop our ability to see options and evaluate alternatives. I believe many of the thinking skills associated with creativity need to be carefully nurtured by active adult involvement in their deep thinking (see Chapter 5). Young children have a natural curiosity and desire to learn. They also have powerful imaginations with an almost limitless capacity to develop new ideas. But creative and critical thinking are skills that are emerging and need to be nurtured and extended as valuable skills that impact on all learning.

Photography as a tool to make thinking visible

As children are often deeply focused and engaged during the process, photography provides a stimulating way to initiate dialogue about work afterwards. It is so true that a picture is worth a thousand words and reviewing images provides a powerful way to reconnect with all the processes involved. Images can be taken by the practitioner or the child. Images taken by children often resonate more and stimulate even more dialogue, but children are often too engrossed to be able to switch between taking pictures and their work. Reviewing images allows analysis of their creative and critical thinking processes as well as being able to reflect on metacognitive understanding.

Brain development

The high levels of engagement and deep learning are clear indicators of significant brain development. When children are deeply engrossed, facing challenges, solving problems and expressing their imagination, and using the cognitive processes of creative and critical thinking, they are literally building new neural pathways. The developmental psychologist Alison Gopnik wrote extensively about this neurological development (Gopnik 2009). As a kinaesthetic activity, woodwork also stimulates brain development through movement and tactile experiences, sending messages between skin, muscles, joints and the brain.

EYFS prime curriculum areas

Personal, social and emotional development

> The emotional impact of woodworking is that it gives children that sense of achievement: 'Yes! I can do this!' Experience builds skills and knowledge which strengthens understanding.
>
> Terry Gould, early years consultant and Ofsted inspector

Learning and development

Working with wood is not about what the children make but what actually happens inside the child. Many educationalists have advocated that it has the potential to develop a sense of self and how children feel about themselves. Otto Salomon (1891) wrote about this extensively as well as the team at Harvard University's Project Zero.

We provide children tools to work with, but they are in turn developing tools within that they can use in a multitude of different situations. As Piaget stated, active experiential learning will 'lead the child to construct for himself the tools that will transform him from the inside' (Piaget 1973: 121).

As we will see in this section, woodwork has a significant impact on children's personal, social and emotional development. Woodwork has a significant impact on well-being, with children becoming more confident and levels of self-esteem raised.

As children become more skilled and competent, they gain confidence in their abilities and develop an identity as a maker. The processes encourage metacognition and self-regulation as well as pride in process and product. This develops a dispositional attitude which can impact on all areas of learning.

There are many important elements that help explain why woodwork is so effective in this area of child development:

- ▶ feeling valued
- ▶ trying new experiences
- ▶ gaining new skills
- ▶ being motivated
- ▶ developing independence

Learning and development

- developing confidence
- developing agency
- developing persistence
- taking risks
- concentration and engagement
- developing resilience
- therapeutic benefits and mindfulness
- developing social skills and collaboration
- perspective and empathy
- self-regulation, self-care and awareness of others
- pride in their achievements
- metacognition.

Feeling valued

Children immediately feel valued and feel a sense of responsibility when given the opportunity to work with real tools. They feel valued by being respected and trusted. When children are engaged with real experiences it develops their sense of autonomy and they feel empowered. This has a visible impact on their self-esteem. The fact that they are taking responsibility in working with real tools also seems to be reflected in their desire to take their work seriously.

Trying new experiences

For young children this will be their first experience of woodwork. Being unfamiliar and outside their comfort zone, it can feel a risk just taking part. As with any new experience, young children

Learning and development

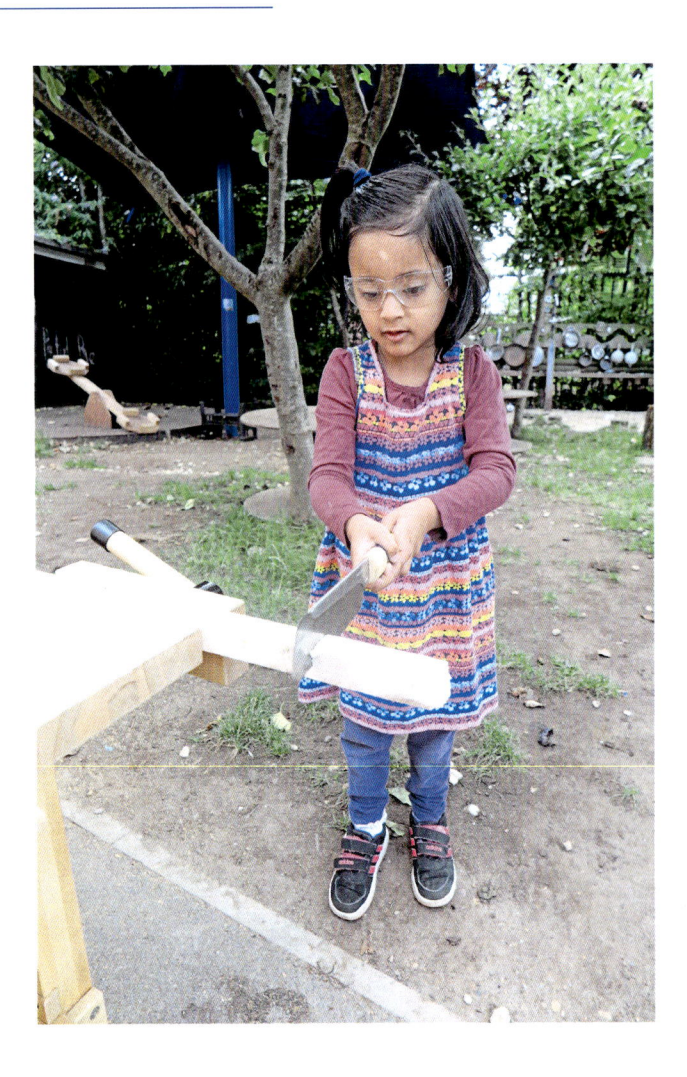

may initially be apprehensive. With woodwork this is no different; most children have never experienced using tools, and moreover they may previously have been told not to touch them.

With the choice of soft balsa wood to start with and ergonomic tools, children find it easy to learn the skills and rapidly become confident hammering in nails and using the screwdriver. This gives a great sense of achievement, overcoming what they perceived to be challenging, once again boosting self-esteem and confidence. As they go on to master more tools and techniques they take great pride in accomplishing increasingly complex tasks. As children progress they will demonstrate a confidence to try new things and ideas, taking delight in new experiences. Woodwork sparks children's curiosity and their keenness to explore.

Gaining new skills

With woodwork there are many skills to learn. There are many tools to learn how to use and techniques to master. We all feel good about ourselves as we learn new skills. This is no different with children – the acquisition of new skills is a significant boost to self-esteem. 'I can do it all on my own!' says Kaya, with a big smile, after screwing into the wood.

Being motivated

Curiosity is a catalyst for motivation. Children are curious and inquisitive about how the tools work and what they can do, they are curious about wood and its possibilities, they are curious to discover how they can join and construct. Children show high levels of motivation, with a strong sense of purpose, whether in becoming familiar with the drill or having a desire to complete their model or project.

Learning and development

Developing independence

Children become more independent as they exercise choice and make decisions. Woodwork is kept open-ended to encourage curiosity and self-motivation. Children are encouraged to be autonomous and use the majority of the tools and resources independently. Children are also encouraged to find their voice, to communicate their ideas, express opinions and to come up with their own solutions to problems. Woodwork lends itself to solitary play, and this enhances children's individual confidence to act on their own decisions. They also learn to self-manage and organise themselves within the woodworking area. Children are empowered, as they can shape the outcome and make an impact on the world.

Developing confidence

Children's confidence in their own ability grows as they master skills and techniques. During their constructions many challenges and questions spontaneously arise that provide opportunities for children to analyse and refine problems and discover solutions for them. This process reinforces children's capabilities as confident investigators, problem solvers and decision-makers. They develop a confident, can-do approach, and are not easily put off by setbacks. Children also gain confidence in asking for help, seeking support and guidance when they need it. As children progress, tackling more complex tasks, this will once again strengthen their confidence, as they build on previous learning. Woodwork also provides opportunities for children to pass on their skills to others. They are excited to teach other children and it really makes them *own* the skill. This again does a lot to contribute to confidence building.

Learning and development

Developing agency

Agency is choosing to act – the power to do something that has an impact. Children learn how things work and discover that they can shape the world around them by making. This imparts an optimistic 'can-do' attitude and imbues children with a strong sense of agency – having a proactive disposition towards the world so they can impart their unique expression. Having a sense of agency empowers young children to feel capable, to believe that they have the ability to create – that they can make choices about what they can do and how they can impact on and change their world. Agency is clearly developed by children planning their own projects, discovering their own solutions, learning through solving problems as opposed to through didactic teaching. Through their sense of agency they will be developing an identity as a maker. The can-do, resourceful attitude associated with agency will extend into other areas and empower children that they can make changes and challenge structures and systems.

Developing persistence

Woodwork also develops children's persistence and perseverance. Many of the tasks involved take time and are not always easy. Things break, split and just don't always go to plan. Children seem to respond to the authentic nature of woodwork and are motivated to persevere, rising to the challenge to work on difficult techniques and find solutions to problems. Sometimes woodwork can be frustrating but children often show sustained interest and a determination to keep going.

The obstacles and challenges can become an attraction of woodwork, with children becoming fascinated by testing out many possibilities and different solutions.

Persistence also often leads on to resourcefulness, as children work around the lack of a certain material, or come up with an alternative method to enable them to keep working.

Children will persist physically: sawing through a large section, hammering in a big nail, drilling a deep hole; or cognitively: working out how to join a mast to their boat, how best to make the propeller turn, or make their model balance standing up. Children will often work on projects and models for extended periods of time, returning to work in progress the next day or even over several sessions.

Persistence can lead on to doing things with care, putting your best effort in, persevering to find the best solution, striving for quality, which will have an impact on how they feel about their work and the pride they take in their product. This attention to craft is sometimes referred to as integrity. This will involve being patient, taking time, being resilient, persevering, paying attention to detail as well as showing some passion and dedication. Quality is an element that young children can understand and aspire to. It is further developed through the analytical reflective process.

Taking risks

For many children woodwork will be a totally new experience. They learn that not knowing and being uncertain are part of the process of being an effective learner. Being willing to try new things provides a foundation for future learning.

As well as learning about how to manage physical risks in terms of safety, children develop their emotional attitude to risk. They confront the fear of the unknown, the risk of failure, feeling incompetent or being embarrassed. Children learn, develop and grow by experiencing challenge and confronting their fears. Children need to take emotional risks. Are we prepared to try a new tool? Are we prepared to take the risk to try something new, to try new challenges that are outside our comfort zone? Are we prepared to learn new techniques? Are we prepared to make mistakes? Are we prepared to suggest creative ideas? Are we prepared to express these ideas in physical form? Are we unafraid to try things that have not been done before?

These characteristics depend on overall well-being, confidence and self-esteem and are so crucial for effective learning. We only fail when we stop trying. Our mistakes provide opportunities for us to learn, grow and develop. The role we play in nurturing and supporting children to become confident and resilient is so important. We need to be attentive, sensitive and encouraging (see Chapter 5).

Children also learn to manage the physical risk of working with tools, by experiencing this risk in a controlled environment. The biggest risk to children is that they do not get to experience risk, and so do not learn how to make judgements and so in turn become more prone to accidents. When children make judgements about potential risk when using tools they develop confidence and learn not be overly timid.

Concentration and engagement

Children's tongues are often sticking out whilst woodworking! Current thinking in psychological research attributes this to a high level concentration when a child is trying to complete a challenging task that involves both cognitive and fine motor skills. The tongue action is thought to either help us focus or provide a visual message to others not to disturb. Another neurological theory is that the hand and mouth nerves are located closely in the brain and one often interacts with the other.

Children show high levels of engagement, remaining focused on their work for extended periods of time, regularly in excess of an hour. Children's focus and persistence impacts on developing

Learning and development

sustained concentration. There are two layers to their concentration and focus. First there is the need to concentrate due to the nature of working with tools, and second, as their models evolve, there is deep level thinking as they express their imagination and work out how best to join and resolve their desired project. Many teachers have reported that these extended periods of concentration have impacted on the general level of focus in the classroom.

Developing resilience

Woodwork can also be seen to strengthen children's resilience. Whilst woodworking there are many challenges and setbacks as things don't go to plan. The wood may split, a thumb may get banged, or a wheel just keeps falling off! These mistakes are opportunities to learn. It only becomes a failure if you stop trying. With woodwork children are highly motivated and have a real desire to complete tasks, and they determinedly persist to resolve their work even when it requires considerable physical effort. Models can often break, and after the initial disappointment children will again resolve how to make their work more robust. This process helps them feel more in control and further builds resilience.

Therapeutic benefits and mindfulness

When adults undergo woodwork training they often mention how therapeutic woodworking feels. The same is apparent for young children who become deeply engaged in working holistically with their hands and minds absorbed in their creative flow. There is an atmosphere of being actively busy but at the same time being calm, and children are not easily distracted. This is an emotional state in which children feel happy, contented and fulfilled.

Developing social skills and collaboration

Woodwork also helps children cooperate with others. They learn to share and take turns, negotiate and support each other. When children discuss and plan projects together, their social skills develop as well as their understanding of how others think. They learn the value of sharing ideas and see how others solve problems and the value of providing feedback.

Mutual encouragement and support is often visible. It is also quite common for children to offer advice and spot when someone is having difficulty in achieving what they want to achieve. They encourage and assist. They will often notice that it would be helpful to lend an extra hand in a particular situation. They often become the teacher – and demonstrate a particular skill, technique or how to use a new tool. Children will also collaborate by finding and sharing resources even when working independently.

Collaboration is often cited as one of the crucial learning skills that is needed in our contemporary economy, so opportunities to develop and extend this should always be seized. I also believe we have a responsibility to share knowledge. It is part of being a learning community, so encouraging children to do this is clearly beneficial for all. In the wider maker community there is a wonderful ethos developing of cooperation, sharing of information and exchange of techniques. Cooperation fosters a culture of generosity, receiving help and support, of offering advice and assistance. Children discover that they can learn from everyone and give back to others. Later in the book I talk about collaborative project learning, which focuses on children working closely together to solve authentic challenges (see Chapter 7).

In the *Makerspace Playbook* (2012) the collaborative element of making is summarised thus:

> fostering the maker mindset is a fundamentally human project – to support the growth and development of another person, not just physically but mentally and emotionally. It should focus on the whole person because any truly creative enterprise requires all of us, not just part. It should also be rooted in the kind of sharing of knowledge and skills that humans do best face to face.
>
> (Makerspace Playbook 2013)

Perspective and empathy

Making in general allows us to see things from others' perspectives as we observe them create and solve problems. This develops young children's ability to see the world from other people's viewpoints, which helps them to understand things in new ways. Seeing other perspectives encourages children to question their own assumptions. Perspective will also develop through close collaboration on projects as children explore ideas, negotiate and work together. The processes will also provide opportunities for children to experience and understand the feelings of others, developing empathy.

Self-regulation, self-care and awareness of others

Woodwork promotes self-regulation – the ability to monitor and control behaviour and emotion in order to meet the demands of the situation. Children will regulate their behaviour in many ways during a woodworking session; for example, being able to regain focus after being distracted, or managing frustration when struggling to complete a task.

Aggressive behaviour is a rare occurrence at the workbench. With children being deeply absorbed in their work and feeling empowered by using real tools they feel confident and strong without confronting or disturbing others. When children feel competent and fulfilled they rarely argue or interfere with each other.

Children also develop their sense of responsibility and self-care as they understand the need to use potentially dangerous tools safely. Children are taking risks in a controlled environment, assessing risk themselves and making judgements, learning how to keep themselves safe.

Children develop an understanding of the importance of taking responsibility for their own bodies and the safety of others. This strengthens self-awareness as children assess potential dangers, and it fosters a sense of responsibility for their own actions. In working with wood there clearly need to be some rules. They need to know tools can hurt them. They learn to understand the need for boundaries to protect themselves and keep others safe from potential harm; for example, being aware that they need to keep their fingers clear when hammering hard and that they need to wear safety glasses to protect their eyes.

Children develop their increasing understanding of how rules and boundaries help them to work together safely. They grow to understand the need to work within certain limits and treat tools with respect. Children who typically have difficulty managing their behaviour are also often so keen to have their turn that they are careful to adhere to the rules and boundaries.

Pride in their achievements

Children get immense personal satisfaction from woodwork, as can clearly be seen from their facial expressions. Not only do they very much enjoy the process, taking pleasure in gaining more complex skills and resolving their work, the physicality of working with wood, sawing and noisy banging, but their satisfaction in their accomplishment and resulting creations is clearly visible to anyone observing. They show such excitement as they share them with parents and those important to them, and I regularly have children or parents tell me years later that they still have their model at home! The delight, satisfaction and pride in their own creations is clearly visible. The combination of these elements again helps build self-esteem and confidence.

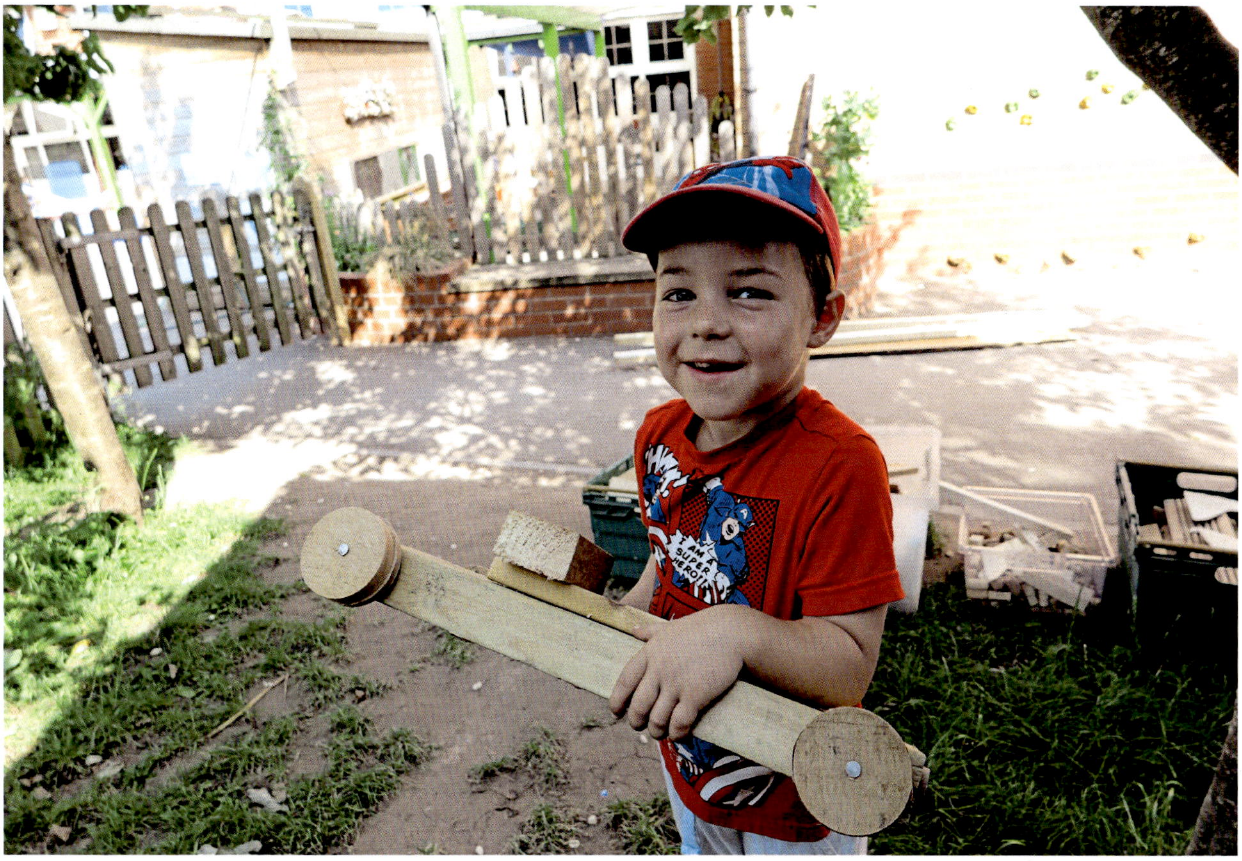

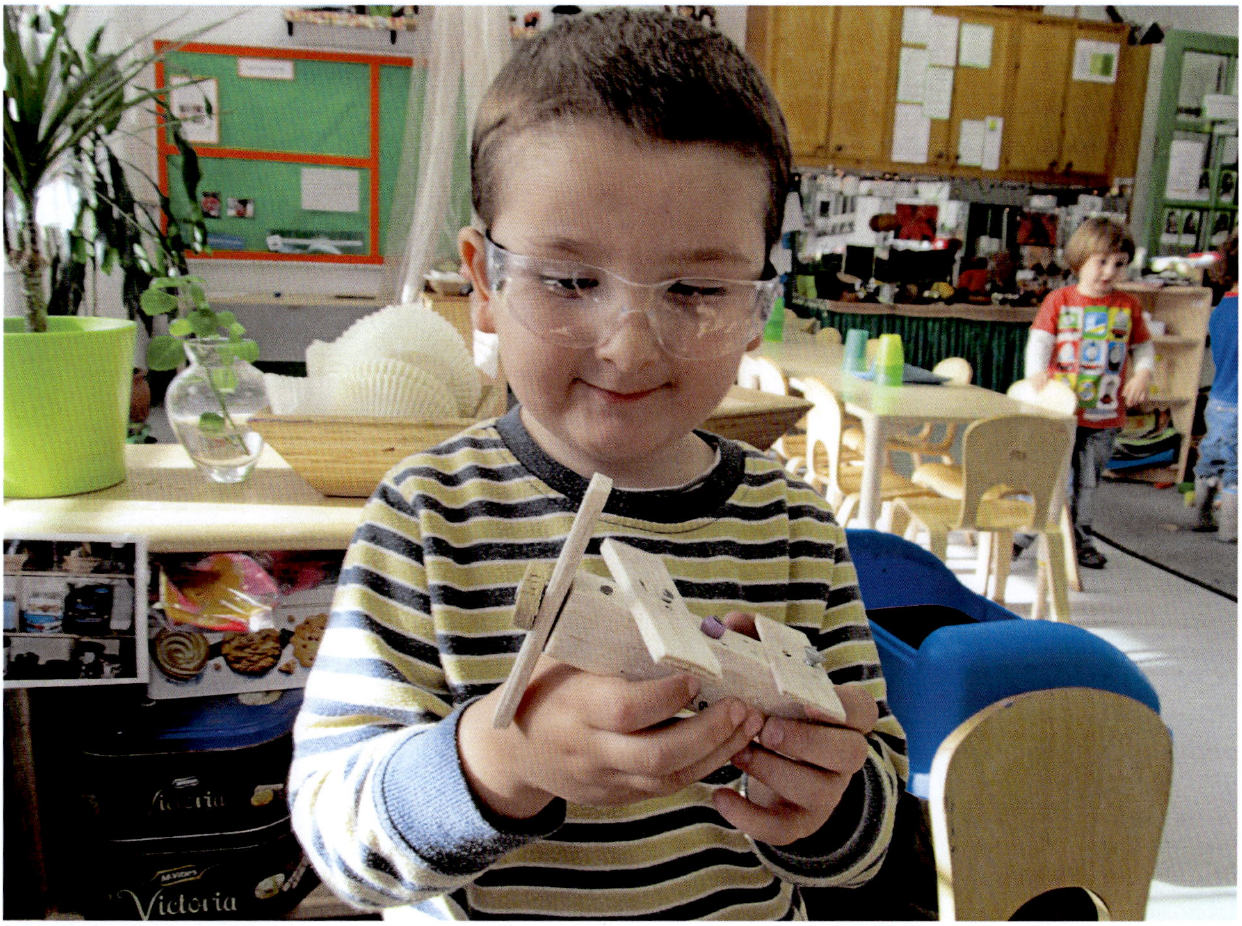

Learning and development

Metacognition

Metacognition is the capability to be aware of, and understand, our own learning processes. Woodwork can play an integral role in helping children become more aware of their own personal way of learning and to think about their own learning process. The opportunities available to develop understanding of process and reflect and analyse at numerous stages allow children to gain a robust understanding of their learning processes. They can reflect on techniques learnt, see how persistence paid off, think about how things could have been done differently, how learning built on previous experience and how connecting different areas of learning was beneficial.

Woodwork provides another context in which children can share learning with each other. Older children or children who are more experienced in woodwork will be observed and copied by younger children and equally older children will take pleasure in offering advice and suggestions to less experienced children who are perhaps having difficulty in achieving what they set out to create. This gives them the experience of perceiving themselves as teachers, having some knowledge and skills that can be shared with others.

The multiple benefits for personal, social and emotional development are clear, especially in terms of confidence and self-esteem. Of course, the experience will be different for every child, but it really can make such a noticeable difference for many children.

Physical development

Woodwork provides many opportunities for physical development as children learn to handle tools safely and with increasing control.

Source: © Community Playthings

Learning and development

Woodwork helps children to:

- develop hand–eye coordination
- learn to handle tools safely with increasing control
- refine balance to develop the poise and stance
- develop agility and dexterity, manipulative skills, and muscular strength
- develop fine motor skills and gross motor skills
- develop rich range of movements
- develop precision and accuracy
- develop core strength
- develop spatial awareness and associated positional language
- develop understanding of physical space and needs of others
- develop awareness through the senses.

Hand–eye coordination is intrinsic to woodwork and children gain increasing control over their bodies as they develop agility and dexterity, manipulative skills, and muscular strength. They refine their balance as they develop the poise and stance required to operate the tools in the most effective way. Proprioception and kinaesthesia are also developed with the children's increasing ability to sense position and develop awareness of motion. Lower arm, wrist and hand control are all developed. This manual dexterity is beneficial in so many ways; for example, learning to use cutlery, kitchen utensils, scissors or supporting early mark-making with pens and paint brushes.

Woodwork incorporates fine motor skills (holding a nail, screwing) and gross motor skills (hammering, sawing). There are many different types of movement such as pushing/pulling (saw, file) and rotating

39

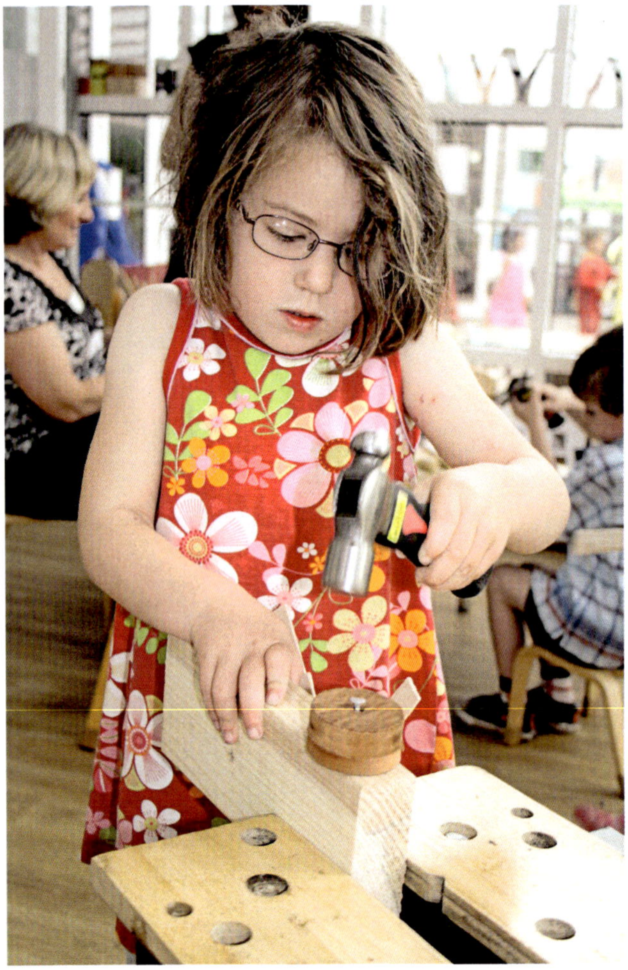

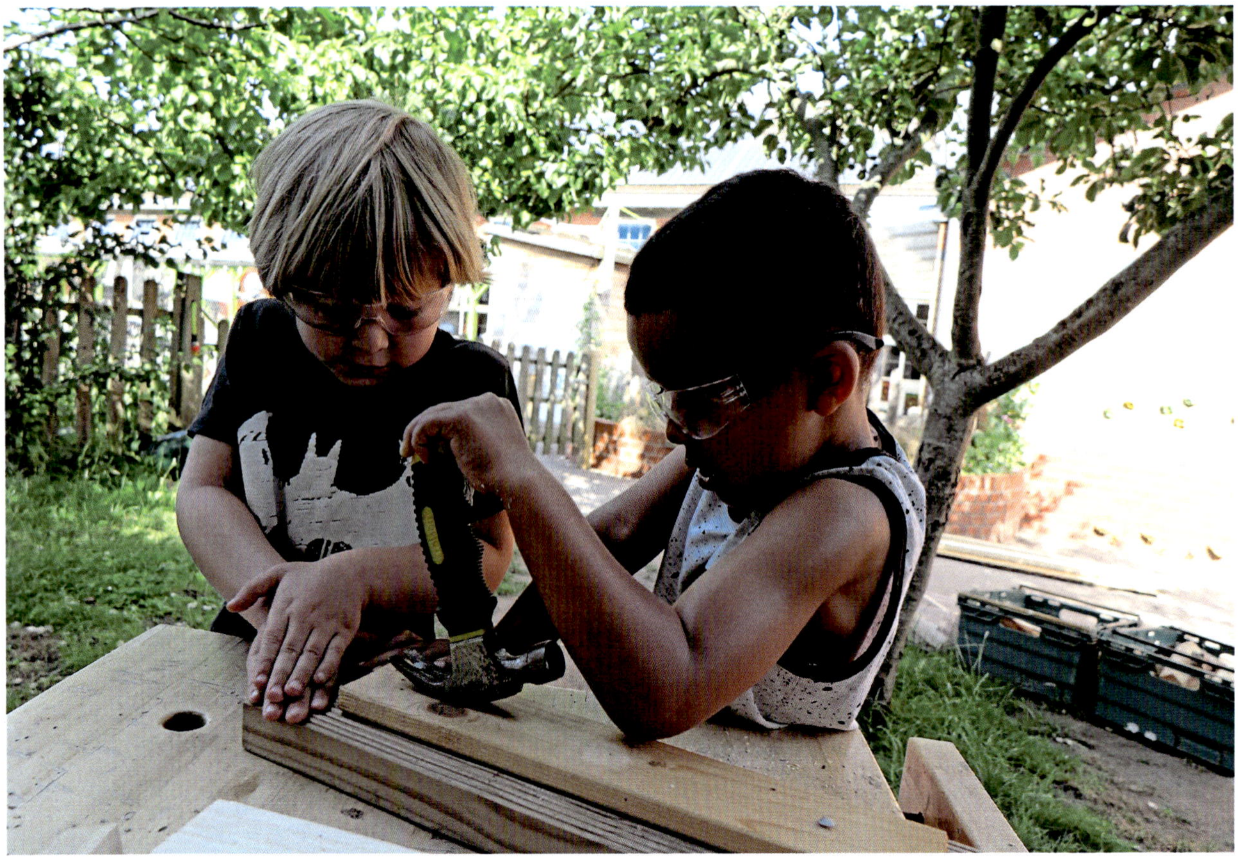

(screwdriver, drill, wrench, vice) and levering (claw hammer, Japanese nail puller) and rubbing (sandpaper). Hand–eye coordination is developed, for example, whilst hammering or threading a nut on a bolt. One-handed tools (screwdriver, wrench) and two-handed tools (hand drill) are experienced. Using tools develops children's spatial awareness and associated positional language.

Woodwork encourages precision, for example, when keeping a nail upright or cutting along a desired line. It also requires using a variety of degrees of force, for example, gentle initial hammering, then more robust hammering to drive the nail into the wood. With sawing, children will refine their action to get just the right pressure to get a smooth and steady cut.

As children become more familiar with the tools they become more adept, adjusting their position and stance to use their muscles more effectively. They learn to adjust their posture when sawing, positioning the left leg forward and the right leg back to be more efficient, enhancing their control and strength (vice versa for left-handed children).

Children's core strength is developed as they use the various tools, such as hammering, rotating the screwdriver or sawing. The delight on a child's face when they have persevered cutting through a section of wood is a wonder to behold: a real mixture of pride and surprise that they could actually make it happen.

Children develop their awareness of the effect of their physical presence on others through understanding the need to work at a safe distance from each other. They also learn how to transport tools safely, walk with tools, carry them at their side and not pass them with sharp edges facing forward.

Woodwork also helps develop children's senses as they experience the different textures of wood, and the associated smells and various sounds that come from the woodworking area.

Learning and development

Woodwork is a kinaesthetic experience that embeds a deep memory as the whole body learns together. Experience of using tools becomes part of children's physical vocabulary.

Communication and language

Woodwork stimulates communication and language development. There are countless opportunities for dialogue, and language is extended as children acquire and practise vocabulary.

- language
- active listening
- communication
- non-verbal communication.

Language

Language develops as children learn the names of the different tools and materials. They will learn vocabulary relating to the processes involved and through discussing health and safety.

Initial discussions can be had about the nature of wood. What is it? Where does it come from? What is made of wood? What is wood like? These conversations will contribute to extending their vocabulary. Relevant vocabulary will develop in all areas of learning from mathematical thinking to problem-solving. As children create and reflect on their work it will develop their ability to express and describe their creative and critical thinking.

Make time for children to talk about their work, talking about how they worked safely and the processes involved. This can also be done with a larger group and can be an effective way to

Learning and development

share learning and exchange ideas. It gives children opportunity to reflect on their work and articulate this confidently. New technical and descriptive vocabulary can also be introduced to enable the children to talk about their work in more depth. Vocabulary and dialogue also evolve from subsequent play as children develop narratives involving their plane, robot or hedgehog.

Children in their early years will have very different starting levels of language. Language has such a strong impact on all learning that it is crucial to ensure that we really encourage language development and make time to really focus on children with less language ability by making time for sustained conversations to explore ideas.

Active listening

The teaching process of learning to use tools safely is quite didactic. We are not going to have children explore how to use a saw! This will require active listening and interpretation, which will build their ability to understand and implement instructions.

Communication

In project development children will express ideas, discuss, reflect and modify their plans as they evolve. Natural conversation occurs among adults and children in the woodwork area. Children will use different forms of expression to clarify their thinking, ideas and understanding. They will share skills and processes with each other, negotiate as they share and take turns, or help each other with solving problems or sharing previous experiences.

But it is also true that often children are really in a state of flow, deeply absorbed in their work and may simply be too busy to talk much. A useful tool is to have a children's camera close by so they can document the progress of their work. Later, when these images are reviewed, it is amazing just how much the children will have to say about their photographs as they explain the process

Learning and development

and how they overcame challenges and resolved their work. This is so much more effective than if the adult takes the images as children feel empowered by having ownership over the photographs.

Non-verbal communication

Children will learn skills and techniques through non-verbal communication as they closely observe other children working. Children with less experience will learn from more experienced children as they watch and take in different techniques. This is almost learning by osmosis – it is common to see a child often carefully observing another child using a particular tool or, for example, smoothing an edge with sandpaper. Children also develop non-verbal responsive and reciprocal behaviour, picking up visual signs to share, take turns and offer help.

The explanation of tools can also be demonstrated visually and children with little language comprehension still gain a full understanding of the methods involved.

EYFS specific curriculum areas

Mathematics

Learning and development

All the mathematical concepts that children need to develop in the early years could be developed at the woodwork bench. Much of the mathematical learning that takes place is coincidental, occurring as children resolve practical problems. It is a natural, authentic way for children to develop their mathematical knowledge and understanding.

There are endless opportunities to explore numeracy and shape, space and measure. Many mathematical concepts are involved, including matching, classification, counting, measuring, proportion, comparison, size, weight and balance, and two- and three-dimensional shapes.

Below I will look at:

▶ numeracy
▶ shape, space and measure
▶ extending mathematical thinking.

Numeracy

Woodwork will encourage the spontaneous use of number names and number language. Children will be able to represent numbers with objects (for example, the number of nails or screws). This encourages them to match number and quantity. Counting quantity, for example, the number of sections of wood used, gives opportunities to work towards exploring numbers up to 20 and concepts such as one more and one less. There are opportunities to sort the various types of materials being used. Children can count out from a larger quantity, for example, counting six nails from a tub full of hundreds of nails.

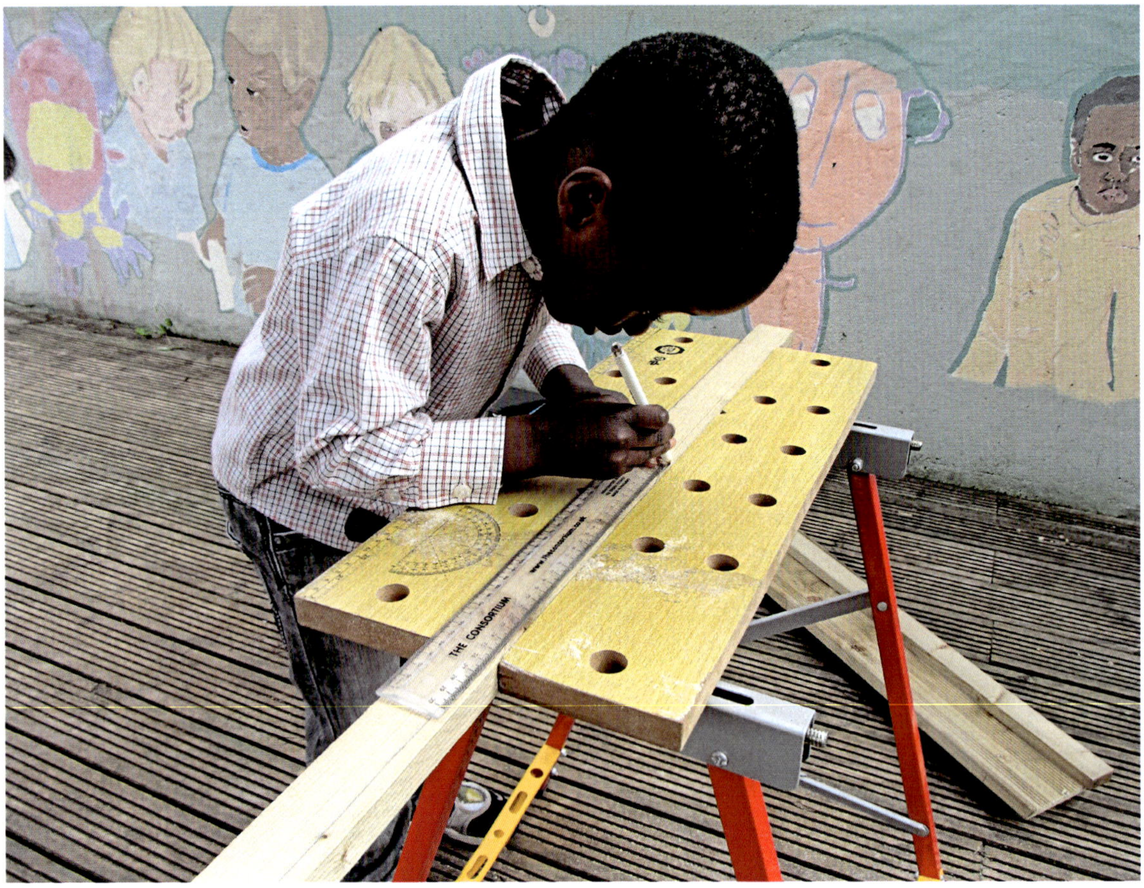
THE CONSORTIUM

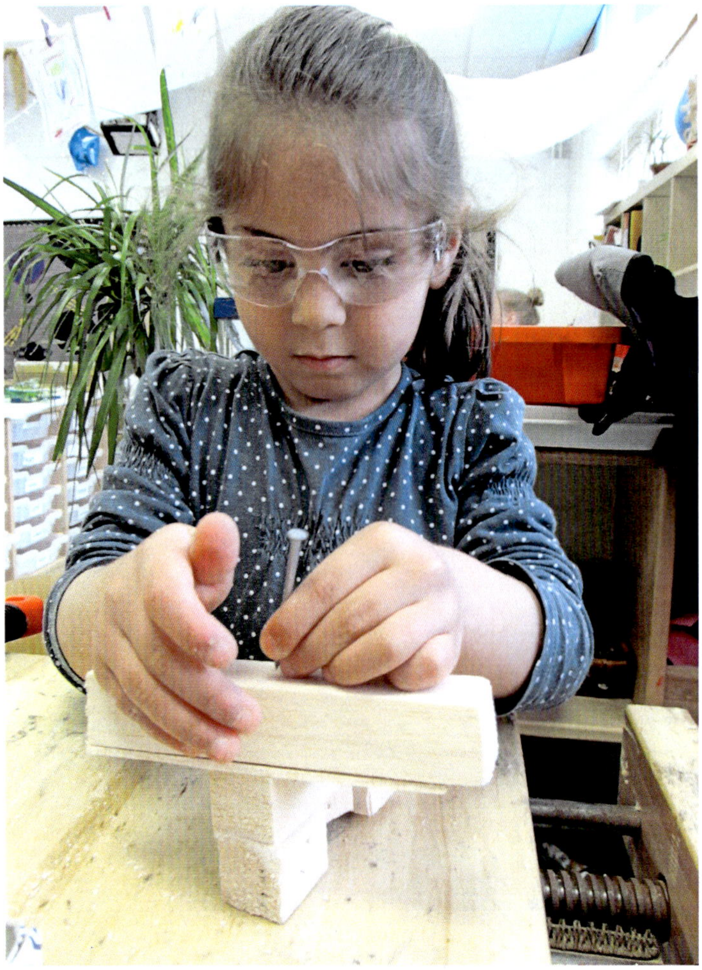

There are opportunities for speculation and estimation and then for checking by counting. Numbers can be associated with length, for example, with the use of the tape measure. Basic mathematical concepts such as adding and subtracting come into play as wood is joined or screws removed. There are opportunities to explore concepts such as halving and doubling by cutting wood in two or joining to equal sections. There are also many opportunities for mathematical problem-solving as the children work out how to use the resources effectively to express their imagination, for example, working out how deep to drill a hole.

Shape, space and measure

Woodwork also provides many opportunities to explore shape, space and measure. Woodwork encourages three-dimensional thinking as children work with shape and create arrangements, developing an understanding of the properties of shapes, angles and spatial relationships. They notice sides, corners, edges, and a variety of shapes. Their understanding develops as they identify, name and describe these shapes and properties.

There are many opportunities to explore and compare size: big/small, long/short, thick/thin, wide/narrow, and these concepts can be further explored with the use of a basic measure. Concepts of weight and height are discussed: heavy/light, tall/short, high/low. Lines can be explored: straight/curved, sides/corner, flat/angle, surface/edge. Children encounter spatial thinking in terms of orientation and position: upright/vertical, horizontal/sloping, under/above, behind/next to. There are many opportunities to categorise, sort and compare according to the shape and size.

Estimating is often involved in woodwork, for example, thinking about the best length of nail to use to join two sections of wood together. Understanding of measure can be supported by using a variety of measuring devices and using different units, including non-standard units. The more opportunities children have to measure for a real purpose the better. This is learning in context.

Extending mathematical thinking

Our role as a teacher in extending thinking is very much about tuning in and showing genuine interest in children's work and noticing when they are using mathematical thinking skills, and to then encourage and develop these. This way our interventions are relevant and have meaning. We need to encourage mathematical problem-solving by asking open-ended questions to support children's learning. Incorporate number language into your interactions, count in a variety of different situations and expand their numeracy vocabulary by using words such as less, fewer, etc. We can encourage the children to speculate in various situations, for example, estimating the age of a tree section and then checking by counting the rings.

Resources

Have pen and paper available to allow children to represent their mathematical thinking through graphics. Encourage them to take some photographs of their emerging models at different stages so they can reflect on the mathematical concepts they have explored.

Also provide: fabric tape measures, rulers, folding rulers, set squares, scales, children's cameras, different-sized tree rings, screws and nails in a variety of lengths, wood in a variety of shapes and sizes, including circles.

Learning and development

Understanding the world

Children's understanding of the world, knowledge of how things work and their scientific thinking are all developed in a multitude of different ways through woodwork. Certain knowledge will be specific to wood and other materials used and some knowledge will also be in relation to the use of tools.

- ▶ knowledge and understanding of wood and trees
- ▶ properties of materials
- ▶ wood products and people who work with wood
- ▶ technology
- ▶ cause and effect
- ▶ Science, Technology, Engineering and Maths (STEM)
- ▶ deconstruction.

Knowledge and understanding of wood and trees

Becoming familiar with wood and trees is part of making sense of the world. Trees are essential to life on our planet, and children are fascinated to learn about the many types, and their different uses and how they grow. Even young children can begin to appreciate the interconnectedness of life and our dependence on the oxygen released into the atmosphere by trees and other plants. Find out together about animals that live in trees, and trees that provide fruit and nuts. Explore how trees grow starting with a seed or sapling. Explore the seasons and life-cycles of trees. There are many fiction and non-fiction books that can support this learning (see Resources and Suppliers).

Take children into the woods to investigate trees – the trunk, bark, branches, leaves and roots – and describe the textures – rough, knobbly, smooth – and smells (such as the sweet smell of cedar). Talk about shapes and patterns, make bark rubbings, build a small fire, use branches to make dens. All of these activities will contribute to building their knowledge. Observe the wind moving trees, listen to the sounds of crunching leaves, snapping twigs and listen to the wind swaying leaves and branches. As an aid to observation, suggest children use a camera to capture images of trees.

Leaves could be investigated on a light box, examining the vein structures and colours. Make prints with leaves (print leaf patterns using a hammer block with muslin/white fabric and paint).

Properties of materials

Children can investigate wood as a material by researching its many properties. For example, wood burns (fires to keep warm, to cook on, charcoal), wood floats (boats, 'pooh sticks'). Learning often takes wonderful tangents and digressions as children follow their insatiable curiosity. Exploring floating could lead to making boats, which may lead to exploring sails and wind.

Children gain an intrinsic appreciation of materials. They learn that the way materials are used is determined by their properties. Children need to be given time to examine wood and test it. Explore its strength by trying to snap and break different sections. Test the hardness. Explore its weight by comparing it with that of other materials. Test how durable it is – by rubbing it, scraping it, sanding it and cutting it. Observe how it reacts with water – absorb, repel, go soggy, float. Discover what sounds it can make.

Children can explore different types of wood, as well as comparing natural wood with MDF and plywood, etc. Children can examine sawdust and shavings.

Wood products and people who work with wood

We can think about how trees are felled, dried and sawn into planks and then transported to a timber yard or hardware store. We can learn about how wood is transformed into a variety

Learning and development

of products. We are never far from wood and wooden objects in our daily lives, both indoors and outdoors. We can start by examining all the wooden objects around us, drawing children's attention to the versatility of wood. This could be supported by the use of a children's camera. We can think about the many people who work with wood: lumberjacks, designers, craftspeople, instrument makers, carpenters and builders, etc. Viewing a video clip of a construction site or saw mill, for example, may be helpful.

Children will develop their understanding of the connection between the natural and made worlds, and of human dependence on nature. This helps them to understand that they can make an impact on the world, and that they can create, repair, and deconstruct.

Technology

Woodwork is simple technology. Technology ('science of craft', from Greek) is the collection of techniques and processes used in the production of goods. Technology is about making things, putting ideas into practice, discovering the possibilities and limitations of materials and tools, and being creative to overcome problems. At the heart of technology is exploration – exploring cause and effect, just as a young toddler explores this through heuristic play.

It is easy to think of technology as solely referring to high-tech electronic devices and computer equipment, but simple tools are in fact a basic technology and have also played a significant part in developing the sophisticated technological world of today.

Children gain a scientific and technological understanding of tools and how they work, for example, by experiencing that the movement and weight of the hammer forces the nail into the wood, or seeing how the claw hammer or Japanese nail-puller work as levers that can slowly lever nails out of the wood, or seeing how turning the crank handle of a drill rotates the drill bit.

Children may make connections with other tools they have seen, such as an egg whisk. This develops their understanding of technology and the underlying scientific concepts.

Cause and effect

Children learn about scientific principles through cause and effect, discovering what causes things to happen. Seeing that a nail has split a piece of wood, for example, or that a section of wood attached with one nail may move whereas with two nails it is fixed firmly. They will witness how turning the crank rotates the drill bit. How the drill bit heats up with friction. How the spirals on a screw help it go into the wood. How rubbing with sandpaper creates dust and warms the wood. How a clamp or vice applies force to hold things steady. They can discover how best to allow a wheel to rotate on its axel. How to correct the angle of a leaning nail. How to remove a nail by using a lever. Movement is explored as children work with the various tools, for example, they will be exploring pushing and pulling or rotational movement through twisting and turning.

As their experience of working with tools and wood evolves they will be furthering their scientific understanding, expanding their knowledge, and developing a sense of what tools are the most suitable for a desired task and what type of wood or additional materials would work best. They will quickly discover if a section of wood is too hard or how a very thin section of wood easily splits.

Science, Technology, Engineering and Maths (STEM)

Many schools use STEM, a way of teaching that provides an integrated approach across the disciplines of science, technology, engineering and maths – as each area reinforces the others. Again, woodwork can be seen as an ideal medium for this cross-curricular learning, as children develop their understanding of wheels, axels and levers, for example. To really enable children to understand STEM concepts we need to provide authentic real experiences, not abstract alternatives. Many schools are not currently providing children with the STEM learning experiences that they desperately need, and woodwork, as it offers many avenues of exploration and investigation, can directly link to all STEM subjects. Through hands-on learning, children are much more likely to develop an interest in and pursue STEM subjects – thus once again woodwork could be seen as being beneficial to the economic narrative.

Deconstruction

Deconstruction (such as disassembling a tricycle, for example) deepens children's understanding of how things are made. As they break the object down into parts, they can investigate each component and discover how they were assembled, building knowledge of how things are manufactured. They will discover how elements interact. They can think about the purpose of each component and the complexity of what is needed to make an appliance function.

Deconstruction encourages children to slow down and observe, to look deeper, to be curious and question. Looking – close and mindful observation – is crucial, and to do this we need sustained time to notice the details, the complexities and the design. Thoughtful observation will initiate investigations, with the potential to open up many new lines of enquiry. They may become fascinated by the fact that a speaker is magnetic and go on to explore magnetism; they may be curious about the coloured wires and go on to investigate further by making a simple circuit. Seeing how cogs work together may draw children's interest to explore rotational movement. Every time we have deconstructed an appliance it has led on to other rich lines of enquiry.

Children will also develop a heightened sensitivity to design, and will develop a critical eye, allowing them to tinker with or ponder on how objects or systems could be improved or redesigned, as opposed to more passive 'consumer disengagement'.

Caution must be exercised when deconstructing. There are a number of safety measures that should be put in place such as always initially removing any plugs and avoiding appliances that contain large capacitors as these can still contain charge. There is more advice and information about safe deconstruction in the Deconstruction project in Chapter 7 (p. 157). In the Resources and Suppliers section there are links to general safety advice for deconstructing. If in any doubt it is better to avoid electrical appliances and stick to more mechanical objects.

Expressive arts and design

Woodwork provides children with a wonderful medium through which they can express their imagination through art and design.

- ▶ creative expression
- ▶ design and construction
- ▶ set tasks
- ▶ open-ended enquiry
- ▶ collaborative work
- ▶ aesthetics
- ▶ craft sense

Creative expression

Woodwork allows children to express their creativity and imagination in another medium. Initial emphasis is on developing skills and experimenting with possibilities. Children then go on to express their imagination in a variety of creative ways by producing work that they personally find interesting. The nature of woodwork is very open-ended, allowing children many possibilities to express themselves in new and unique ways. The resulting work varies enormously, ranging from symbolic and representational, to abstract, to work containing narrative. Abstract work is sometimes in relief as children use sections of wood to create a picture but mostly they create more three-dimensional sculptural work.

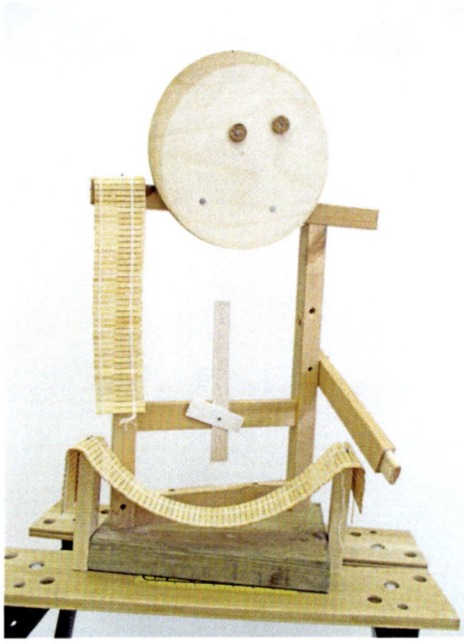
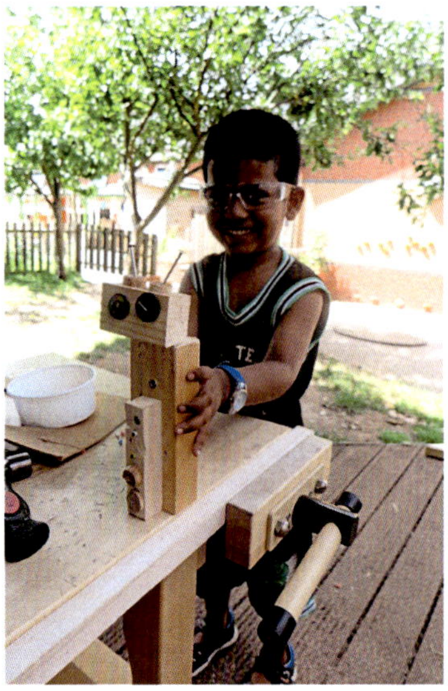
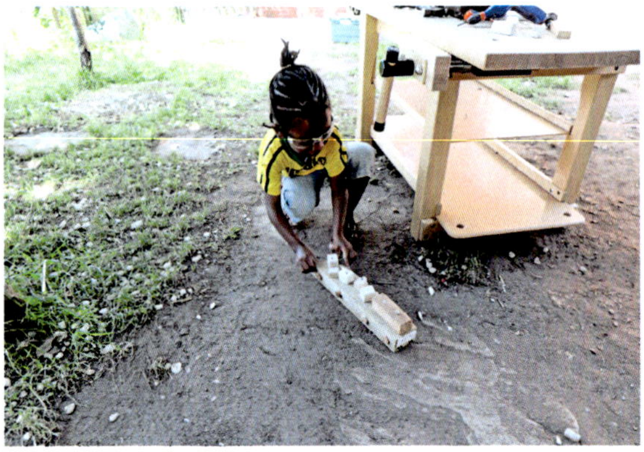
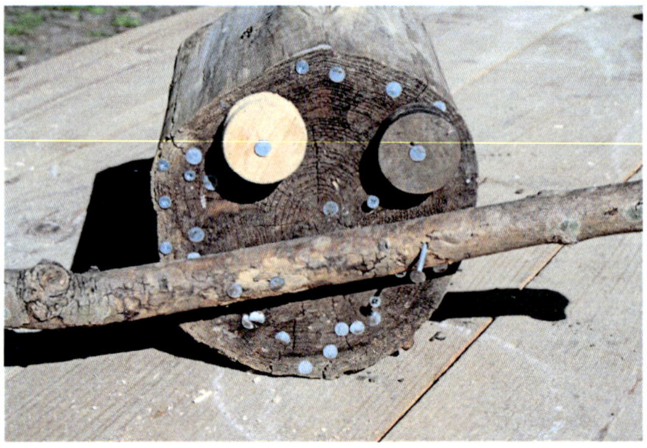
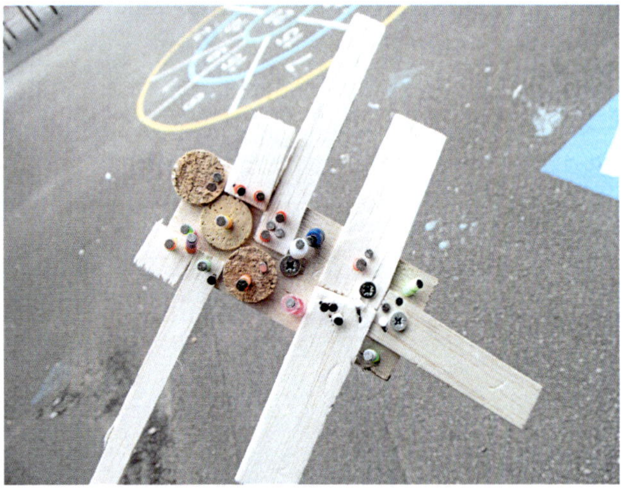
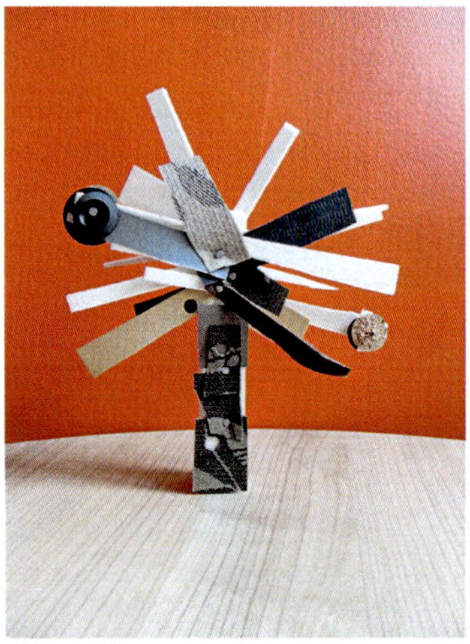
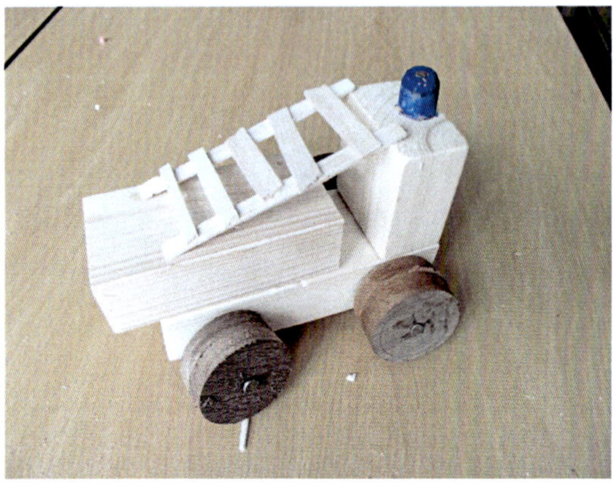
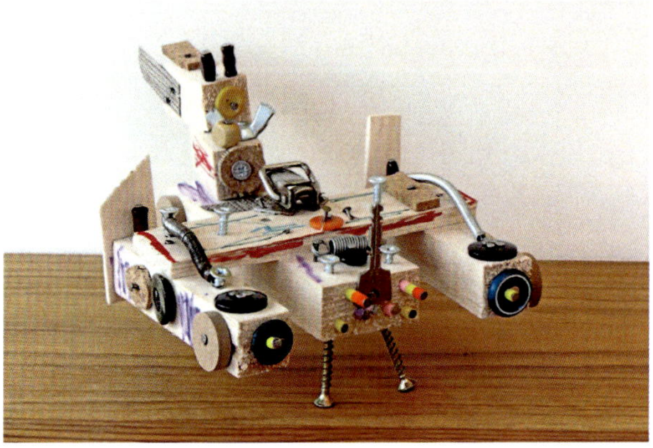

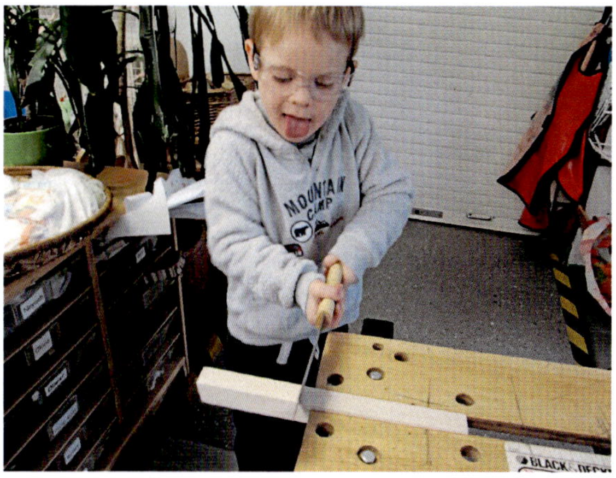
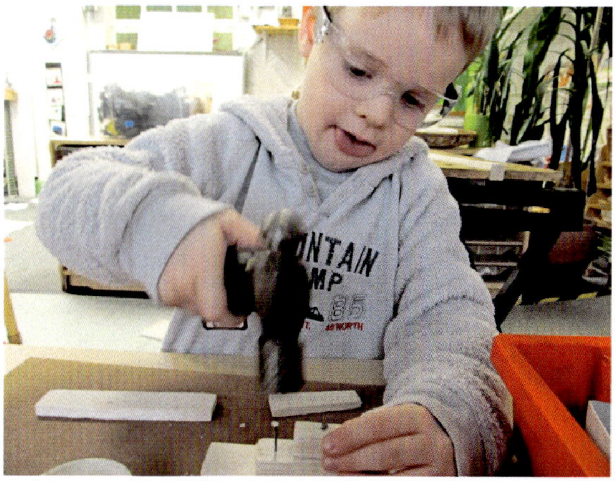
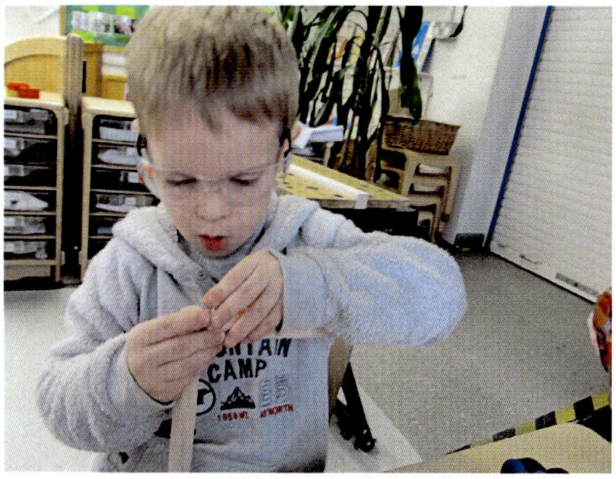
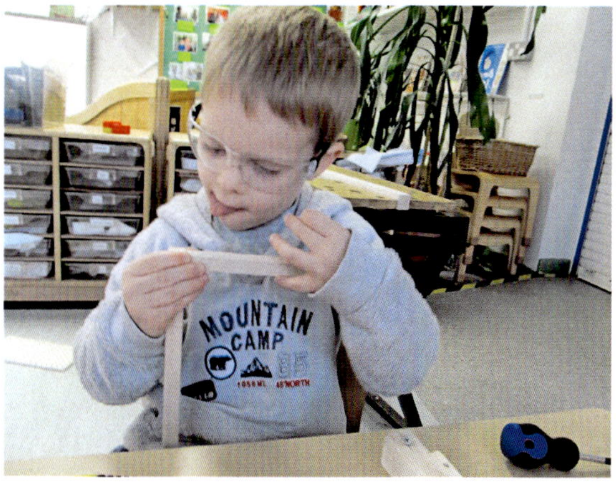
MOUNTAIN
CAMP
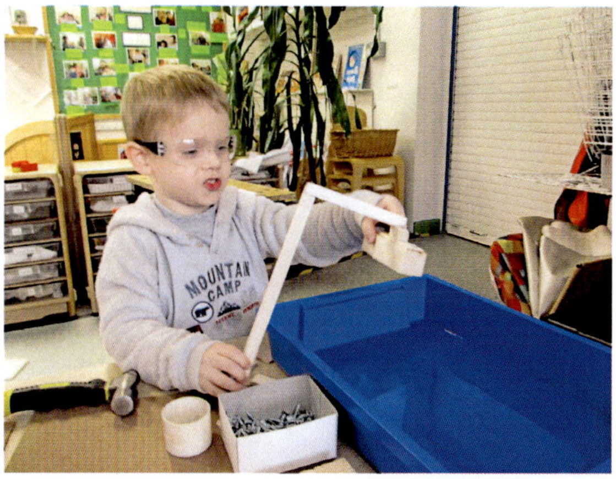
MOUNTAIN
CAMP
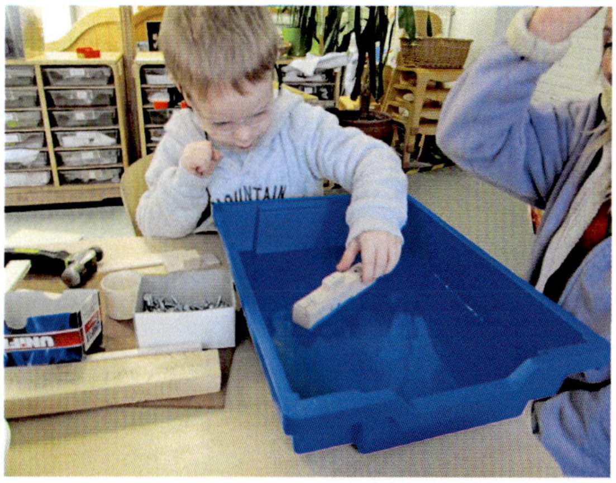
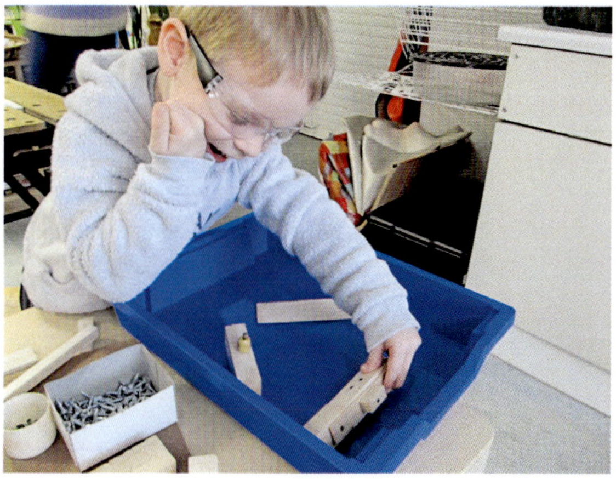
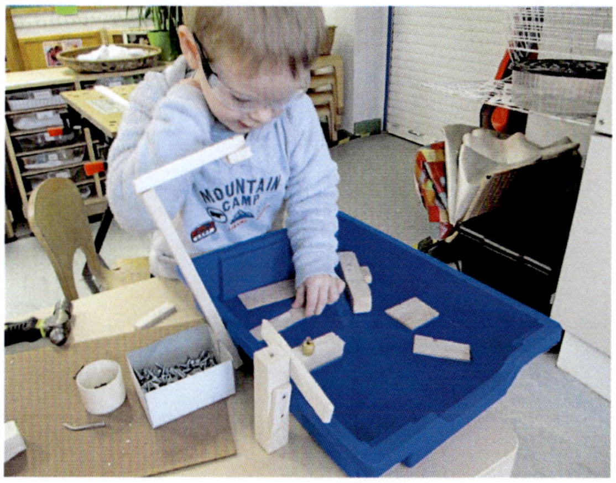

Learning and development

Case study 3.1 Max and the *Titanic*

On p.55 is a pictorial example of work that contains a strong narrative. Max had been fascinated by the *Titanic* for some time. As soon as it was his turn in the woodwork area he started to make the ship – adding a propeller, an engine room and a cabin for the captain. He then decided he needed to make a crane to lift the *Titanic* into the ocean. All the while he had to make choices and problem-solve how best to join the various elements. We then filled up a tray of water and the *Titanic* was launched. Max experimented with making waves and then re-enacted the *Titanic* capsizing. He also experimented to see if he could make wood sink. Max then decided he needed to quickly make some life boats – these were duly made and then sent to the rescue. Max thought that the lifeboats may run out of petrol – so then started making a wind-powered petrol station to enable the life boats to refuel. The entire time Max was transfixed, being deeply engaged in the flow of his creating. Eventually, he was satisfied with his play and dismantled all the models completely and moved on to play outdoors.

Design and construction

Design and practical skills are combined in the woodwork process. Design involves defining the task, making a plan of action, deciding how to proceed, and refining and responding accordingly as the work evolves. The practical skills or craft transform the designs into things. These processes go back and forth as work is often fluid and evolving as children adapt, refine and change it as it progresses. Older children may also wish to draw some initial designs to help articulate their ideas.

The processes involved in woodwork develop children's knowledge of construction. In woodwork they will inevitably join and construct in a variety of different ways. They discover that wood sections with flat edges are easier to connect than angled pieces. They discover how to make joins strong and robust, or work out how to make their model stand up on its own. As they construct, children are designers, architects, builders and sculptors.

Set tasks

It is important not to set projects whereby all the children create the same object. They should not make from pre-cut kits (such as birdhouse kits) or make models simply by copying an example model. The secret to children remaining really engaged in woodwork is that they are following their own interests and solving their own problems to create their work. When children are set specific projects, such as making bird boxes or key holders, many will lose interest and others will be frustrated by having to follow narrow instructions as these projects do not allow them to work at their own ability level. Set projects inevitably have more emphasis on the product than on the process. All exploration becomes more meaningful when it has been initiated and is led by the children.

Open-ended enquiry

Woodwork provides a wonderful way to support open-ended learning and self-initiated enquiry – essentially play! Have a wide range of resources available to allow plenty of possibilities and options for tinkering. Provide a mixture of additional materials to combine with wood, such as bits of fabric, buttons and beads, string, and so forth. It is a delight to see the resulting pieces of work all being so individual and unique. Children can further develop their models by painting or by gluing on other elements.

Throughout the process children will be using their imagination as they search for the most suitable shapes and combinations in a box of offcuts to express their ideas, seeing possibilities in an odd offcut, for example, 'This could make a good trunk for my elephant!'

Other expressive explorations may emerge, for example, as children stamp patterns on wood, print with blocks wrapped in string, mix sawdust with paint to create a textural paint, or create artwork with shavings.

Collaborative work

Children may also wish to work together or in groups to work on a particular project. Cooperation is needed as children discuss ideas, and resolve problems together and refine their design. These ideas can evolve from previous learning, chance events, current interests or a problem posed by children. Collaborative work can also be planned and initiated by teachers but in a very flexible and inclusive way, allowing children to have as much control as possible of the process. We can always tell if this type of project is working by observing the levels of engagement and whether children are absorbed. The adult role can be very much about providing the necessary resources, posing questions to open up thinking, sharing knowledge and skills and partnering the children in exploring their imagination and creative forms.

Aesthetics

I believe aesthetics are very important and often overlooked. Many early educational pioneers (Froebel, Montessori) talked at length about the importance of beauty, and Dewey talked about the need to endow ordinary experience with the aesthetic, but in recent years beauty seems to be given less value as an aspect of educational experience.

Working with wood has the potential to develop children's sense of aesthetics. Working with a natural material encourages a rich sensibility. The feel and smell of wood, the textures, the grain, the bark, the rich colour palate, the warmth, the way it can be altered, creating dust when sanded, changing shape when filed or sawn: all of these things contribute to the development of children's aesthetic awareness.

Aesthetics have the potential to be transformational: beauty can elevate the soul and lift the spirits and impact on our well-being. Working with natural wood and creating objects will emotionally, aesthetically, and intellectually nurture young children as they strive to make sense of the world in which they live. Appreciation of wood will enhance respect for nature and also for human creations.

There are some who advocate that children should only work with natural wood, avoiding other materials. This can have value, but at the expense of the rich creative possibilities of mixed media work.

We must consider that visual language is actually children's first language and they are powerful visual thinkers, constantly absorbing and interpreting the visual world around them. Children exhibit an extraordinary sense of aesthetics in the way that they construct and think about three-dimensional form. I have often been taken aback by the way children use their spatial awareness in constructing small sculptures.

> Having eyes, but not seeing beauty; having ears, but not hearing music; having minds, but not perceiving truth; having hearts that are never moved and therefore never set on fire. These are the things to fear, said the headmaster.
>
> (Kuroyanagi 1996: 80)

Craft sense

Woodwork is a wonderful medium for developing 'craft sense'. Craft sense is a term sometimes referred to by Sloyd educators – it really embraces craft, design and technology as well as children's reflective understandings of the processes involved. Craft sense is about *making* and then evaluating the production process. Envisioning is central to the process; what might happen? How would it have been if we had tried a different approach? Children set their own goals, explore ideas about how to realise these, then plan, experiment, implement and evaluate. Through reflection, children add new knowledge to their cognitive schemata. The heart of developing craft sense is to tune into this process and make time for evaluation of all processes involved. A camera can be a useful tool to support this analysis. Visualisation of the learning processes embeds learning. Reflecting back on the images later can stimulate dialogue and children can order the images according to the process they followed. Deep-level focus and involvement, metacognition and self-regulation are integral to developing craft sense. Another important aspect is *transfer*, in which children use previous knowledge gained for planning new projects, then once again monitor and adjust actions in responce to the new challenges arising from the new project. Attention is also directed towards children expressing what they need to learn to accomplish a certain project, which again develops their skills of metacognition.

Literacy

There are many books available that enable children to read and listen to stories about wood. There are books about the uses of wood, carpentry and different people that work with wood, types of trees and forestry. There are also a number of songs that can relate to woodworking. In the resources section there are some examples of books and songs.

Literacy is about understanding and expressing thoughts through the written word. In woodwork children express ideas in a concrete physical way. This is part of the mental foundation they build that leads towards expressing ideas in the more abstract medium of writing.

Children could make their own books about what they have made, including photographs, labelled drawings and writing. Older children may wish to extend narratives incorporated with their model with creative writing. Young children can use their emerging mark-making skills to express design ideas and develop plans. There are also opportunities for mark-making on the models as an additional element.

The fine motor manipulative skills acquired through woodworking will also help develop children's fine motor control needed for handwriting. The finger, wrist and arm control gained all contribute to children's emerging mark-making and subsequent writing skills.

Learning and development

Skills for life: beyond the curriculum

Woodwork leaves a deep memory. Once children have learnt to use tools they become part of their vocabulary. Many children do not experience using tools at all throughout their entire education. With many primary and secondary schools not providing woodwork, the early years could be their only opportunity. Working with tools develops skills for life, whether for fixing a bike, home DIY or just the sheer joy of making.

Many children will need to use tools in their future jobs and many professions require work with tools to develop ideas. Many children will go on to work in vocational trades and there are an infinite number of other jobs that require the use of tools.

We are living in rapidly changing times, more so than in any previous time in history, with global economic shifts, technological innovations, natural resource depletion, significant population growth and environmental change. Many jobs that early years children will be doing in the future do not currently exist. Being adaptable, innovative and able to think creatively about new solutions will be more important than ever. Woodwork is an activity that strongly enhances these skills by developing creative thinking and problem-solving skills.

Sustainability

Woodwork builds children's ability to design and make. It develops the ability to repair. Both of these attributes are important tools to counteract characteristics of our consumer society, through making and repairing rather than consuming and disposing.

By just passively consuming, children are removed from design. Through making and deconstruction, children discover how things are made, see the elements of design and develop a sensitivity to material, its functional possibilities and the designed elements of an object.

There are also many opportunities for children to gain environmental understanding and learn to respect the natural world. Early years children are developing their fundamental attitudes and values, so any opportunity to embed thinking around sustainability should be embraced.

Understanding where wood comes from is another important aspect: seeing the beauty of wood and how long trees take to grow can help children respect and understand the value of wood as a material and the need for us to take responsibility for our shared environment.

The majority of wood used will be recycled, using offcuts. It is great to be able to utilise waste materials. If buying wood, try to source it from responsibly managed forestation. Balsa wood is more problematic: it is a fast-growing tree, harvested and replanted, but being equatorial it does have a large carbon footprint. Use it sparingly for the initial stages, then move straight on to more sustainable soft wood.

Education for Sustainable Development (ESD), in which teachers develop an understanding of environmental and sustainability issues, also acknowledges that woodwork develops many of the skills that are important to sustainability: these include critical thinking and reflection, systemic thinking, looking for connections and solutions to problems, promoting dialogue and negotiation and decision-making when working on group projects, and envisioning – imagining the future. Woodwork can also be seen to support Eco-schools' sustainability agenda.

> Young children appreciate the beauty of nature and the world surrounding them through engaging in Woodwork. I do believe Woodwork is the bridge between children and the world. Woodwork is the heart of Education for Sustainable Development and it invites children and adults to engage in dialogue for the future.
>
> Dr Mari Mori, Professor at Tsurukawa College, Tokyo, Japan

Learning and development

Observation and assessment

Observing and monitoring progress

Woodwork provides us with many opportunities to observe and monitor progress – across all areas of learning.

Woodwork particularly gives insight into children's creative and critical thinking and their underlying learning dispositions. It is a great opportunity to really get to observe some of these more complex areas of learning and development. In the Resources section there is a link to a useful document: 'Monitoring Progression in Creative and Critical Thinking'.[2] It allows us to really tune in to the thinking elements involved and to ensure that progression is taking place.

Monitoring progression is important – we need to know children are making progress from their starting points. We need to ensure disadvantaged children are catching up. We need to know who to focus attention on and what elements of learning need developing.

Observing development and learning through woodwork will also highlight to others the learning associated and raise awareness of the rich potential of woodwork. In this context quality documentation and individual learning stories will help to raise woodwork's profile.

Schema

Woodwork also provides an opportunity to become more aware of children's schemas – behaviour where children repeat certain actions. Children often repeat actions to practice and embed what they know, building neurological connections in the process, and this is an important aspect in children's development. Early schemas such as banging, rotation, positioning, orientation, connection and disconnection are all very much visible and further developed through tool use and working with wood.

Learning and development

Skills checklist

On a more practical note there is also value in assessing the basic skills of tool use – by having a checklist to mark off who has learnt what, so that we know who is ready to work more independently. This is particularly useful when children start at different times during the year. Keep this quite simple, focusing on the four basic tools: hammer, screwdriver, saw and hand drill. Some schools have a passport or certificate system showing that the children have these skills and are ready to work independently. Personally, I prefer to stick to a subtle checklist to avoid external motivation in terms of reward.

Case study 3.2 is included to demonstrate just how cross-curricular woodwork can be, and the benefits for children's learning and development in all areas.

Case study 3.2 Sustained concentration and engagement

We access woodwork as part of the setting's core provision. We have a workbench with an integrated vice and storage for tools, wood and resources that we share with the three other nursery rooms. The workbench is usually outside with a table to the side of it, on which we lay out the wood and other resources like beads and corks. However, some children prefer to work indoors so we move it between locations. There is always an adult at the woodworking area who is on hand to offer support and talk through things with the children.

When I first introduced the children to the concept of woodwork, I talked to them as a class, taking them through the safety aspects and showing them the tools. We then tried out the tools in small groups of three and now children are free to access woodwork as and when they choose.

It has been a huge success. Children now work largely independently, always with an adult on hand to talk through their ideas and problem-solve. One child, who spent a lot of time playing alone, has really come out of himself as a result of the woodwork. His language skills have developed and he's much more confident to try new things.

This week, he spent the morning working on a creation. He picked up two pieces of balsa wood, examined them and said they were going to be the legs. He then put them in the vice and chose another thin piece of wood. He said, 'I'm going to make a dragon'. I watched him try to connect the piece of wood to the legs with a nail. It wasn't working, so I asked him to look at the depth of the wood and the size of the nail. He realised he needed a bigger nail and when it worked he was really proud of himself.

He then chose some small pieces of wood for wings and tried to screw them in with a screwdriver but it didn't work. So we worked out another plan to fasten the wings. When he finished it and put eyes on, he decided he didn't want to keep it so he took it apart and put all the pieces back into their places and moved on to make a dinosaur using all his accumulated knowledge and skills.

This extended level of concentration is not unique to this child. All children, of both genders, participate in woodwork with the same levels of concentration. Their levels of critical thinking and ability to manage their own risks have increased tenfold due to working with wood, and it's built up their fine and gross motor control.

Liberty Fletcher-Gardiner, class teacher at St Werburgh's Park Nursery School, Bristol

My wood split so I had to fix it with a bigger bit and I used even bigger nails, but it still broke so I made a hole in the wood first and then it worked.

Sara, age 4

Notes

1 The pupil premium is additional funding for publicly funded schools in England to raise the attainment of disadvantaged pupils of all abilities and to close the gaps between them and their peers. Department of Education. www.gov.uk/guidance/pupil-premium-information-for-schools-and-alternative-provision-settings (accessed on 13 July 2017).
2 'Monitoring Progression in Creative and Critical Thinking' form, available from http://irresistible-learning.co.uk/resources (accessed on 13 July 2017).

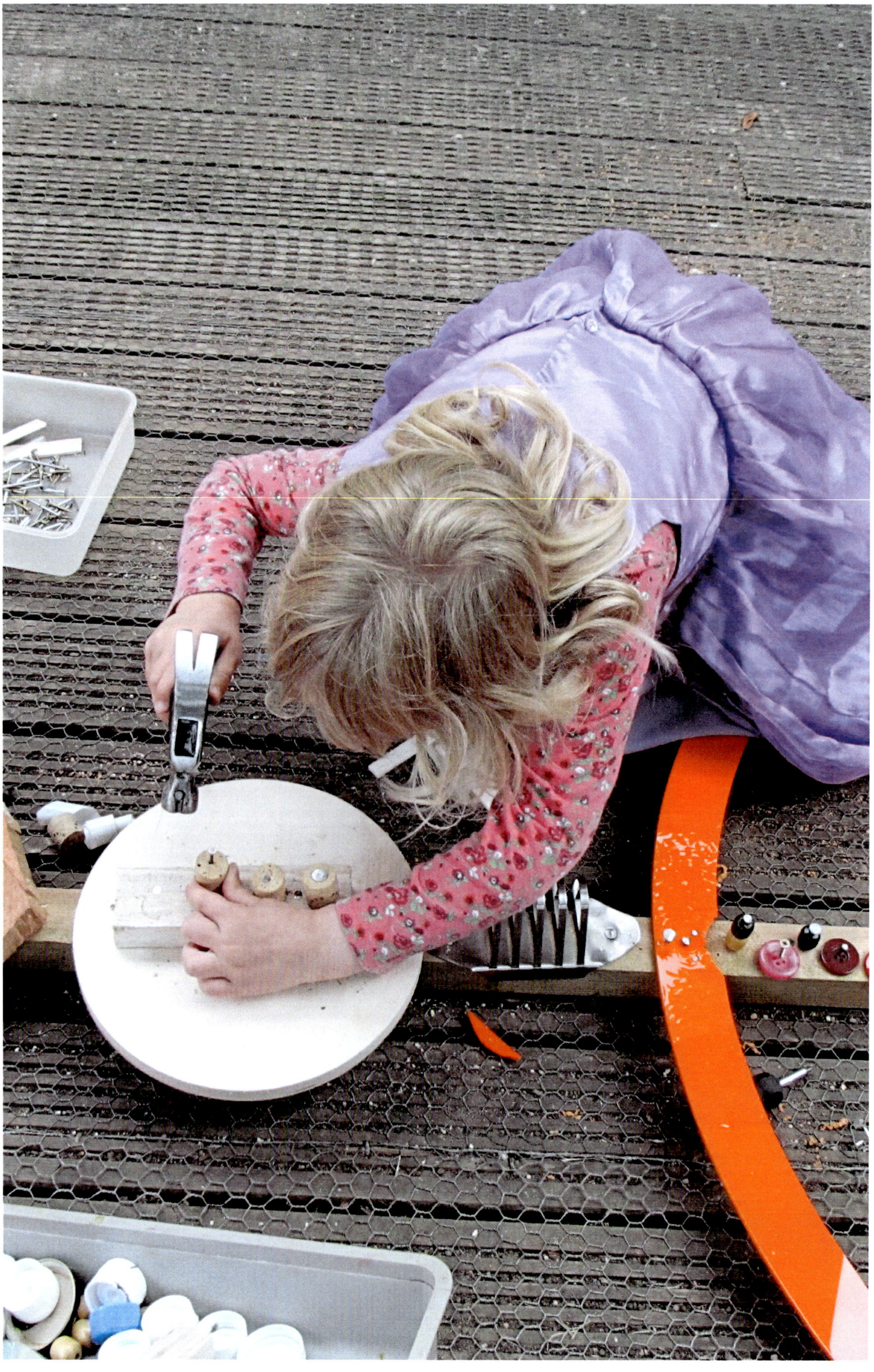

CHAPTER 4

Equal opportunities

> Having the opportunity to explore wood through bespoke and focused woodwork sessions has enabled young children, aged 3 to 5 years, to create the unimaginable by following their interests. I continue to be amazed at the confidence of young children using real tools and creating unique structures that enhances their communication and language, their physical skills and personal and social development. Every child should have the opportunity to work and explore with wood.
>
> Dr Lesley Curtis OBE, head teacher, Everton Nursery School and Family Centre, Liverpool

Chapter overview

In this chapter I look at the importance of inclusion and providing equal opportunities for all children. I explore best practice to ensure we are proactive in tackling disadvantage and challenging stereotypes. I explain how woodwork can be a powerful medium with which to deeply engage all children.

Disadvantaged children: diminishing differences – closing the gap ▸ 68
Gender ▸ 69
Special educational needs and disabilities (SEND) ▸ 70
English as an additional language (EAL) ▸ 72
Left-handed children ▸ 72

Equal opportunities

I believe it is fundamentally important that all children in a setting have access to learn and benefit from the basic skills of woodwork. After being introduced to the basic skills, children should be able to choose for themselves whether they want to pursue this interest. Ensure that initially the basic woodworking skills are introduced to all children so they can then make an informed decision if they wish to pursue this interest.

Disadvantaged children: diminishing differences – closing the gap

Many children entering early childhood education will already be significantly disadvantaged by family circumstance. This could be for a number of reasons such as poverty, debt, mental or other health issues, housing issues, abuse, neglect or being in care. The effect is often that children have fewer positive first-hand experiences, fewer interactions and lower levels of language as well as having poorer diet and less exercise. These children can often have poor communication skills, lower levels of concentration, and lower self-esteem and self-confidence. This will in turn affect their core dispositions for learning, especially their levels of curiosity, resilience and empathy. We need to know children's starting points and do our utmost to redress disadvantage. I believe it is crucial to be aware of children's initial learning dispositions and their levels of creative and critical thinking when they first arrive in the setting. In the Resources and Suppliers section there is a link to a monitoring sheet that is designed to track development to ensure that children are making progress *and catching up*.

In this context, woodwork can provide a wonderful medium for capturing children's curiosity. But it goes way beyond that. Disadvantaged children need more attention, more conversation, more modelling of creative and critical thinking skills. Woodwork can help so much to develop emerging thinking skills and rekindle positive learning dispositions.

Equal opportunities

Gender

Young children will already have been subjected to a vast amount of social conditioning, absorbing beliefs and expectations from roles portrayed in stories, television and advertising, and observed in family and friends. This has had the effect of stereotyping woodwork as a male activity for many young children.

There is absolutely no gender difference in terms of children's desire to do woodwork once they have gained the initial skills. Both boys and girls take enormous delight in the joy of woodwork and both genders are equally competent. In fact, it is very hard to predict which individuals will particularly thrive. Teachers are often surprised by who responds particularly positively to the experience of woodwork – it seems to bring out thinking and learning not often visible in the classroom. It is not unusual for a 3-year-old girl who is perhaps not particularly outgoing or physical to actually flourish working with tools, showing great delight and competency in her work.

It is important to ensure all children get introductory sessions to woodwork where they learn how to use the basic tools. Then they are able to decide based on experience if they would like to continue and extend this area of work. If we initially just asked who would like to try woodwork it is quite likely that the boys could take over the woodworking area, making it harder for girls to join in. In addition, children who may be apprehensive about starting to use tools also get the encouragement they need to build their confidence and overcome any fears. It is also worth considering having male and female teachers facilitate woodwork sessions to avoid further stereotyping and provide positive role modelling. It could also be an idea to have some images on the wall of male and female construction workers and carpenters.

Equal opportunities

In recent years much has been written about the need to engage boys in meaningful activity. Woodwork certainly captivates boys, who become deeply engaged and focused at the woodwork table for long periods of time. However, this should absolutely not be at the expense of girls getting the opportunity to do woodwork.

Special educational needs and disabilities (SEND)

Children with additional needs and disabilities should also be given the opportunity of woodwork but they may need extra support. This obviously depends on the needs of the individual child but with careful planning and enough staff support children can participate and gain enormously from the experiences that woodwork has to offer. Seeing the delight and satisfaction of a severely visually impaired girl hammering a nail into a block of wood, or seeing a child with dyspraxia persist in carefully holding a nail upright, certainly only go to emphasise the importance of making opportunities available to all children. Staff have commented that certain children have found working with wood very therapeutic and relaxing, sometimes repeating simple tasks such as hammering or sanding for considerable time.

We need to ensure woodwork is made as inclusive as possible. It is important to discover what adaptations or additions are necessary to provide suitable challenges and experiences, and to allow as much equal access as is reasonably possible. The wide range of movement within woodwork helps children with their ability to sense position and their awareness of motion (proprioception and kinaesthesia). Responding to the needs of children with special educational needs means we need to be continuously re-evaluating what is working and what improvements and refinements can be made to ensure successful inclusivity and to provide targeted development opportunities.

Some children find great difficulty in concentrating for any length of time in many areas of their learning for a number of different reasons, such as attention deficit hyperactivity disorder (ADHD). Teachers are often surprised by how woodwork has really engaged these children, drawing in their curiosity, with children showing focused attention for impressive stretches of time. For some, woodwork has proved to be the key that unlocks their excitement about learning. These children seem particularly drawn to working with tools and to three-dimensional constructing.

Case study 4.1 Engaging and capturing interest

Callum joined the school in the spring term of reception year. We were told that he had never completed a whole day at school because of behavioural issues. He also had a thick file with numerous reports concluding that he had ADHD. As he walked into the class, he noticed that the door to the outside area was open and he ran out. He looked back to see who was going to come and drag him back but this did not happen. The children in this school had the choice to learn indoors or outside – Callum had made his choice. Once outside he immediately noticed the woodwork benches and wandered over. An adult came alongside him, explained the very simple rules and carefully introduced the tools to Callum who quickly got the hang of them. Callum was then silent and still as he watched the children working.

Again, the adult prompted him, saying, 'There is a space on this bench if you would like a turn.' Within a week, he could use all the tools with ease and was beginning to plan what he was going to make. Each day his mum rang the office to check whether she needed to pick him up and each day she was shocked to hear that he was showing great concentration and was following the agreed rules. Callum was never sent home for the remainder of that year. The woodwork proved that he did not in fact have ADHD. In his previous schools, the problem was that he was being asked to do things that were developmentally inappropriate and that did not interest him. Once he found the woodwork, he found a way to satisfy his innate desire to learn – being active, challenging and real.

Anna Ephgrave, early years consultant, former assistant head teacher, Cartherhatch Infant School

Case study 4.2 The challenge of woodwork for everyone

Suggesting that you want to spend your class budget on a fully stocked woodworking bench may not be the most radical but in the special needs unit where I was it was certainly a first! Attitudes of other adults varied from astonishment to sceptical support. The head teacher took the risk and sanctioned the spending.

The group of ten children in the class were cautious and wary of the new equipment. The children were all around 4–5 years old. The three girls and seven boys had a range of special educational needs, some with diagnosis, others still being assessed. Their needs included ADHD, ASD, Asperger's, epilepsy, learning difficulties, language delay, and Fragile X.

Initially, they explored the empty bench and then went on to working with balsa wood and glue. As their interest in the wood grew they began exploring using the glue to join different sized pieces together. As their confidence also grew, individuals became frustrated when they couldn't make the pieces the size they wanted. We talked together about what tool might be helpful and went on to use a saw to cut wood.

(continued)

(continued)

So there we were, all eager and excited about sawing balsa wood! There was one important rule, if you want to use the saw you have to be alongside the adult. Each child had support to develop the skills of putting the balsa wood into the vice and cutting it to the size they wanted with the saw.

For many weeks the children were thrilled to cut the balsa wood and make boats to sail in the water tray, planes to add to the airport, cars to race, pretty things, useful things, weird things and loads of fun things! Then Josh got in a grump, 'This is not real woodwork! We should have hammers and nails'. Other children agreed and we then introduced hammers and nails. Again each child had support to practise holding the panel pins and correctly hammering them into the balsa wood. One child initiated the chant 'tap tap, tap tap, hammer hammer' to link with the first little taps to make the pin steady in the wood and the bigger tap to really knock it in.

The creations got bigger and more complex and soon the need for measuring became crucial to the success of some of the models. Parents also began to show an interest and spend time with their child at the woodwork bench anytime they visited the setting.

The benefits for the children, in my opinion, were much greater than the skills of using tools and joining bits of wood. There was a real sense from the children and parents that they were being trusted and were able to deal with risk/danger in a mature way. They also began to notice wood in their environment, whether in the setting, at home or during outings. This led us to find out about where wood comes from. We progressed to trying to hammer panel pins into samples of different woods but the children's decision was that they wanted to stick with using balsa wood for their modelling making for the time being. With the correct support, woodwork can certainly be a very rewarding experience for children with complex needs.

Kay Mathieson, early years consultant

English as an additional language (EAL)

Children with English as an additional language usually have no difficulty understanding the processes involved in woodwork as the introduction of tools and their safe use can all be clearly visually demonstrated. You can often see them visibly relax as they realise they will not be dependent on understanding English. It may be useful to visually explain certain processes on a one-to-one basis to ensure understanding and correct safe use of tools. It is important to continue to use dialogue throughout to ensure children are hearing and building their language knowledge. The earlier they learn to communicate in English the better for enabling deeper conversations about their work, but in the interim period it's surprising just how much sustained shared thinking can be achieved non-verbally.

Left-handed children

Because the majority of people are right-handed, most everyday items have been mass-produced with right-handers in mind, but we need to bear in mind that approximately 10 per cent of the population are left-handed. Left-handed children will find it more difficult to work with right-handed tools. They can feel awkward or uncomfortable to use.

To take a common example, right-handed scissors are designed so that a right-handed user can easily see the line being cut along, whereas a left-handed user may not be able to see as well. A right-handed action with such scissors tends to force the blades together, producing a more effective and cleaner cut, whereas a left-hander's cutting action may force the blades apart, reducing the effectiveness and often resulting in ragged or creased cut. The moulding of the handles may also be less comfortable for a left-hander than a right-hander. A right-hander can easily see how this feels by using regular scissors with the left hand.

Fortunately, the basic woodworking tools can be used by both left- and right-handers. There is a difference with some tools in their ergonomics – for example, with the screwdriver when we screw the thread is such that we use the most powerful rotational movement of the wrist as we tighten the screw, but this is the opposite rotational twist for a left-hander.

This is the same with the drill: manageable but not quite as ergonomic, as it is less easy to generate strength. The handle will be on the wrong side, requiring that the drill is turned around, which in turn means that the moulding is not comfortable. Left-handed screwdrivers and drills are not available.

The location of a vice on a workbench can be set up to be more suitable to a dominant hand when sawing, allowing the free hand the potential to hold the bench. It is a good idea to have a workbench with two vices making it suitable for both right- and left-handers. For right-handers a vice is best located to the right side of the workbench and vice versa for left-handers. The posture when sawing is also different with the reversed position of feet.

Many objects are subtly more difficult to use for left-handers – another example is the retracting tape measure, which is designed to be held in the left hand and pulled out with the right so that way the numbers are the correct way up. The mouldings on some saw handles and the shapes of many wrenches, spanners and pliers are also designed with right-handers in mind.

So it is worth being aware that some tools will be more awkward for left-handed children. It is worth remembering that in the early years children can still be working out which is their dominant hand and will often switch freely between hands as they are still discovering which works most effectively for them. If we notice a child struggling with a particular task it may be worth suggesting that they try their other hand. There are no specific left-handed woodwork tools available.

> I made an aeroplane with a window and a blaster. It was difficult to join the blaster – I had to use this bit of wood here to fix it to both sides. I'm going to paint it now with fire coming out of the blaster.
>
> Freddie, age 4

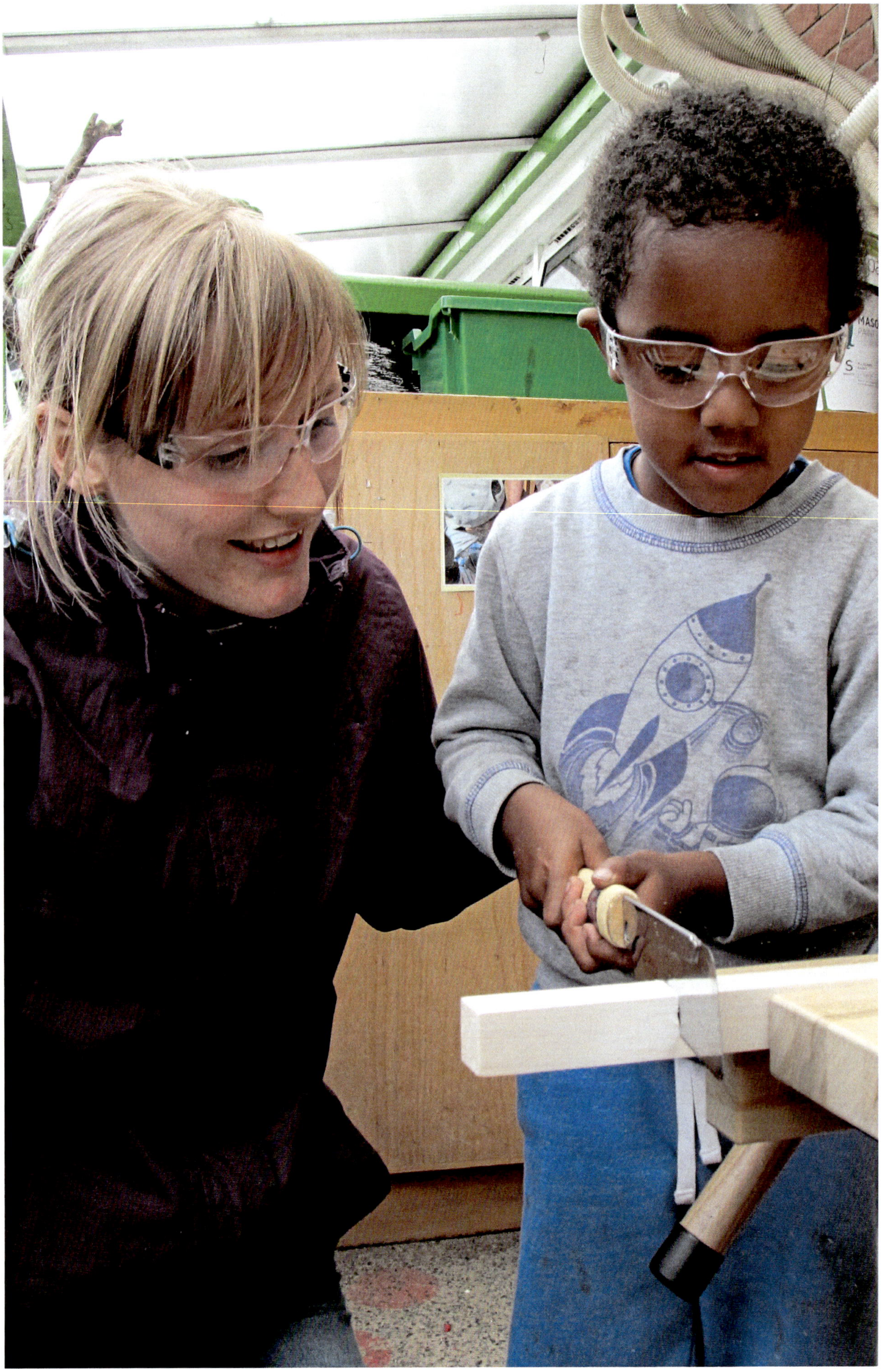

CHAPTER 5

Adult support

Deep engagement or involvement indicates brain activity and progress. This is seen continuously at the woodwork bench. Children are developing perseverance, confidence and problem-solving, driven by their innate desire to master their woodwork skills. Woodwork is one activity that will develop children in a holistic, challenging and exciting way.

Anna Ephgrave, early years consultant

Chapter overview

In this chapter I look at the role of the teacher in supporting woodwork. I look at how the woodwork area is best managed and discuss provision, looking at woodwork 'sessions' and woodwork as continuous provision – where it is always available. I talk about the importance of really getting involved in children's thinking processes, by encouraging their creative and critical thinking skills. In addition, I also look at the benefits of involving parents and carers.

Staffing of activity 'sessions' and continuous provision ▸ 76

Adult role in supporting learning ▸ 78

Involving parents and carers ▸ 83

Adult support

Source: © Community Playthings

Staffing of activity 'sessions' and continuous provision

Introducing children to tools

Children are initially introduced to woodwork in small groups. I recommend a ratio of 1 adult to 3 children for all tools.

The ratio of 1 to 3 is maintained until the children are confident with using tools. After that you will be able to relax the ratios as you feel more assured of their competency. Clearly there is a difference in ability between children who are three and five, and younger children will need higher ratios maintained for longer. The exception is the saw, which is always monitored on a one-to-one basis (see section on the saw, p. 126). You will also need to decide how the children will access the woodworking area once the children have successfully learnt to use the basic tools independently. Will it be available for certain session times or will it be available all the time as part of continuous provision?

Adult supported woodworking sessions:

> The majority of settings choose to provide woodwork for time-limited periods to ensure they can have a teacher supporting the activity and also because of the high demand on resources. Settings feel more comfortable having a teacher closely monitoring the woodworking area at all times so that they can ensure safety, provide a greater range of tools, and are readily available when needed for practical assistance and to extend thinking.

Adult support

Woodwork session with adult in proximity:

> It is also an option to monitor these sessions with a teacher in proximity. This way the teacher can be available when needed and can also keep an eye out. This usually works better in the indoor classroom environment where the woodwork area can be seen easily at all times. When the woodwork area is outdoors and more children can access the area it is often best being monitored more closely.

Continuous provision:

> Woodwork can also be set up as part of continuous provision whereby it is always available. There will need to be limits to the number of children working in the woodwork area and a limit of two to three children at a time working at a workbench (depending on the size), but because woodwork is available all the time it is less likely that there will be a rush for the bench and crowding. Continuous provision of woodwork can only work after all the children have had clear instruction on how to use the tools and have demonstrated competency. With children joining the setting throughout the year this has to be monitored carefully to ensure children have had their introductory sessions.

In an ideal world the most effective way to implement woodwork would be as part of continuous provision, just as we do for other resources such as painting and block play, but the understandable practicalities make it difficult to achieve for many settings. With continuous provision children do benefit from extended time to develop and build skills. It also allows movement between different areas to facilitate making connections with different areas of learning. This arrangement requires that the area is in an easily visible location and set up with tools and consumables that are easily accessible in containers and boxes. It can be quite demanding on supplies and consumables, which will regularly need replenishing.

While continuous provision of woodwork is not directly monitored, it is still important a teacher is in the vicinity to keep an eye on the area. Children will still need to ask for adult supervision to use the saw and the adult also needs to check that the vice is fully tight before sawing commences. With continuous provision it is important that teachers do still interact when appropriate, showing genuine interest, offering encouragement and extending thinking.

Some children enjoy the freedom to work more independently whereas other children will need more support, without which they could become frustrated and lose interest. It takes great sensitivity on the part of the teacher to gauge when it is appropriate to offer support and guidance. Striking this balance is something that is developed over time and we have all intervened too soon at some stage.

In my experience, settings that provide the continuous provision of woodwork do so by limiting tools and resources available, and it often is mainly hammering into sections of wood. Clearly, if this is the case there needs to be additional sessions when woodwork can be explored in more depth.

Which set-up works best for you very much depends on your particular setting, the space and work surfaces available, and the age and ability of the children. Younger children (3) will need to be closely monitored at all times whereas older children (5) will be able to carry out many of the tasks more independently.

Some settings opt for a combination by providing a limited amount of resources for continuous provision and then offering a wider variety of tools and materials for more focused woodwork 'sessions'. Either way, it is important to decide on the number of children you feel comfortable working with within the available space to ensure it is not overcrowded and to ensure you can provide each child with the attention they may require. In all situations inappropriate behaviour cannot be tolerated and children will have to leave the area if they are not working safely.

Taking turns

Woodworking is very popular and I find we often need to have a rota. However, I do not limit the time children have available to work in the area, feeling that giving children limited time slots would curtail their creative expression and progression. To be told after 30 minutes that it is time to stop can be incredibly frustrating for young children. One setting I visited in Japan had each child make a small wooden rectangle, which they painted on one side, with their name on the other. They then drilled a hole in the rectangle and the finished articles were all hung up on hooks on a board. When the children had finished their turn at woodwork they turned their rectangle over to the painted side and in that way it was easy for everyone to keep a check on who had had their turn.

Staff confidence and competency

Staff have to feel comfortable working with tools themselves. It is unfair to expect staff to teach basic skills or extend children's learning when they themselves have little experience and have had no training to support woodwork provision. We don't need to be proficient DIYers or carpenters, we just need to know how to use the basic tools safely and to be aware of some simple techniques. All staff should have basic woodwork training so that they feel confident working with all the tools and also really understand the value of woodwork. For more information on staff training, see Chapter 8.

Apart from this basic knowledge, it is really about applying teaching techniques that are applicable right across the curriculum. Some schools have opted to use their caretaker to deliver woodworking sessions – however, I believe the skill set of trained educational practitioners is very important to support children's learning effectively.

> I tried different ways to join the top . . . in the end I used a drill and a really long screw.
>
> (Mica, age 4)

Adult role in supporting learning

There are many aspects to our role both pedagogically and practically in ensuring that woodwork is successful and safe.

High expectations

The teacher's expectations of children affects both the quality of provision and the outcomes. We need to believe in the high capability and potential of children to construct their own learning. Children are naturally curious and imaginative and have an innate desire to learn. We need to capture this enthusiasm by allowing them to be at the centre of their learning, to follow their interests and to make decisions.

We need to respect and recognise each child as an individual and use careful observation to support their effective development and extend their thinking. We need to allow children to grow at their own pace and provide challenges appropriate to each child's stage of development.

Understanding the value

Valuing the importance and uniqueness of woodwork and understanding the rich educational learning involved spanning all areas of curriculum will enhance the experience for the child. A greater understanding of the pedagogy underpinning woodwork will contribute to the teacher's commitment and enthusiasm.

Pedagogy

Teaching is: 'not only of how much he shall demand from the children, but of how much he shall tell them, and how much he shall not tell them. The best teacher is the one that teaches least' (*Sloyd* Educator, Otto Salomon 1891: 14).

Woodwork provides rich experiential learning – learning by doing. Progressive education, championed by Dewey, advocated this type of learning, as opposed to the prevailing model at the time that children were buckets that needed to be filled up with information. Progressive education valued self-directed learning, children making their own choices and decisions, and children finding their own solutions to problems and reflecting on their learning, all of which are integral to creative woodwork. Woodwork is a great medium for giving children opportunities to think – and we must allow them the space in which to do this. As Piaget once wrote, *'Each time one prematurely teaches a child something he could have discovered himself, that child is kept from inventing it and consequently from understanding it completely'* (Piaget 1970: 715). Our role as educator is to provide the conditions in which the child can flourish and to show great sensitivity as to how we interact. Below, I talk in more detail about interaction. We also need to be flexible and tolerant. Woodwork can be messy and noisy and we constantly need to respond to children's plans and time frames to allow them to work at their own pace and give time to develop and finish work. We also need to be flexible in our pedagogical roles, at times admitting we do not have the answer, at times working alongside, scaffolding and modelling, sometimes being didactic (as we teach how to use a saw safely, for example) and at other times adding new information and context. It is a complex mixture and a balance is found over time.

Adult support

> If I can ask my own questions, try out my ideas, experience what's around me, share what I find;
>
> If I have plenty of time for my special pace, a nourishing space, things to transform;
>
> If you'll be my patient friend, trusted guide, fellow investigator, partner in learning;
>
> Then I will explore the world, discover my voice and tell you what I know in a hundred languages.
>
> (Houk, Gandini and Malaguzzi 1998: 293)

Practicalities: resourcing

Part of the adult role is to ensure the woodwork area is well stocked and ready for action. This is often easier said than done. Children can get through a lot of wood and supplementary materials as well as consumables such as nails and screws. We need to keep a good overview of what needs replenishing. It can be frustrating to find no nails left. It makes sense to have a dedicated member of staff to keep an overview of resources. It is likely that much of the wood you use will be donated by parents or sourced from offcuts. These will need checking over and preparing, possibly cutting into smaller sizes ready for the children to use (a battery-operated jigsaw can be very useful for doing this quickly). Tools will also require regular checking to ensure they are safe. (See health and safety section in Chapter 8.)

Health and safety

It is our responsibility to ensure health and safety measures are in place and are adhered to at all times. We also need to ensure a risk assessment has been completed. We need to monitor woodwork provision to ensure safety is maintained at all times and that tools remain in the woodworking area. Health and safety is explored in detail in Chapter 8.

Introducing tools

It is our role to introduce the tools to the children. We need to explain and demonstrate their appropriate and safe use. This will include how to look after them and carry them. This is explained in depth in Chapter 6.

Physical support

At times children will need some physical support. For example, an adult may need to provide an additional hand to steady wood whilst a nail is being removed or a hole being drilled. Sometimes, all that is needed is a little extra strength to help complete a task: getting the screw in that little bit further or ensuring the vice is tightly clamped. But for the majority of tasks it is incredible just how persistent and tenacious young children can be as they determinedly saw through a large log or drill a deep hole.

Interaction

It is a fundamental part of our role at times to be actively involved in children's learning through woodwork. There needs to be dialogue that helps to scaffold the learning and extend children's thinking.

We need to show genuine interest in their work through careful observation and talk. Children's engagement is often shortened and their thinking less complex without some adult interest and encouragement. It is important to respect their choices and decisions, but also provide open questions to expand their thinking. As children explore their ideas they

Adult support

will be presented with many problems: What can I use best to represent my idea? How could I join these two together? How can I get this nail out? Which wood section would be best for this?

When they are following their own ideas and making their own decisions, they will be looking for solutions to their own problems. We can work with them together in this process to help them develop their creative and critical thinking skills. This process of sustained shared thinking involves saying the right thing at the right time. It's about keeping the dialogue open by asking open questions to promote deep thinking and to extend and develop thinking. This encompasses different aspects such as encouraging them to think of alternative ideas, to speculate about what might happen, and to reflect on and evaluate their work, perhaps thinking about whether they could have done anything differently.

Throughout the process we need to ensure that children remain the protagonists in their own learning by allowing them to ask their own questions, pose possible solutions, find their voice and develop their confidence. We must be careful not to offer too much information and disempower the child by taking over and making decisions for them.

Sometimes, children can remain working within their comfort zone and on occasion our role can be to introduce new challenges, raise questions and encourage them to explore new skills and concepts.

When giving encouragement and praising children, try and be clear in what you are praising and focus on their processes as opposed to the product. Example: 'That's wonderful you persevered for so long to make sure the wheel stayed on,' or, 'I can tell you have thought really hard to come up with other ideas for joining the mast'.

Adult support

Documentation

It is important to keep in mind the rich learning and development associated with woodwork, discussed in Chapter 3. Create quality documentation to reflect the learning process, highlight the areas of learning covered, focusing especially on creative and critical thinking. Include children's dialogue and how they extended their thinking. Use this material for children's individual learning diaries as well as for documentation that is displayed in the environment. It is important for sustaining woodwork that the rich learning is made visible.

Case study 5.1 Interaction

Massimo: 'I need to put this steering wheel on, how can I fix it?'
Teacher: 'I'm not sure, what ideas have you had?' (Encouraging ideation)
Massimo: 'It looks like it's too thick and there is a hole in it.'
Teacher: 'I wonder what we could use to attach it?' (Exploring possibilities)
Massimo picks up small nail.
Teacher: 'Great, I wonder if it will be long enough?' (Encouraging reflection)
Massimo: 'No, I need a long one' (holding it beside the wheel) 'but it is slipping through the hole.'
Teacher: 'Are there any ways we can stop that?' (Exploring possibilities)
Massimo: 'Yes, I need a really big nail' (meaning with wide head).
Teacher: 'That's a great idea – that would definitely work, but unfortunately that's the biggest nail we have. I wonder if you could do anything else to help it stay on?' (Exploring possibilities)

Massimo:	'Maybe use a cork bit.'
Teacher:	'What do you think would happen if you did that?' (Encouraging speculation)
Massimo:	'It would stop it slipping off.'
Teacher:	'Okay, shall we try and see what happens?' . . .
Massimo:	(Hammers on the steering wheel after carefully positioning the work to be able to hammer effectively – problem-solving several times by trying different positions.) 'Look, it is turning!'
Teacher:	'That's interesting, I wonder why it turns?' (Exploring cause and effect)
Massimo:	'Because it's not too fixed!'
Teacher:	'That's really interesting, it is fixed but not too fixed, allowing it to move. That's great, you will be able to turn round bends now!'
Massimo:	'Not now . . . it's going to be a flying car . . . I need wings!'

Involving parents and carers

Woodwork has proved a wonderful way to engage and share learning with parents. It is good to have parents on board. Initially, some parents may be a little concerned to hear their young child may be working with real tools, so explaining about woodwork at a parents' evening or in a newsletter, highlighting the rich learning and explaining safety measures, can allay fears. An informed parent is easily reassured. It is great to have the support of parents, who may very often be able to contribute offcuts of wood to keep stocks replenished. It can also be helpful to have parent volunteers coming into the class to help in the woodwork area as a way of providing extra support and possibly allowing more children to work at once.

We have also organised days for fathers and mothers to come in and work alongside their children. These have been popular and incredibly successful. Fathers in particular felt more comfortable coming in, perhaps feeling they could be more 'useful' in this context and have welcomed this opportunity. When we first started this initiative I was taken aback by how much parents tried to direct the children's creations, making decisions for them and often doing the majority of the making too. It almost felt like it was a competition between parents!

We now use these parent sessions as a valuable opportunity to share pedagogy of how children learn best. At the beginning of the session we have a talk with parents about the importance of respecting the children's ideas and ability with tools and with the parent role as being supportive and nurturing. The feedback from parents has been that they have really appreciated being given the opportunity to think more about how we support children's learning

Adult support

and encourage creativity. They also comment on their delight in witnessing their children working so competently with the tools to express their ideas. The experience challenged their perceptions of what children are capable of. This type of project makes a positive contribution to building a strong school community.

There are many families that have also decided to make woodwork available at home with a few simple tools. The feedback has been wonderful, with woodwork providing an opportunity for parents and children to have quality time together, and children greatly enjoying tinkering with wood. Any opportunity to engage children in anything other than the screen must be grasped!

I can do it all! I can saw big bits of wood and use big nails.

Max, age 4

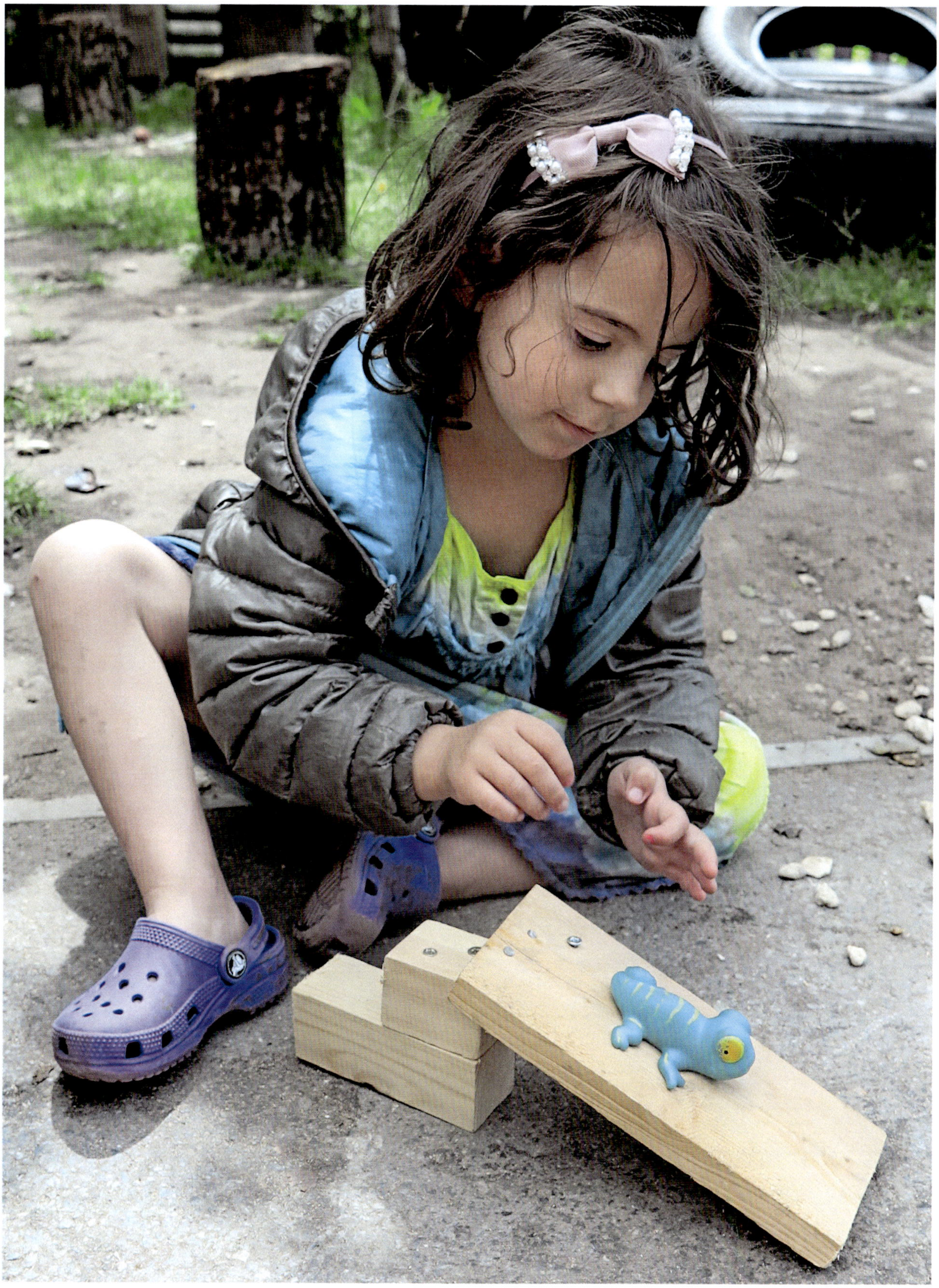

Source: © Community Playthings

CHAPTER 6

Getting started

Woodwork is a gradual process. Of children being taught woodwork skills and then being given the opportunities to practise and build on those skills.

Terry Gould, Ofsted inspector

Chapter overview

In this chapter we look at all the practicalities of what you need to know to get started. I start by looking at what age to introduce woodwork, then look at the different layers of progression as children develop their knowledge and skills. I explain ideas for starting to work with wood, exploring wood as a material, and then talk in depth about setting up a woodworking area. I then discuss types of wood and all the tools that can be included in the toolkit and how to safely work with them.

What age to start? ▶ 88	
Stages of development ▶ 89	
Investigating wood ▶ 94	
Establishing a woodworking area ▶ 97	
Workbench ▶ 100	
Types of wood and other materials ▶ 104	
How to introduce tools ▶ 112	
Tools and equipment ▶ 115	
How to use tools ▶ 116	
Consumables ▶ 135	

Getting started

What age to start?

I recommend introducing woodwork to children in their pre-school year. In the UK that is the year in which they turn four. At this age they will have developed the maturity and physical coordination to be able to successfully work with basic tools. Their developmental stage at three and four years old is also perfectly suited to the learning and development associated with woodwork. This book focuses on introducing woodwork to children aged three to five but there is clearly a large spectrum of capability within this age range. Skills that a 5-year-old may acquire straightaway will take longer with younger children, who often need more time to develop skills and repeat processes in order to embed their learning.

Younger children

Right from birth I would recommend providing young children with wooden objects to play with. Being a natural product, wood is very sensory, interesting to touch, has a certain warmth, and rich visual detail and often has a pleasant smell.

I would recommend encouraging heuristic play, having a variety of wooden objects for young hands to experience and play with. Young children love to feel, smell, taste, touch and handle natural wood. In terms of their environment it is also good to expose them to natural materials as much as possible, through choices of wooden flooring, chairs, storage and so on.

A peg hammer bench is very popular with young children (1–3 years) and builds hand–eye coordination and develops motor skills. Having a set of play tools can be a good resource to encourage role play.

Providing a collection of natural wood blocks and tree sections can provide a great way to start exploring wood and to experiment with placing and arranging and basic construction. It is worth ensuring that these are smooth and well sanded to prevent any splinters. They can also promote language development around the vocabulary of wood and its properties.

I do not encourage using real tools with children younger than three. The risks of injury are increased as their coordination is still developing and their behaviour can be less predictable. Some children will be ready as they near their preschool year and with the correct supervision some could accomplish some basic tasks. If you do wish to consider this I would suggest working with ratios of 1:1 or 1:2. Another option could be to do preliminary work such as hammering golf tees into clay or a pumpkin. Younger children could also do some simple construction with small wooden sections and glue. On balance, I believe it is good practice to wait for the pre-school year and it gives younger children something to look forward to doing when they move up a year.

Stages of development

Getting started

I am still, after all my years of woodworking with young children, taken aback by just how competent they become by the end of the year. Having had regular opportunities to work with wood throughout the year, children rapidly build on previous learning and develop a whole set of skills that enable them to accomplish ambitious projects. This is achieved with a combination of their enhanced creative and critical thinking skills and their increased dexterity and deftness in working with their hands to manipulate tools.

Gaining familiarity with wood by exploring its context and properties

Initially, to set the scene, embrace a thematic approach whereby children explore wood in the wider context. Encourage them to share what they already know about wood, exploring its properties and researching contexts such as where wood comes from, uses of wood, things around us made of wood and people who work with wood. It could also be a possibility to take some trips out visiting a park to look at the trees, visiting the hardware store or wood yard or visiting a local carpenter or wood carver.

Induction to tools and safety: embedding skills

Discuss the basic tools and talk about the importance of safety measures. This is followed by demonstrating use of the tools, and children having their first experience of using a hammer, screwdriver and saw. (On how to discuss safety, see Chapter 8.)

As children are mastering their techniques, their interest in the tools increases. They are curious about wood as a material and the way tools work, often asking questions: What is the round ball (pein) on the hammer for? They are captivated by the process of sawing and fascinated by the falling sawdust. They are delighted that they can screw the screw into the wood and then unscrew it again.

Tinkering

Tinkering is an attitude – a playful way to explore or solve problems through direct experience, experimentation and discovery with materials and tools.

Tinkering is the next stage, whereby children really start to explore possibilities of working with tools and wood using their heads, hearts and hands. Tinkering demands time, as children almost literally think with their hands. Children need to be unhurried and able to work at their own pace, giving them time to pose questions, find solutions, form new ideas, make new connections, test things out, try alternatives, explore and invent. They will begin to explore, combining sections of wood, often without a product in mind but just enjoying experimenting with joining different pieces together in different ways. The result may resemble some object or remind the children of something, leading them to name it ('It's my power boat').

I strongly recommend that you do not set projects, such as making a tree cookie or simple bird box. This may work for some children but for many they will lose interest if they have to make someone else's idea and can easily become frustrated having to follow instructions. We need to allow children to experiment with the possibilities to create their own learning.

Tinkering can be defined as: 'Exploring with tools, to improve in a casual way with experimental efforts'. Another definition I came across was: 'Keeping busy in a useless or desultory way, lacking purpose or plan' – here I would argue that the etymologist has clearly missed the point

Getting started

as this is the time when the mind plays with ideas and possibilities – the very heart of creativity! Tinkering is slowing down and acting on curiosity, inquiring and sometimes getting results sometimes failing.

Tinkering is really important – allowing the children to explore how the tools work and what they can do, what they can make them do, working out what works and what doesn't, and learning by trial and error. There will be lots of failures for every success and persistence is key. The only real failure occurs when we stop trying. Children need time to converse with tools.

It is also a time experiment with materials. Children can discover how different woods respond to the tools and finding out about the differences and similarities between materials such as plastic, leather and wood. Children learn to have a dialogue with materials – as they ask questions of the material, finding out to how it responds to various inputs and experimenting with possibilities.

Tinkering is play. Fergus Hughes defined play as having the elements of freedom of choice, personal enjoyment and focus on the activity as an end in itself rather than on its outcomes (Hughes 1991) – all of which are very true in relation to tinkering.

Tinkering is of immense value in itself and does not need to be superseded by more 'end-product' work. But in many cases children's explorations will lead on to other lines of enquiry which will create a desire to make.

Construction

Once children feel more confident using tools and combining various elements, specific ideas may begin to emerge and they may start to plan and envisage a product. Older children may wish to use their mark-making skills to draw out a basic plan or vision of what they wish to create. Then they are off – there's no stopping them! These designs often transform as their work progresses and as other ideas are added but sometimes children complete their original intention. Their engagement is very much in the process as they constantly have to figure out ways to work towards their ideas. Children create a variety of different models and it's a joy to see a wide variation in expressive imagination. Some make models that contain narratives: their work becomes the starting point for stories or becomes a prop for role-play or drama. The beauty of woodwork is that there are multiple layers of learning as at any of the developmental stages new tools and skills can be introduced that are appropriate and meaningful to children's progression.

Children often continue to work on their models in different ways, perhaps painting with watercolour or acrylic (I often mix PVA glue with acrylic paint to give the paint more of a shine). They may wish to use glue to add other elements or decorative features.

Collaborative extended learning projects

Once children are competent they may very well have a desire for other challenges. We can use woodwork skills for many collaborative extended learning projects. These can evolve in response to children's interests, such as deciding to make a scarecrow to protect their garden, or in response to something that actually needs making or repairing within the setting. These authentic learning experiences deeply engage children and they enjoy seeing them through to the end and take great pride in their achievements. (Examples of projects are discussed in detail in Chapter 7.)

It is worth remembering these are typical stages in the process of becoming confident makers but in reality learning often takes wonderful digressions as children's curiosity and interest is sparked in another direction. It is important to follow their lead for that is where their energy and focus is. For Michelle, who decides to collect the sawdust and mix it with paint, it is the beginning of another journey. Ricardo, when making a boat, tests it in water and becomes fascinated by the fact that it floats. He then starts exploring concepts of floating and sinking with different materials, beginning a new journey entirely. Their curiosity becomes the spirit of enquiry and these new journeys must be nurtured and encouraged.

Every child is unique

As with every activity, children's ability and engagement varies. Children's ability will also vary greatly with age, background and previous experience. Some children will progress quickly and have a strong desire to learn how to use new tools, whereas others may wish to go at a slower pace, exploring simple processes for longer periods of time. Interest can also vary according to energy levels and time of day. We need to be responsive to the children in an individual way. Some children simply won't be able to get enough of woodworking and others may be content with shorter periods. However, it has been our experience that woodwork provides an experience which is pretty much universally enjoyed by all children.

Summary of progression in woodwork

- ▶ familiarity with wood by exploring the context and properties
- ▶ knowledge of basic tools
- ▶ understanding safety and risk
    - ▷ personal protection
    - ▷ thinking of others
    - ▷ safe use of tools and workbench
    - ▷ keeping safe in the woodwork area
- ▶ learning techniques and skills
- ▶ practising skills and techniques

Getting started

- tinkering: open-ended exploration – exploring possibilities of materials and tools. Starting to combine wood sections
- construction: creating unique work that is representational, symbolic or abstract
- introduction of more complex skills
- increasing complexity and further development of creative/critical thinking
- collaborative extended learning projects involving high-level thinking.

Investigating wood

Wood and trees

Start by investigating wood. This could involve researching and sharing knowledge, and thinking about where wood comes from. Research can include learning about forests and felling, finding out about different types of trees, thinking about how they grow, life cycles and seasons. It's a great opportunity to get out into the woods, investigate trees and the many elements such as leaves, bark, fruit, seeds and roots. Children could create a mind map or poster to collate all their knowledge.

Teachers could set up displays in the classroom – a selection of natural wood, perhaps including sawdust, tree rings, shavings, twigs, leaves, seeds, conkers and driftwood. Another display could contain various products made from wood, such as wooden spoons, pencils, wooden bowl, a chair and beads. Images of people who work directly with wood such as construction workers, carpenters and craftspeople can also be added.

Wood that has been dried and prepared by being machined into rectangular sections can seem quite abstract and hard to relate to an actual living tree. It is a good idea to develop understanding that this wood does come from inside the tree. I have a large tree ring section from which I have cut out a small block of wood to help illustrate this and help children to make the connection

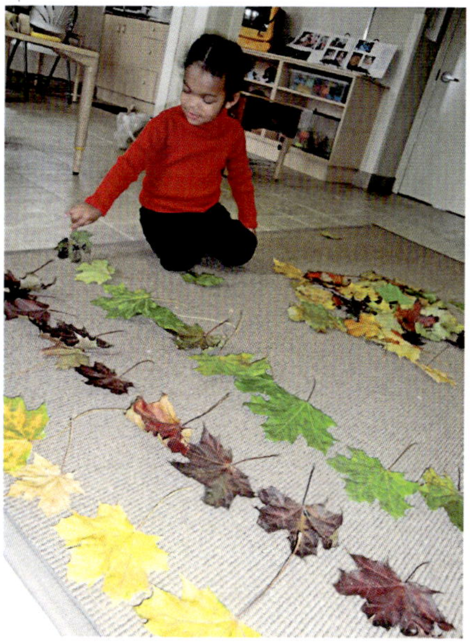

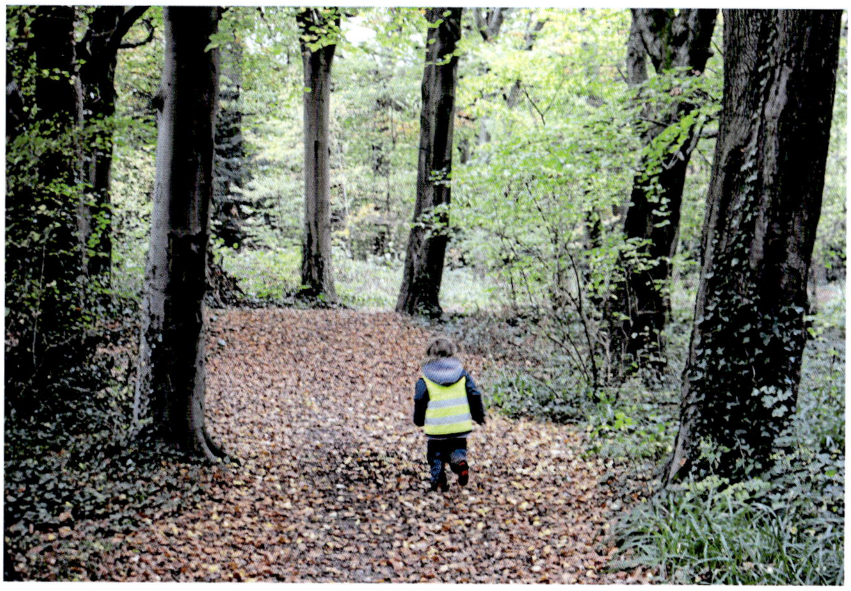

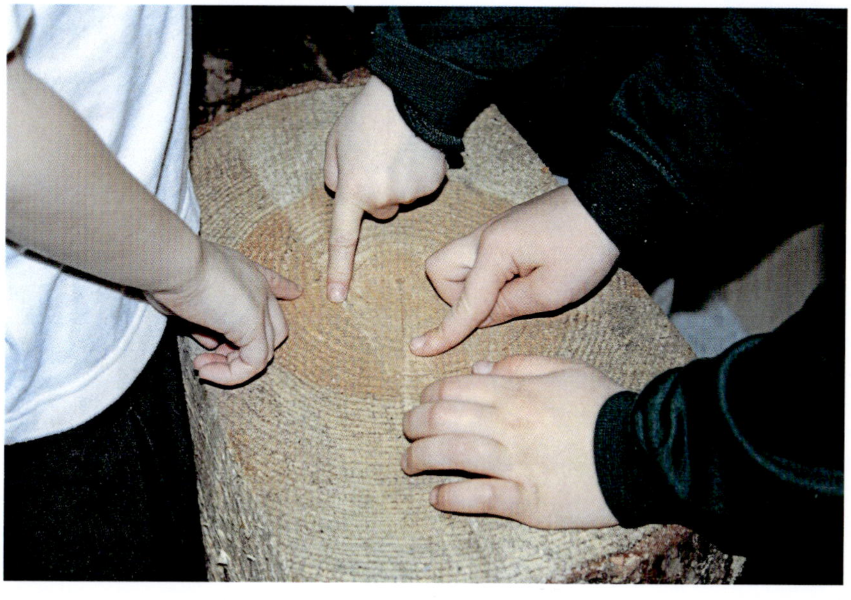

Getting started

between wood and trees. Children can also be involved in planting trees and this can develop further understanding. Making comparisons between trees planted in previous years helps children get an insight into their slow rate of growth. Young children become quite curious about ages of trees and this all goes to deepen their understanding of the growth of living things.

During this initial research, learning can extend in all sorts of directions, for example, exploring different leaves in detail on a light box and examining the different colours and vein structures; exploring making prints with leaves; investigating the different things that grow on trees or animals that live in trees and experiencing the smells of freshly sawn wood.

Wood as material

Another aspect of investigating wood can be exploring it as a material. Here again we can start by children sharing what they already know and then extending this knowledge by researching together. We are investigating the 'woodness' of wood. What is distinctive about it? What are its properties? We can explore the grain, the smell, the textures, the weight, compare dried wood to wet greenwood, and make comparisons between different types of wood. We can find out that wood floats, that wood burns and turns into ashes or charcoal, we can investigate its strength, discover that it creates sawdust when cut, that it gets hot when rubbed, and so on.

Explorations can be extended in a number of different directions. Perhaps after burning wood the burnt wood can be used to make charcoal drawings. Talking about wood and paper may lead on to trying to make paper or creating with papier-mâché, or to a discussion about recycling paper and how recycled paper can be transformed into other products. The possibilities are endless but it's important to follow the children's natural curiosity and interest.

Throughout this initial period of investigation and exploration children will be developing their understanding, expanding their vocabulary and becoming more familiar with the notion of wood and its potential. It provides a great building block from which to move on to working directly with tools on wood.

Establishing a woodworking area

The first thing to decide upon is a suitable space. This depends very much upon your setting and there are several factors to take into account, such as: how many children will have access to the area, how it will be supervised, whether younger children also access the area, and the particular cohort of children. It is good to try and choose an area where there are few distractions as the children really need to be focused and keep looking at their work when they are hammering! It can also be frustrating for a child woodworking who is trying to concentrate and focus on their woodwork if there are constant distractions. The woodworking area should also be located in an area where there are fewer passing children.

Woodwork can work equally well indoors and outdoors. Working outdoors in general is preferable and I encourage outdoor learning as much as possible. Being active, fresh air and natural daylight only go to enhance learning. Woodwork is not an aerobic activity – there are short bursts of activity interspersed with longer inactive periods when children are thinking and making decisions. If it is very cold, children can get cold quickly by not moving around much. Wearing several layers of clothing can restrict movement and wearing gloves is not advisable as children's fine motor control is diminished, so when it's cold it is advisable to set up indoors.

Woodwork also works very well indoors, for example, when located in a quiet corner of the classroom. There are many schools that provide woodwork as part of their core provision and

Getting started

where every classroom has a small woodworking station. In Fife in Scotland, woodwork forms part of their core provision in every early years setting with every classroom having a small woodworking area. Woodwork is not as noisy as many people might imagine as much of the time children are thinking and problem-solving rather than continuously hammering! But clearly at times it can be very noisy with all the sounds of purposeful work. The noise level may be a factor in deciding how many children you have working at one time. Robust sturdy tables tend to absorb some of the sound whereas more flimsy tables seem to vibrate and increase noise levels. There will certainly be some clearing up to do with sawdust on the floor but tidying will certainly be no more than with many other activities.

Children can work standing up or sitting down depending on the height of the work surface. Many classroom tables are too low to be worked at comfortably standing up. Workbenches are generally higher and are stood at. I find many children prefer to sit at a table during the first sessions so they can really take their time to explore working with the tools and really focus. Certain processes such as sawing should always be done while standing. Once children have mastered basic skills and can get busy working on their own projects they tend to work in a position that best suits them, with most choosing to stand up as they can get more power into their actions. Occasionally some work directly on the ground if it better suits the particular task.

The woodworking area also should be set up on a hard surface where fallen nails and screws can be easily picked up. A large magnet makes this task much easier! It is worth thinking about keeping the block area some distance from the woodwork area to avoid expensive blocks becoming part of children's creations!

Some settings choose to have their woodwork area gated to restrict access. This can prevent toddlers entering the area and can also be used to limit the distractions of other children and to limit the number of children working at one time. Again, this will depend very much on your particular setting and what works best for you.

The area could also have some images of people who work professionally with wood, images of construction, and images of the children's own learning journeys with wood.

It is essential that the woodworking area has at least one workbench with a vice to enable sawing and to allow wood to be clamped for drilling. The tools, wood and other resources will need to be organised in a coherent manner and be easily visible and accessible for children. Depending on your set-up, tools could be arranged on the wall with tool silhouettes to aid returning them to the original place, or kept in boxes ready to be brought out when needed. The woodworking

Getting started

area will also need to have a plentiful supply of wood in a variety of shapes and sizes, mixed media resources such as corks and buttons, and lots of nails and screws. Children need to be able to see and touch what is available in order to make the most of the resources. Having a wide selection of materials will enhance children's experience – and this will often mean dedicating as much space to storage as workspace.

Storage of tools should also be considered; however, this will depend a lot upon your particular set-up – tools may be brought out for a woodworking session or could be arranged on a wall panel with their silhouettes as described above. Whatever the set-up, keeping tools organised and ensuring that they get returned to their designated place is crucial. It is also worthwhile having a space available for the storage of work in progress, as children often want to return to their work.

The woodwork area can clearly contribute to providing an outstanding enabling environment.

Workbench

A sturdy workbench is very much recommended. Wood being sawn must always be tightly clamped in a vice. The workbench should be solidly built and be heavy enough so that it does not move about when the children are sawing. Lighter workbenches could have a concrete block placed underneath or be fixed permanently to the ground. There are a number of educational suppliers that produce workbenches at a height suitable for young children.

An ideal workbench would have a flat working surface made from hard wood and have at least two vices. It can be useful to have a recess in the centre to hold nails and screws, and storage

Source: © Community Playthings

space underneath. Workbenches are fairly expensive but it is an investment that will last many years. Children very quickly become adept at using the vice, winding it anti-clockwise to open it and clockwise to close it, but it will need an adult to check that it is tight. In addition to having vices, a workbench could also incorporate a bench hold-down clamp – useful for holding down work when drilling.

101

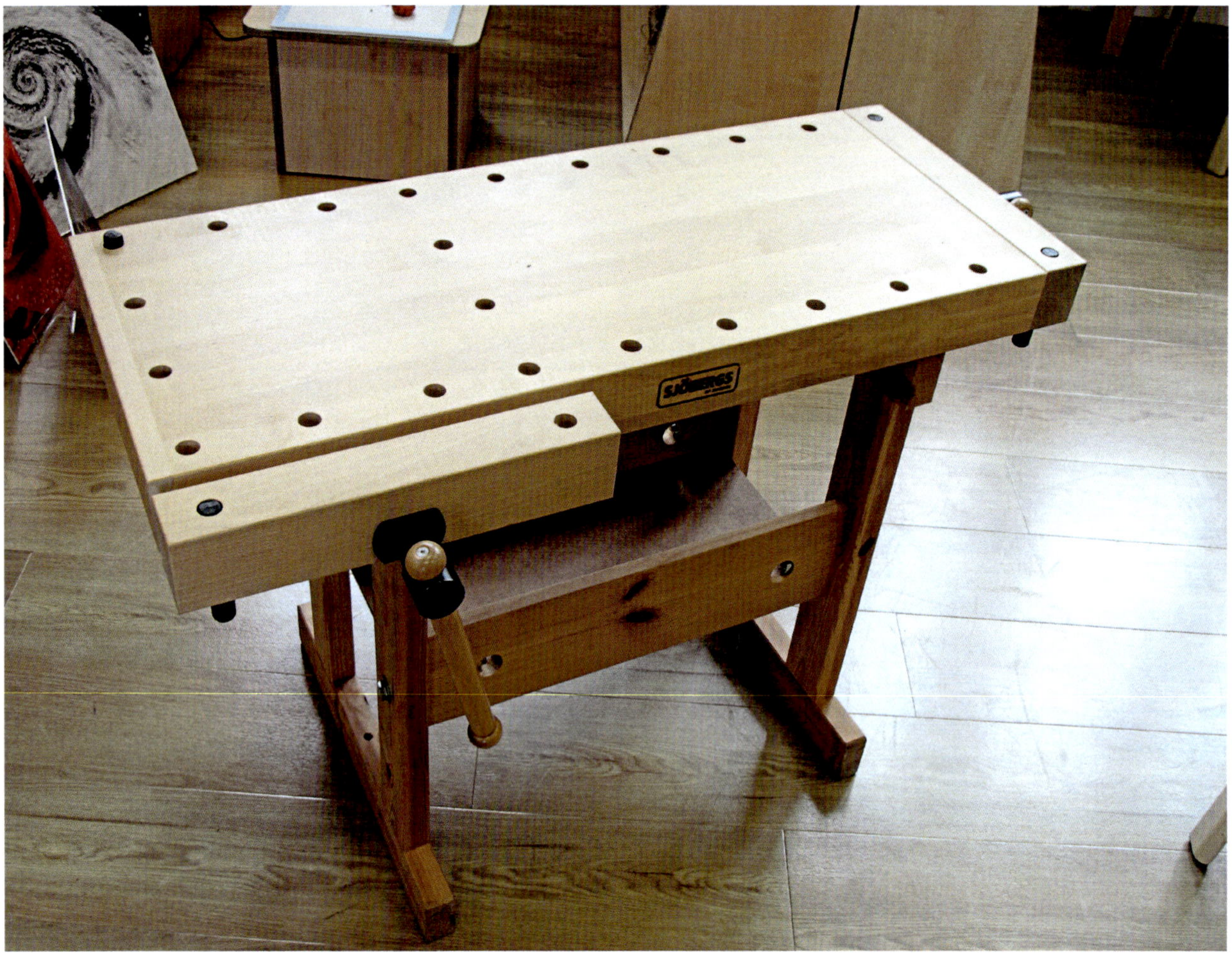

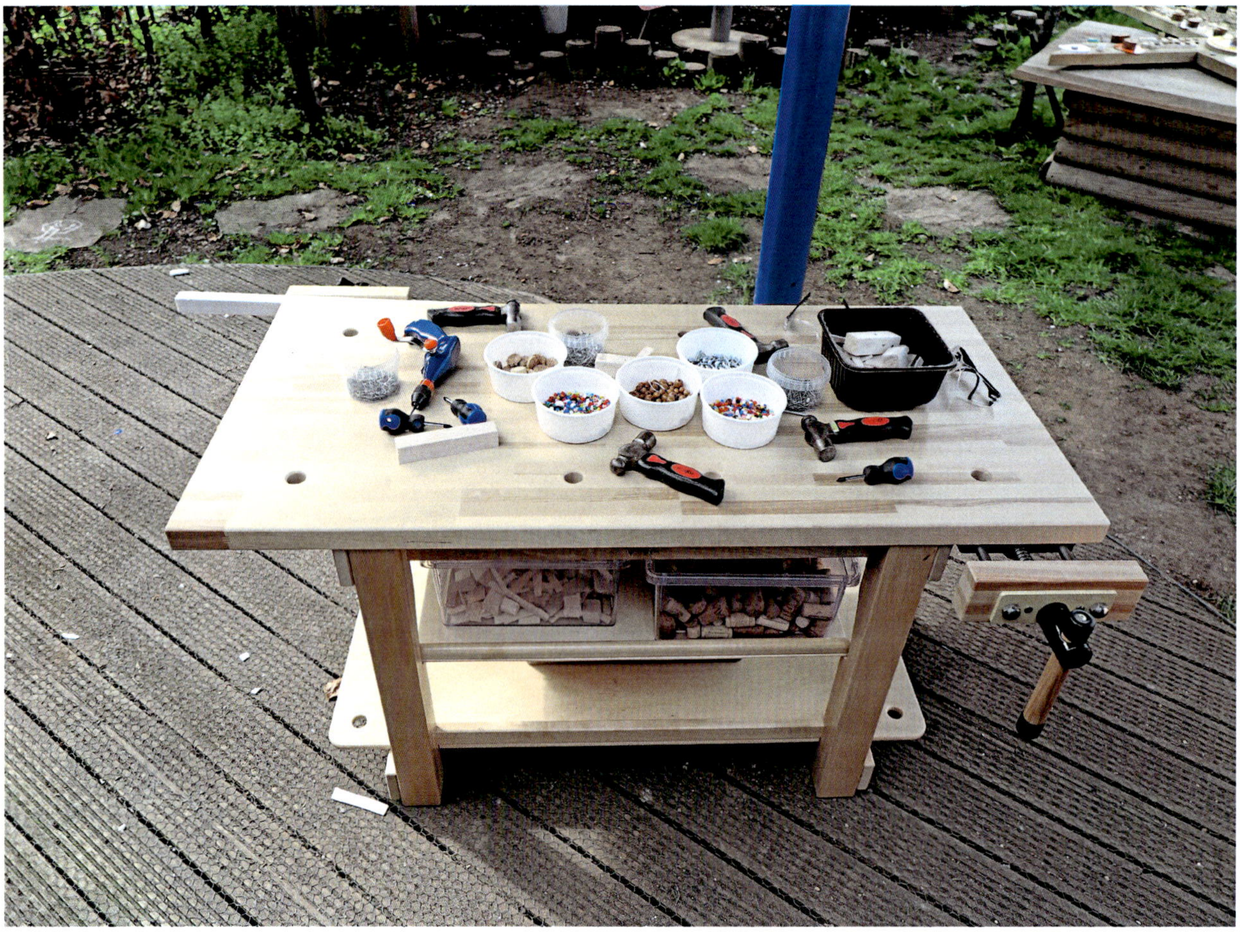

For those on tight budgets an alternative solution is to use an old robust kitchen table, cutting down the legs so the table top is at the correct height and then adding a vice or two. A woodworker's vice, with wooden jaws and flush with the surface of the table, is preferable to a raised engineer's vice. (However, an engineer's vice is much easier to attach to a table as it is fixed to the top surface.) Some vices incorporate a quick-release button, which is a useful feature. Another option is to purchase an adult workbench and simply cut the legs down to the correct height.

A workbench that is approximately 1,200mm × 600mm is suitable for 2–4 children depending on the tasks they are undertaking. I would recommend a working height of approximately 610mm. Sawing works best when the saw is angled slightly downhill just below waist height, and hammering at waist height. For the supporting adult it will mean a lot of kneeling – knee pads are a worthwhile investment!

There are a couple of solutions available for pack-away settings where transporting a heavy workbench is not possible. The Stanley quick-close vice is an ingenious vice that can be attached to most tables with small clamps. It closes with a pumping action and holds the wood firmly and is then released by simply raising the handle slightly. Another clamp-on vice is the portable bench vice – which is an engineer's style vice with an attached clamp underneath to secure it to a table.

Pack-away settings may also wish to consider a collapsible workbench such as a 'Workmate'. These are light and transportable but they are flimsy and not very stable, requiring considerable adult support to stop them moving whilst children are sawing. Stability generally increases with cost but that usually also increases their weight. There is also a collapsible vice called the 'Triton', which is much more stable and robust and comes with a corresponding price tag.

G-clamps can also be used to hold wood. It is not recommended to hold wood to be sawn with G-clamps. G-clamps are suitable both on the workbench and on a table to hold work steady to be drilled. As with the vice the supporting adult should ensure it is tight.

Getting started

Work surfaces

In addition to the workbench, tables are good for general working. Children can do work such as hammering and screwing on old tables or even classroom tables if protected with some thin wooden mats. For the mats, I suggest using 5mm MDF with dimensions of approximately 40cm × 40cm. Most hardware stores can cut these for a relatively low cost. Tables need to be sturdy and rigid. Any give or flexibility lessens the impact of hammering as some of the energy is absorbed by the table, making hammering harder work. (There is a similar effect if the table is positioned on a carpet.) G-clamps, as mentioned above, can be used on the table to hold wood for drilling.

A number of suppliers making workbenches for young children are listed in the Resources and suppliers section.

Types of wood and other materials

Balsa wood

There is no substitute for initially using balsa wood in the early stages of learning skills. It allows techniques to be easily mastered and leads to a smooth transition to working with harder wood. It is very soft and easy to hammer into, thus the children quickly gain confidence and in no time they will be knocking in nail after nail. It's also perfect for learning to screw and saw. The drawback with balsa wood is that it is expensive (due to low worldwide stocks) so it is best used sparingly and only for the introductory stages as the basic skills are acquired. Then have the children move straight on to 'soft wood' such as pine.

Getting started

Some practitioners have experimented with alternatives to balsa wood such as using pumpkins, thick cardboard, dense foam block, clay in a box or a shoebox filled with cardboard, for developing the initial skills of hammering, screwing and drilling, but I really believe that balsa wood is the most effective, especially as it provides an authentic and aesthetic experience of working with real wood and subsequently transferring skills to other woods becomes easier.

Balsa wood's name comes from the Spanish for 'raft'. It's a fast growing tree, reaching a height of 30 metres, and is grown in South America and Indonesia. It's an evergreen and is actually classified as a hardwood due to its leaf shape. It has large cells that contain water, which once dried form spaces, leaving the wood with a low density but high strength.

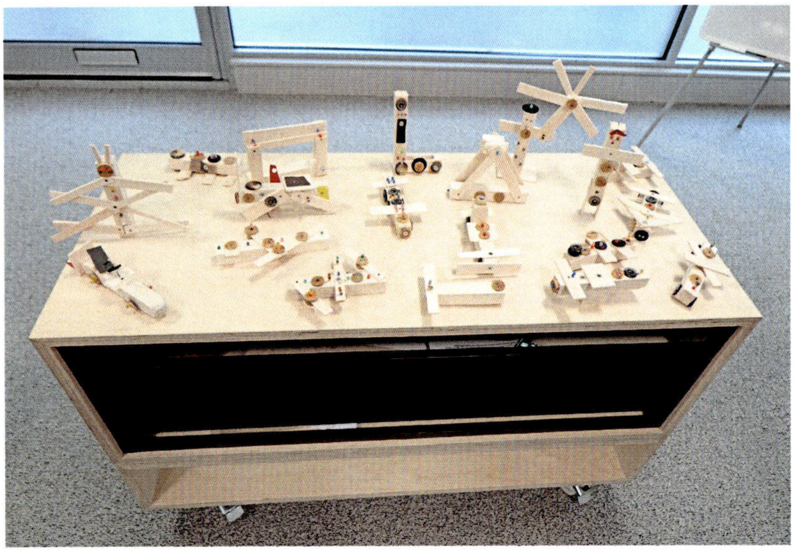

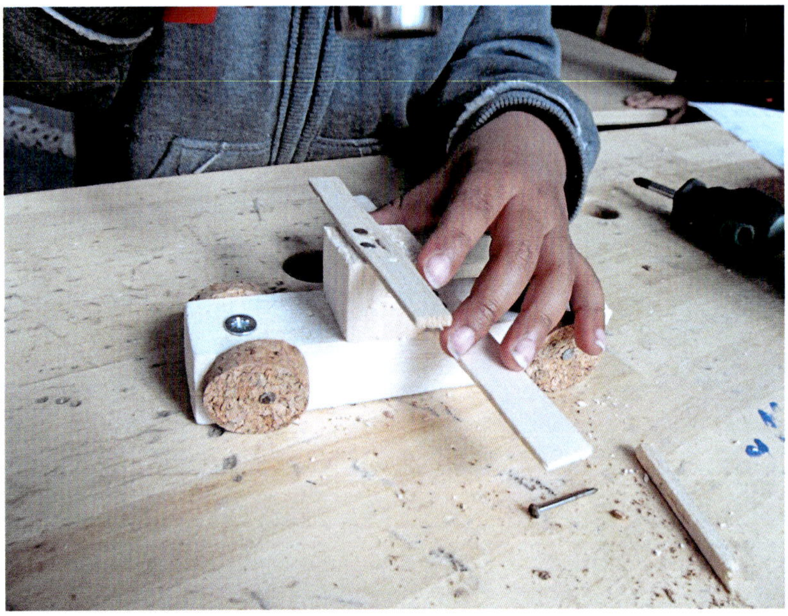

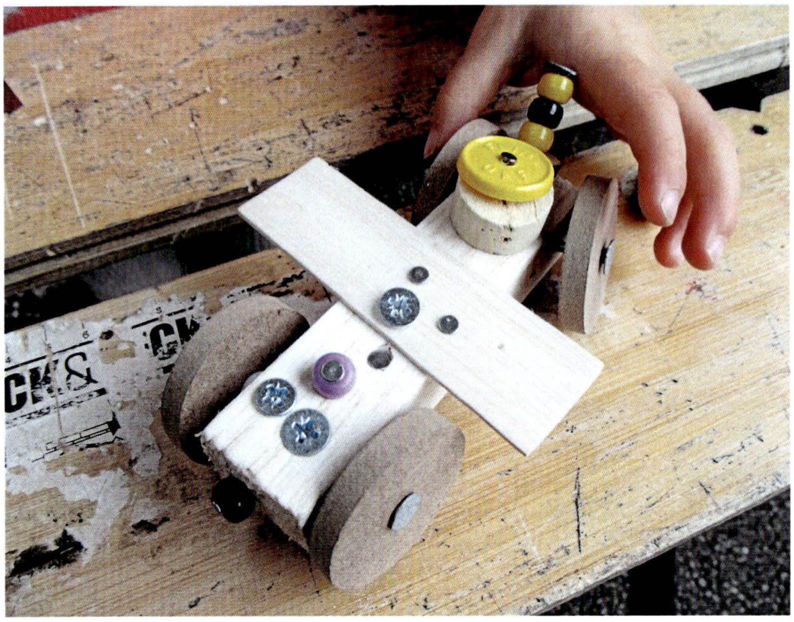

Getting started

There is clearly a high carbon footprint associated with importing wood so using balsa wood sparingly is strongly advised. If you feel uncomfortable using balsa wood for ecological reasons, or if it is hard to source, the alternative would be to source the softest wood available in your country. In the UK that would be poplar, lime or cedar and these would need to be prepared by a specialist supplier. Another option would be to use small blocks of pine and have the children just work initially on the end grain side, which is easier to work, being easier to hammer into, but it still would need to be drilled before screwing.

Young children (3–4) may well need a few sessions with balsa wood to become confident in their skills whereas an older child (aged 5) may just need a short session to learn basic skills then be ready to move immediately on to soft woods (like pine).

Balsa wood bundles can be bought from a number of suppliers. (See Resources and suppliers.) Lengths of 25mm × 25mm box sections and thin sheets (3–4mm thick) are perfect to start with. These sheets can be cut into smaller sections and are good for joining to the box sections with nails or screws.

The 25mm box section is also great to learn to saw with, but very quickly children will gain confidence and will want to move on to cut much thicker wood!

Softwood

Softwoods are significantly harder than balsa wood. If children initially started with softwoods it is quite likely that some will struggle to master the techniques and be deterred from continuing.

As children move on to readily available pine, the possibilities rapidly expand and they are able to create more interesting work. They will certainly develop their hand and arm muscles. After experiencing working with balsa wood it is merely a matter of applying the same techniques, but hammering harder when using nails or drilling small holes first when using screws. One way to test if wood is soft enough is to see if your fingernail indents and leaves a mark as you

Getting started

scrape it across the surface. Pine, cedar, fir, larch, redwood, poplar, lime and spruce are all good for children to work with. Pine is by far the most readily available and easiest to source. Even pine can vary considerably in hardness. Most varieties grown these days are fast growing and therefore softer. Generally, if the growth rings are close together the wood will be harder. It should be noted that the knots in wood are much harder and it is best to advise children to avoid them as they are very difficult to nail and screw into or saw through.

Softwood can be bought from all timber merchants and comes in all sorts of shapes and sizes. Pine is still relatively expensive as a disposable early years resource, but you should be able to get more than enough offcuts by sourcing from carpenters and builders. I get offcuts from a local pine bed workshop who are glad to see their waste get put to good use. Timber cutting services will also have a whole load of offcuts that they will happily donate to schools. We regularly put out appeals to parents asking for donations of softwood and in that way always have a plentiful supply. If buying pine, it is easy to find sustainably grown wood from tree farms to ensure an endless supply, meaning you're not contributing to deforestation and will always have a supply of wood for your projects.

If you do buy wood I would suggest buying lengths of '2 by 1' (25mm × 50mm) and an assortment of trim (such as 40mm × 10mm) and then cutting them up in advance into smaller manageable sections ready for the children to use. Dowel is also useful in a selection of diameters and children can easily saw it into the lengths they require. Dowel can make excellent wheels.

Hardwood

Hardwoods are best avoided. These include tropical hardwoods and indigenous hardwoods such as oak, ash, birch and beech – they are difficult to work with and can be frustrating for young children to saw and hammer and drill into. There is also a higher risk of nails rebounding. Certain tropical hardwoods also have a toxicity associated with the wood dust.

Plywood

Plywood is made of thin sheets of wood laminate that are glued together. It tends to splinter very easily and the splinters tend to be quite sharp and long so it is best avoided. It is also hard for young children to hammer into. Being relatively hard, due to being combined with glue, plywood also tends to dull saws very quickly.

Preformed wood – MDF, hardboard

Preformed wood such as hardboard and MDF should not be cut in school. MDF does not contain the level of toxins it used to but it does create an irritating fine dust when sawn, which should certainly not be inhaled. For this reason MDF should not be cut by children. If used at all the preformed wood should be presented as ready cut shapes prepared off-site with the operator wearing a dust mask. I often do this as it is easy to make some wavy shapes with a jigsaw and these just expand the resources available and add to their options. MDF is also very hard and needs to be drilled before being hammered or screwed. MDF is relatively cheap and is used by many primary and secondary schools in Design and Technology. There are also pre-cut shapes such as wheels available from educational suppliers.

Hardboard is made from pulverised wood. It is easy to hammer into but again best not sawn due to the dust levels. An alternative to MDF or hardboard would be getting thin sheets of cedar from a saw mill – these could then be cut into more interesting shapes with a jigsaw. Cedar is easy to work and also has a wonderful sweet aroma.

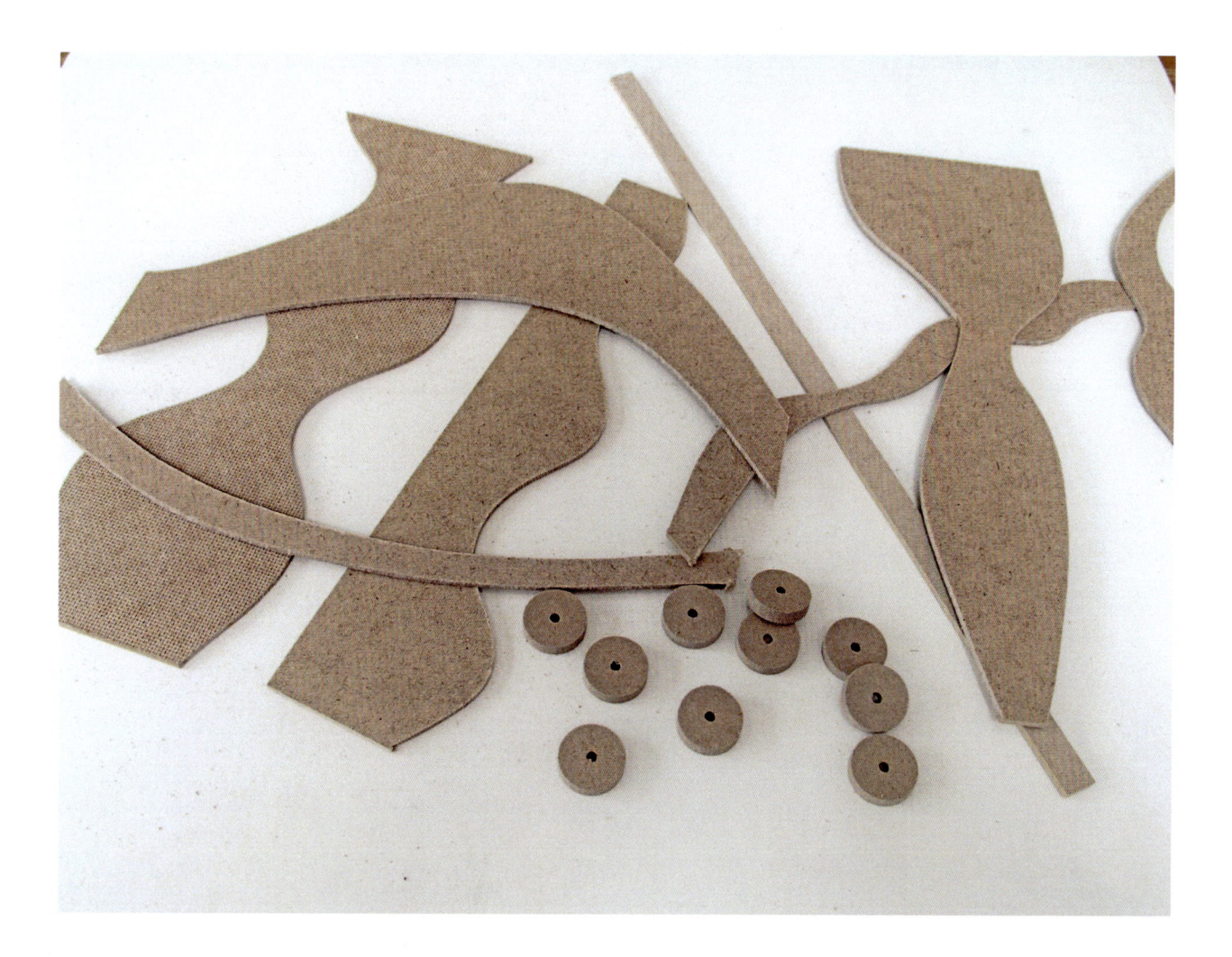

Chemically treated wood

Avoid wood that has been pressure treated with chemicals as a preservative and wood that has been previously painted. It is especially important to check this with donations of wood. These may contain toxins that can be inhaled when the wood is sawn or absorbed when handled.

Cork

Cork is sourced from the Mediterranean cork oak tree and is the primary source of cork products in the world. Cork has a unique set of properties not found in any other naturally existing material. It is lightweight, impermeable to gas and liquid, and soft and buoyant. It's these properties that make it ideal for wine bottles and tile flooring. It is also wonderful for children's woodwork.

It's soft and particularly easy to start a nail off in and hammer into. Corks make great wheels when thinly sliced. I prepare these in advance by going a little upmarket in my wine selection and then slicing the corks up with a sharp kitchen knife like a carrot. There are also several suppliers that sell pre-prepared slices of cork. Cork tiles can also be cut up and combined with other wood.

Natural wood and green wood

Children often bring sections of fallen wood – sticks and branches brought back from Forest School trips and wood collected from the forest can make an interesting addition to the resources available. These are often incorporated into their woodwork – slivers of branch become wheels, peeled bark becomes string, forked twigs become antlers! Combining these different elements helps the children make connections and gain more understanding of the nature and properties of wood in its various forms.

Branches of anything up to 10cm diameter are suitable to be cut into smaller sections. If using narrow sections of branch it can be helpful to drill a small hole before hammering into them as they can often split. If the wood is still green it can make sawing harder as it tends to clog up in the saw cut.

There are lots of possibilities for using twigs and sections of branch and even chestnut cases or conkers can be incorporated into models. A large tree stump can also make a good solid surface for practising hammering and the end grain is very easy to hammer nails into. Elder can be cut into short sections to make beads as the inner pith can be easily removed. Hazel can easily be cut into slivers that could make great wheels. Found wood such as driftwood may not be exactly the shape children require, but is full of wonderful surprises and can be adapted in many ways to suit their designs (or they may adapt their designs to suit the wood!) Children may wish to combine some of their Forest School skills with tools on some of the natural wood, such as stripping bark.

Preparing wood

It can be very helpful to have a battery jigsaw available for an experienced adult to cut up larger wood into small sections ready for the children to use. This is particularly useful with donations of long lengths of wood. This can save a lot of time and energy as well as ensuring there is always a plentiful supply. Small circular discs can also be easily prepared by an adult in advance using thin wood and an electric drill with a hole saw attachment.

Be sure to remove any nails or staples from the wood before it is made available to children. If very splintery, sand the rough edges in advance.

Arranging resources

Rather than having a large pile of offcuts, which can be overwhelming, it is best to sort them into several boxes, making it easier to find a good choice for a particular purpose. Try and provide a wide selection of shapes and sizes of wood as this will offer more options and choice and will help children to be able to realise their ideas.

Additional materials

Getting started

Provide a wide range of additional materials to allow more possibilities and options to express imagination. It also deepens children's knowledge about other materials and encourages making connections with different areas of learning.

It is particularly useful to have circular shapes, as these have so many applications, including wheels, faces, eyes, switches, etc. Packs of MDF wheels can be purchased from many early years education suppliers. Buttons and bottle tops are also useful additions. Bottle tops can be added by drilling small holes in the centre or hammering a small hole through with a large nail first; this makes it easier to get a nail or screw started.

How to introduce tools

> The thrill of being allowed, in a secure way with clear boundaries and support, to use woodwork tools when you are only three or four years old is probably never forgotten. This is high quality learning.
>
> (Tina Bruce 2001)

Additional materials
- pencil, paper, clipboard
- felt-tip pens
- paints
- cork slices
- buttons
- beads
- fabric
- string/wool/ribbon
- leather offcuts
- MDF wheels
- mini branch sections
- blind samples/fabric book samples
- CDs
- pipe cleaners
- dowel
- cotton reels
- rubber bands
- foam
- wire
- glue (PVA)
- nuts and bolts
- fabric dye to colour wood
- hinges and catches
- hooks and eye-hooks
- tape
- metal bottle tops
- tinfoil
- spools
- parts from deconstructed toys – such as wheels from broken cars.

Getting started

Tools should be introduced to children gradually one at a time. We need to teach children the safe use of tools – it's a slow and deliberate process. Start by having a discussion about the safe use of tools, highlighting any potential hazards such as any sharp edges, and thinking together about how to keep safe. Discuss their function, share knowledge and think about potential applications.

It is important to explain that tools have a specific purpose and should be respected. Ensure children understand that the tools must remain within the woodworking area and be returned to where they belong after use. When carrying tools they should be carried carefully at their side.

The emphasis of the first couple of sessions is becoming familiar with the tools, acquiring skills and gaining confidence. Observe and document children's levels of competence to determine when they are ready to take the next steps and are competent to work independently. Below is a suggested order in which to introduce tools. In the following 'tools and equipment' section I explain the correct use of each tool in detail.

Order of introducing the basic tools:

1   Hammer.
2   Screwdriver and bradawl.
3   Saw.
4   Hand drill and G-clamp.

Start by using balsa wood as it is soft and allows all children to master the basic techniques easily. Initially, we introduce the hammer and nails, first hammering the nails into the wood and then starting to join pieces together. At first you can often see on the children's faces that they think this task is going to be a real challenge and are a little apprehensive. Very soon, after getting their first couple of nails in, they are happily banging in nail after nail and you can see their delight and satisfaction.

The second tool to introduce would be the screwdriver, again just screwing screws into the balsa wood and then using the screws to join pieces of wood together. A bradawl is useful at this stage to make the small hole in which to start the screw. These two basic skills, hammering and screwing, providing different ways of joining, already allow much creativity as the children make aeroplanes, sculptures and so on.

The third tool I introduce is the Japanese saw (or other type of pull saw), which the children use to cut short sections of balsa wood; again, using balsa wood this is very easy.

After the children have had a couple of sessions (probably just one session with older children) with the balsa wood practising these techniques, we then move on to using softwood such as pine.

The next tool to introduce would be the hand drill, as screwing into pine is difficult without drilling a pilot hole. We can also introduce the G-clamp at this stage to hold the work firmly whilst being drilled.

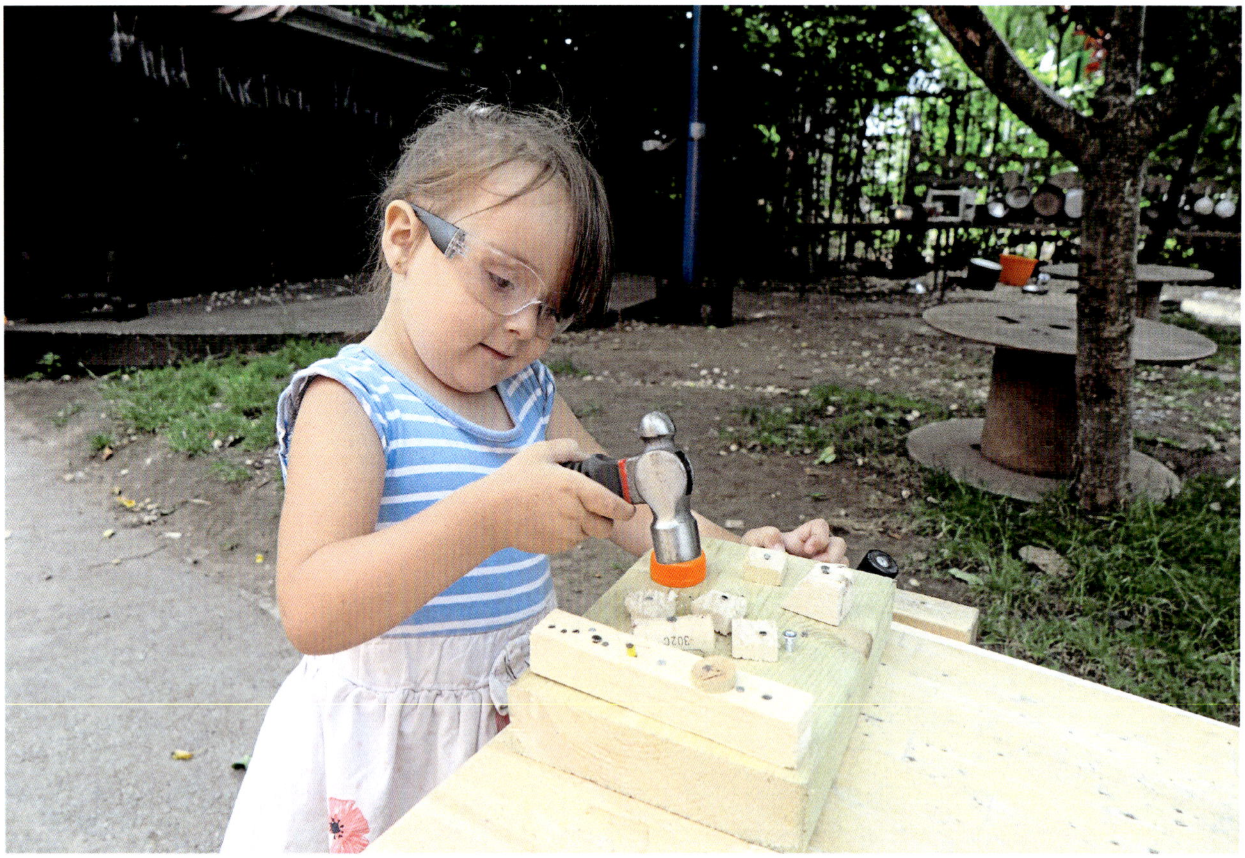

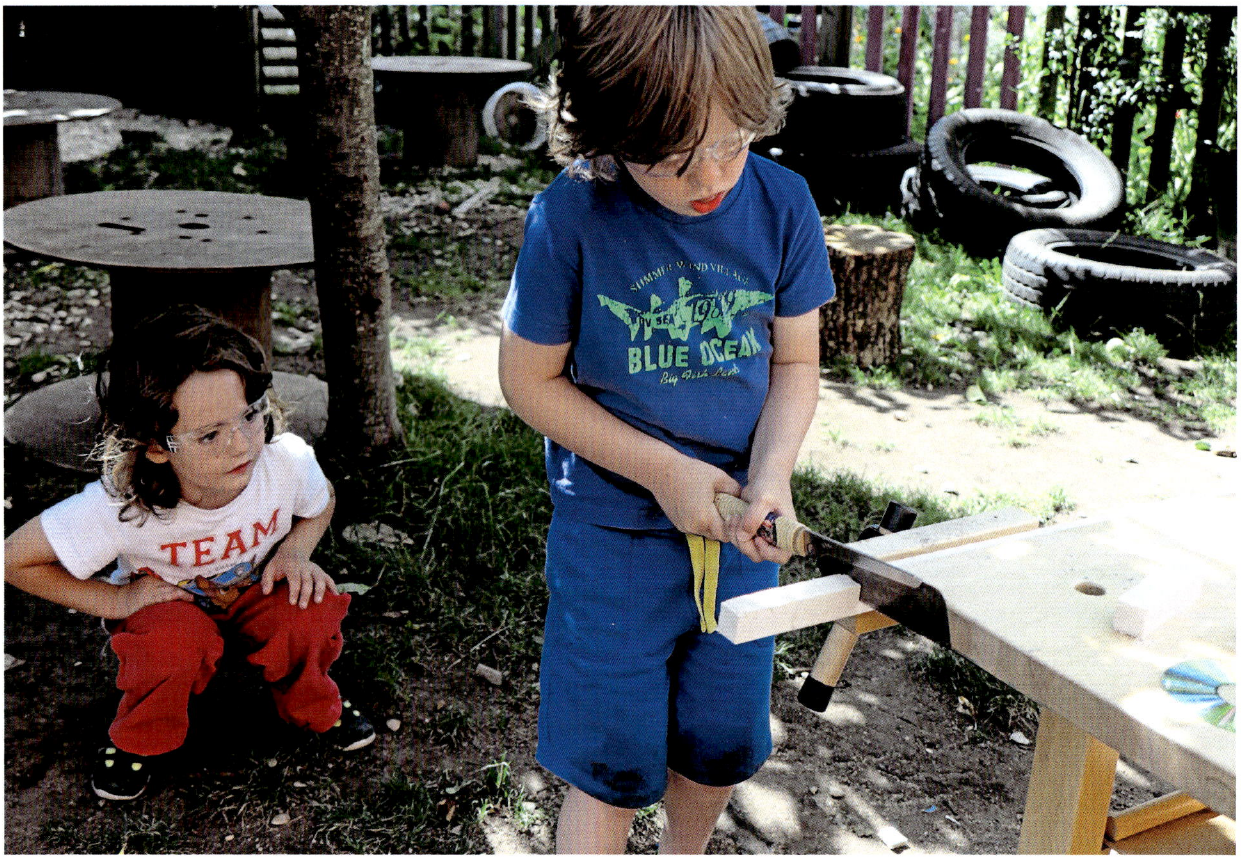
BLUE OCEAN
TEAM

With just these few simple tools young children will be able to accomplish a wide variety of extraordinary creations. Other tools can be introduced over time when they are appropriate and relevant to the children's needs and stage of development. New layers of learning will open up with each new tool and technique that is introduced and gradually a whole wealth of knowledge will be acquired.

Keep a checklist of the basic skills learnt as the children become competent at using a particular tool. Keeping a record allows us to be more confident about letting children work more independently and in larger groups. It is also useful to keep track of who has learnt to use which tool if we have children joining at various times throughout the year.

Tools and equipment

To get started you will need a basic toolkit. Having the most ergonomic and suitably sized tools does make a significant difference and the benefits of this should not be underestimated. For example, a hammer with a short handle, good grip, reasonable weight and a large head would be excellent; however, a long-handled pin hammer with a small head will make tasks more difficult, leading to frustration. Investing in quality tools will be cost-effective in the long term as most tools are extremely durable and last for many years. Using high quality tools shows respect for the children who will be using them and also encourages quality work.

Initially, a basic toolkit is all that is required. Supplementary tools can be added over time as children's knowledge and skills develop.

Basic toolkit

Workbench with vice
Junior safety glasses
Stubby ball-pein hammer
Stubby claw hammer
Pozidriv screwdriver
Hand drill
Japanese saw
Cross-cut saw or large pull saw
G-clamps
Bradawl or awl

Consumables

Sandpaper
Nails
Screws
Drill bits

Supplementary tools

Japanese nail puller, flat nail puller, pincers
Small battery screwdriver and hex shank drill bits
Brace and bit
Palm drill
Gimlet and auger
Surform
Files and rasps
Block plane
Pliers and wire cutters

Getting started

Adjustable wrench and spanners
Large magnet
Rulers and tape measures
Set square
Spirit level

Supplementary consumables

Nuts and bolts
Hooks, eyehooks
Wood glue

How to use tools

My recommendations for the use of tools have evolved from many years' experience of working with young children and observing what works best for them. My priority has always been to use tools that are easy and ergonomic, safe and allow the children to work as independently as possible.

Note: Video clips demonstrating all the tools can be viewed following the link in the Resources and suppliers section. Information on suppliers is also in the Resources and suppliers section (p. 184).

Safety glasses

Safety glasses should be worn at all times by children and teachers. It is important we model good practice. With hammering, there is a very small risk that a nail could rebound toward the eye. This can happen particularly with hard woods, MDF or even hard knots in soft wood. This risk of impact with the eye is eliminated by wearing safety glasses.

If we believe young children are old enough to do woodwork then they are also old enough to learn about looking after and taking responsibility for their bodies with appropriate safety protection. Children also like the role play aspect of wearing eye protection and feeling the part.

Goggles (as opposed to safety glasses) are more problematic as children find them uncomfortable and they are distracted by constantly repositioning them and their peripheral vision is also restricted. This results in children having a diminished experience of woodwork and being potentially more likely to injure themselves. Safety glasses are comfortable and children quickly forget they have them on (the biggest problem is reminding them to take them off at the end of a session!). Small-sized junior safety glasses are now readily available that fit comfortably on even the smallest of heads.

Safety glasses should be looked after carefully and stored individually to avoid them getting scratched, which limits vision. They often require a quick rub down before use to remove finger marks.

Ball-pein hammer

The first tool to introduce is the hammer. Use a short handled ball-pein hammer. The 8oz stubby ball-pein hammer is readily available and is perfectly suited to young children. This hammer is designed for mechanics to get into awkward places but couldn't be more suitable for young children. It is the ideal weight, has good grip and a short handle allowing more control. It has a large face and a ball-pein rather than a claw, thus being safer in case of accidental contact with the user. The round ball-pein end was designed to shape metal, not for trying to hammer nails with! Schools traditionally used long pinhead hammers as they were relatively light, but having a long handle and small face makes them more difficult to control and increases the likeliness of banged fingers. Many schools may already have hammers with long handles. A good trick is to simply cut the handle down making the hammer much more controllable for young children.

I recommend introducing hammering with a 1:3 supervision ratio at the most. This allows the support and guidance to ensure the children develop confidence and are using the hammer correctly and safely. Obviously, with more staff a larger group can work at the same time. We initially use balsa wood blocks (25mm × 25mm) and 25mm round nails with a head. This way the nails do not protrude through the wood.

I start by demonstrating how to hold the hammer in the middle of the handle and showing which part of the hammer (the face) to hit the nail with. I emphasise the importance of looking at where you are hitting all the time and not distracting others whilst they are hammering. We talk about how it might feel if we banged our finger and the importance of not swinging the hammer in a manner that could hurt someone else, especially behind you. Have the children gently feel the point of a nail to raise their awareness of the sharpness and emphasise the need for care. I then demonstrate how to hold a nail with finger and thumb, ensuring it is vertical, and demonstrate giving gentle vertical taps first whilst still holding the nail upright. With these gentle taps, even if they miss and bang their thumb or finger it will not hurt too much. We've all banged our fingers at some stage and as a consequence this makes us more careful in future. Do monitor and stop any over-exuberant hammering.

Once the nail is standing on its own, the children then remove their hand and hold the wood firmly well away from the nail. They can then hammer with more vigour, banging repeatedly until the nail is right in. It is helpful to emphasise the need to hammer from directly above as opposed

Stubby ball-pein hammer

to hitting the nail at an angle, which would make the nail lean over. Ensure that children don't take wild swings with the hammer, and let the weight of the hammer do most of the work. Start by using wrist movement, which allows good control and needs less power, then use forearm action to hit harder. I'd recommend that children don't lift the hammer higher than their head to keep the motion safe and more controllable.

Wood tends to split if we nail too close to the edge and thick nails are also more likely to split wood. To avoid splits a pilot hole can be drilled first. When joining two sections of wood together it can also help to drill a pilot hole in the first piece of wood, which will make it easier and more manageable for the children to insert the nail in the drilled hole and then hammer two pieces together.

Avoid hammering into hardwood, MDF or knots. These are too hard and too challenging for young children, plus there is an increased likelihood of nails rebounding if hit at an angle. Remove protruding nails or hammer the end level to make it safe. To join MDF, drill a pilot hole first.

Some practitioners advocate holding the nail with a pair of pliers or a clothes peg so that the fingers are well away from the hitting area. Young children are more than capable of carefully holding the nail upright and gently tapping until it stands up on its own in the wood. After a short time they will be happily banging in nails independently.

When children are hammering larger nails they will be using considerably more force. It becomes even more important that the hand holding the wood is well away from the nail.

When hammering, ensure children never hold nails by putting them in their mouths. (This practice is used occasionally by adults to hold a nail whilst both hands are occupied – so be aware not to model this behaviour!)

Children will develop concepts and understanding over time. They will learn how to best position the work to be able to hammer effectively, discover that when joining with one nail sections swivel whereas with two nails they are rigid, and work out the best size of nail to effectively join different sections.

A tree stump section can be good for practising hammering as the end grain is easier to hammer into.

Claw hammer

It is also useful to have a short stubby claw hammer in the toolkit for removing nails. The claw is used to lever out a nail by inserting the nail head in between the claws and gently levering the hammer away from the nail. Having a small additional block of wood can be helpful to assist levering the nail fully out of the wood. There are other tools that are also good for removing nails. (See below.)

Stubby claw hammer

Getting started

Japanese nail-puller, flat nail-puller, pincers

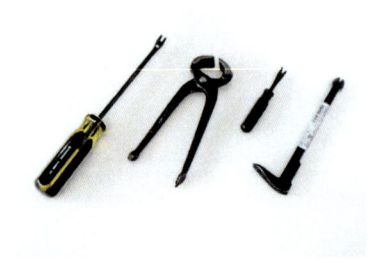

A small Japanese nail-puller is a really wonderful tool and very controllable for young children to lever out nails. It is important to ensure the nail puller is used with a levering in motion rather than yanking as children could potentially pull the tool towards themselves. For this reason I suggest the Japanese nail puller is used when being closely monitored. Another good tool is the flat nail-puller (basically like a flat screwdriver but with a small slot that fits under the head of the nail), which children find easy to use. Pincers are another tool used for removing nails – however, due to the finger trap hazard, only use when closely monitored.

Screwdriver

The screwdriver provides the children with another way of joining pieces of wood. It is best to use short cross head screwdrivers, often referred to as stubby screwdrivers. These are much easier for children to control and learn to use. Slotted or flat blade screwdrivers are more difficult as they easily slide out of the screw slot.

Cross head screwdrivers come in two types: Pozidrive and Phillips head. Pozidrive is the preferred option as it has a firmer grip on the screw and is less likely to slip out. (Phillips head screwdrivers will still work but can be more prone to slip.) Pozidrive is the most common type of screwdriver in Europe. Use a short stubby Pozidrive screwdriver with a head sized PZ2. Screwdrivers' heads come in different sizes and the screwdriver needs to fit the screw head correctly. The PZ2 is a larger size, making it easier for children to manipulate. Ensure the screw size matches the screwdriver head otherwise it will not grip correctly and slip. With the Pozidrive PZ2 screwdriver use screw sizes 8 or 10 (4mm or 5mm) and have a variety of lengths of screws available.

Demonstrate how to turn the screwdriver with a rotational and downward motion and have the children experiment with turning in both directions to see how the screw goes into the wood and

Getting started

how it can be removed. It can help to have the wood they are working on clamped so they can use both hands on the screwdriver. Stubby screwdrivers can also be purchased with a ratchet mechanism, which makes it even easier for young children to use.

It can help to first make a small indentation in the balsa wood to make it easier to start the screw off, and then twisting the screw in slightly with finger and thumb so it stands up. The indentation can be made with large nail or bradawl.

Bradawl or awl

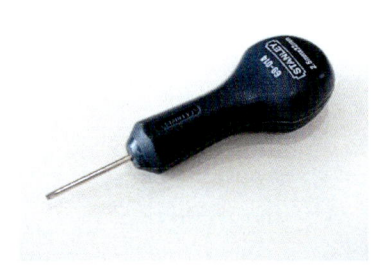

A bradawl or awl is used to poke a small hole in the surface of wood. They either come with a sharp pointed end or with an end similar to a very small flat head screwdriver. The second option is much safer and is readily available. It is best to get a short version so it is more controllable. They are useful to make a small hole for starting screws in soft wood or locating where to start drilling.

Small battery screwdriver

A small battery-operated screwdriver is another possibility to explore. There are several very small models available, such as the 'IXO by Bosch'. They rotate slowly and are quite manageable for young children, and can be particularly helpful if they are screwing in long screws. Children really enjoy having the experience of using a battery-powered tool. Note that only small low torque models are safe for young children as they need to retain a firm grip. Do not use power drills with screwdriver bits.

Small battery-powered screwdriver

Hand drill

Young children find it very easy to screw straight into balsa wood but with softwoods it is necessary to drill a small hole first, otherwise it will be very stiff and hard to turn, which is too difficult for young children.

Getting started

There are several types of hand drill available. Use hand drills with enclosed mechanisms – the 'Draper pistol grip' drill is a good example. With hand drills that have exposed mechanisms there is a small possibility of getting fingers caught in the rotating cogs.

When demonstrating emphasise that the drill needs to be kept vertical at all times, otherwise the drill bits are likely to snap. I purchase extra-short drill bits (stubby drill bits) to lessen the likelihood of snapping the drill bits. Teach the correct use by turning the drill in the right direction. I start with the turning handle at the top and then pushing the crank handle away so it is rotating clockwise. (This would be opposite

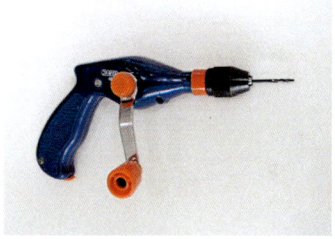

123

Getting started

for a left-hander). Hand drills work best with small diameter drill bits. I recommend short 3mm drill bits, which make a good size hole to start a screw off or to nail into. Smaller drill bits are more likely to snap. For screwing, drills need to be a little smaller than the screw size.

Once a hole has been drilled it can be difficult to remove the drill from the wood. A useful technique is to the rotate the handle in the opposite direction for one turn, which helps release the drill bit, making it easier to lift it out of the hole.

To remove a drill bit, hold the handle so it cannot rotate, then twist the chuck anticlockwise to remove the bit. To insert, place the drill bit into the chuck and tighten it firmly by rotating clockwise whilst the crank handle is kept steady. This should be done by the supporting adult as it needs to be tight.

Depending on how the work is supported it may be necessary to place a sacrificial piece of wood underneath the wood being drilled to protect the workbench or table from being drilled into.

Drill bit depth stop collars can be joined to a drill bit to limit the depth that holes can be drilled – this can be useful to allow drilling of small holes without drilling right into the workbench! These usually come in a pack to fit a variety of different diameter drill bits.

Brace and bit

The brace and bit is another type of drill that is particularly popular with children as it has a very satisfying motion. It has a higher rotational force and can be used by the children to drill wider holes. With the advance of power tools, brace and bit drills have become less common but are still readily available second-hand. Drill bits sized 6mm to 10mm would be ideal for use with these, and being wider are less likely to snap.

Getting started

As these are quite large, children find them more comfortable to use, with the work being drilled on the ground using it in the vertical position. They can also be used horizontally, drilling into work held firmly in the vice. As before, it is important to keep the vertical or horizontal alignment steady whilst drilling.

Palm drill

125

Getting started

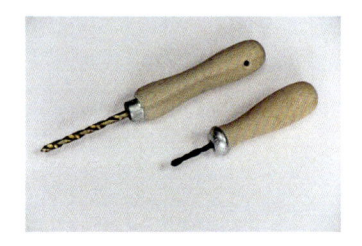

The palm drill is a small non-mechanised hand drill. These are basically a drill bit combined with a handle and can be used by young children to make holes in soft material such as balsa wood, cork or conkers.

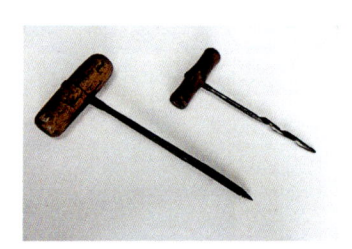

Gimlet and auger

These are small hand tools for making small holes in wood. An auger is slightly larger than a gimlet. They work in the same way, both having a small thread at the end to help them get started and then continue to cut a hole as they are rotated. They can provide an alternative to using a drill to make holes to start screws off.

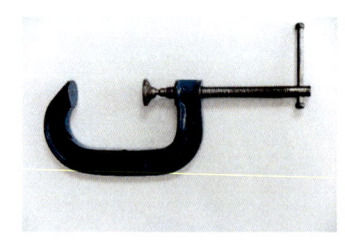

G-clamps

G-clamps have a number of uses and provide a good solid grip. When children are drilling they will have both hands on the drill so the wood they are drilling needs to be held firm. This can be done by clamping the wood in a vice or by using a G-clamp to clamp the wood to the table. Clamps can hold wood firmly while glue sets and can be used to hold wood firm whilst a nail is being removed. G-clamps come in a variety of sizes and need to be large enough to clamp the wood to the table. A clamp with an opening of approximately 100mm (often referred to as being 4 inch) would be useful. These can be operated by children; however, it is important that the supporting adult checks and tightens if necessary.

Saw

126

Many practitioners get a little nervous at the thought of their children using saws and often ask if woodwork can be done without the sawing! The saw is an important addition to a toolkit, allowing the children to have more control over their designs and creations by being able to cut wood to the size they require.

Having the correct saws makes a huge difference. We really want sawing to be as easy as possible so as not to discourage any children. There are so many different types of saw available: coping saws for curves, bow saws for branches, hacksaws for metal, etc., that it can be quite confusing to choose the most suitable.

The toolkit should contain two saws (see below for more details):

1 A small 'dozuki' Japanese pull saw.
2 A larger pull saw for cutting through thicker wood or a standard European cross-cut saw.

Saws clearly need to be sharp to be able to cut wood, so we need to exercise care when handling them. Saws with fine teeth are more suitable, having a smoother action, and are also less likely to cause injury through mishandling.

In all cases it is essential that the wood being cut is held firm in a vice and it is important that the workbench is firm and solid. It may be necessary for the teacher to help steady it if using a light workbench. The wood should be cut close to the workbench so that the wood is held firmly, avoiding vibrations. It is best to cut about 2cm away from where the wood is clamped in the vice. Too close and the saw handle may bang into the table, and too far away and the wood may flex, making the sawing more difficult.

When introducing the saw, show the children how sharp the saw is; allow them to very gently feel the teeth to raise their awareness. Emphasise the need for care.

Getting started

When sawing, one-to-one supervision is required at all times. This is to check that the wood is tightly clamped in the vice and to ensure the child is using the saw correctly and to support them if necessary. But most importantly it is to ensure other children don't pass in front of the saw or try to watch from in front. This is a significant area of risk if a child were to get in front of the saw, so we need to be vigilant. This risk is eliminated by the teacher being positioned directly in front, keeping the area clear. Children love to watch – but ensure they stand well back. It could also be an option to have the workbench positioned so that the saw protrudes towards a wall with no potential for children to access the area of risk. After sawing, the saw should be returned to a safe place – we keep it visible but elevated.

Some practitioners have advocated the hand that is not holding the saw be held behind the back, but this is counter-productive as it is an uncomfortable position and children's balance is affected and they are not able to put as much strength and refinement into their sawing. Others have suggested wearing gloves, but this restricts children's grip and control, which is not helpful. Some saws are best used with two hands and others with one hand – I explain which below.

Small Japanese dozuki pull saw (approx. 160cm blade length)

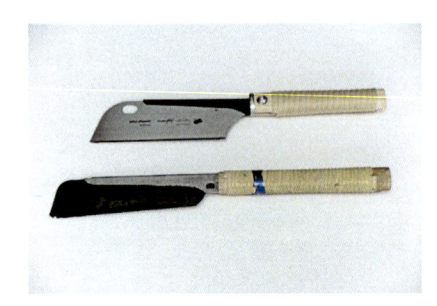

The Japanese saw is an important addition to the toolkit. It is sometimes referred to as a pull saw. Originating in Japan, it is also used widely in the Middle East and is rapidly becoming commonplace with carpenters in Europe. It is a great introductory saw, especially when using soft balsa wood.

Japanese saws differ from European saws as they cut on the pull stroke. Pull saws are more controllable and easier for children to use. The Japanese pull saw's blades are thin and have very fine teeth with the result that children find using it particularly easy. Being thin means that it takes less effort to cut the wood (as less wood is being sawn away). It is held with two hands, which actually helps the children cut in a straight line perpendicular to the wood. There is the added benefit that with both hands safely holding the handle they are away from the cutting area. It can be easier for children to start the cut with a couple of forward strokes (opposite to European saws).

Everyone who uses the Japanese saw is taken aback by just how much easier it is than the European saw, which can tend to snag slightly on the push stroke or will become stiff and hard to push if it is not kept straight. These days many builders and carpenters are moving over to using Japanese saws.

Japanese saws come in three types: ones with teeth on both sides of the blade (ryoba) and others with teeth just on one side (dozuki and kataba). The kataba has no strengthening strip and the blade is very flexible, so best avoided. Children in Japan use saws with teeth on both sides, allowing them to cut through thick pieces of wood. In order to keep risk to a minimum, use Japanese saws with teeth just on one side and the smooth strengthening strip on the top side (dozuki). The limitation with this saw is that the depth of cut is limited by the width of the blade (30mm to 50mm), hence the need for a second saw for deeper cutting work.

To summarise the three types:

Dozuki – teeth on one side with stiffening strip in the top.
Ryoba – teeth on both sides – cross cut and rip.
Kataba – teeth on one side but with no strengthening strip.

I recommend the Dozuki style, 'Ice Bear' brand with a blade length of about 160cm.

Larger pull saw or European cross-cut saw

A larger pull saw is the preferred option, again as it is more manageable for children. They are less common than European cross-cut saws but are still readily available.

This pull saw could be a larger Japanese saw but this time 'kataba' style (without the strengthening strip), or there are many other manufacturers producing these larger type pull saws. The Japanese versions are held with two hands whereas other pull saws often have a mounded handle more suited to one hand. Children are

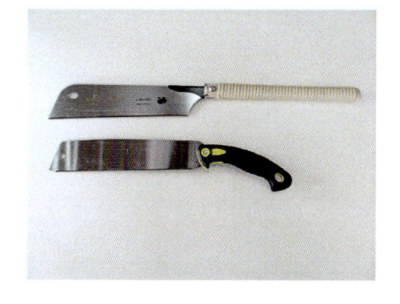

Getting started

capable of using either. These work just the same as the Japanese saws described above but have thicker blades so are more robust and less flexible. They do not have the support 'back' rod that strengthens the blade so they can cut through any thickness of wood (given the strength of the operator!) Cutting on the pull stoke makes them more controllable for young children. A blade with fine teeth and length of 30–40cm would be suitable.

When starting cuts with pull saws it is easier to do a couple of forward strokes to get the groove started.

European cross-cut saw

The European cross-cut saw is a perfectly suitable alternative – and many schools will already have one. I would recommend a small saw with an approximate blade length of 40cm and with relatively fine teeth providing a smoother action and a cleaner cut. The Swedish Bahco tool box saw is a good example of this. The European saw is best used one handed with the other hand holding the workbench to provide balance. Demonstrate how to hold the saw with one hand and show that the other hand must hold the table well away from the saw and the wood being cut.

European saws cut on the forward stroke and are more likely to jam and bow especially if children apply too much

130

pressure. It is important when sawing to keep the saw in a straight line otherwise it easily gets stuck making it hard to push and pull. When sawing, keep the eye, arm and length of the saw all aligned. It can be easier for children to start the cut with a couple of back strokes. Demonstrate how to get into a slow rhythm of strokes and not to use too much pressure. We need just enough pressure for the teeth to cut without getting stuck, letting the saw and time do the majority of the work. Avoid cutting through knots as they are very hard and challenging for young children.

With cross-cut saws the teeth are actually a little wider than the saw blade (called the kerf) to enable the blade to move freely as the cut deepens.

In both cases, with the larger pull-saw and European cross-cut saw ensure that you keep the maximum blade length to approximately 350mm, especially for the younger children (3- and 4-year-olds). Longer saws are heavier and there is increased risk that once the wood is sawn through the saw may swing down back towards the child.

Sawing: general tips

Sawing sometimes can be tricky and some wood is harder to cut than others. The most important thing is that the saw is sharp and sawing is done at a steady speed, without too much effort, letting the blade do the cutting.

Store the saw in an elevated position where the children can see it clearly and then ask for it when they would like to cut. The sawing is then closely supervised and the saw returned to its safe place.

It is a joy to see the delight on a child's face after spending a long time and a lot of hard work sawing through a piece of wood when it finally falls on the floor with a thump! It is amazing just how persistent children can be in cutting large sections of wood. Cutting wood is much easier across the grain than along, and softwood that is grown fast has a more open grain and is easier to cut. Green wood is harder to cut as it tends to clog the saw teeth.

Traditionally, many schools have used junior hacksaws for woodwork. These are designed for cutting metals and plastics and with such a short blade it makes the sawing motion quite un-ergonomic. However, they do work quite well with very soft balsa wood so can be an option for that.

Previously, schools often used a bench hook to support wood being sawn. Its purpose was to provide a stop against which the piece of wood being worked can be firmly held, without having to use a vice, thus saving time. This is not a good option and definitely not recommended for early years children. The hand holding the work can easily lose grip, letting the wood slip, and the sawing is also too close to the hand holding the work.

Getting started

Posture is important when sawing to get the maximum strength into the motion, so standing well positioned and being balanced, with feet apart (left foot forward for right-handers and vice versa for left-handers) and keeping the eye in line with the length of the saw and the cutting line.

Sawing will often leave a rough edge and potential splinters so can need smoothing with sandpaper, a file, a rasp or a surform.

Surform

A surform tool incorporates a strip of perforated sheet metal and resembles a food grater. The rim of each hole is sharpened to form a cutting edge and the strip is mounted in a carriage or handle. The surform is useful for smoothing uneven edges. There are a few different models that are suitable for young children.

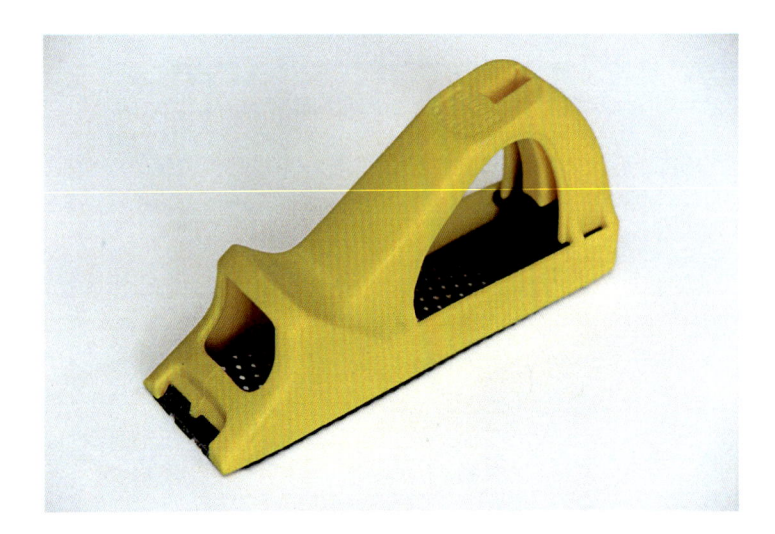

Files and rasps

Files and rasps are good for rounding corners, smoothing edges, or for the general shaping of wood. The file is relatively fine whereas a rasp is coarser. More care needs to be used with the rasp as the teeth are quite aggressive but they do remove wood more easily. The teeth can become clogged with wood so it is good to occasionally brush out the ingrained wood. A selection of three rasps, one round, one flat and one half round would be a great addition to the toolkit.

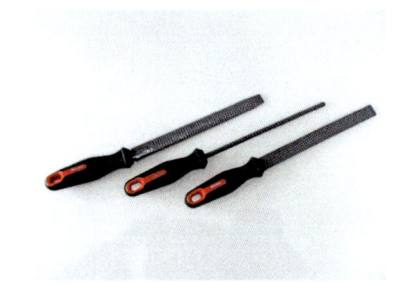

Block plane

The block plane requires more coordination and skill and thus is more suitable for older children. It is best introduced to children who are quite experienced in other woodworking skills. It is a useful tool for shaving layers of wood off the surface to smooth it. Children particularly enjoy the process of using this tool and are drawn to the wonderful shavings it produces, which become a useful byproduct that can be used in many different ways in their creations.

Pliers and wire cutters

Pliers can be useful for a wide variety of tasks and wire cutters are useful to snip lengths of wire. Their use is best monitored closely as there is the potential for fingers to get caught. They are more suited to children who are older and more experienced but do provide a useful addition to the toolkit, especially when combining different materials.

A large magnet

Not an immediately obvious addition to a toolkit but extremely useful! Nails and screws will rattle off tables and at the end of a session we need to collect these up, especially as younger children may very well be sharing the space. I used to ask children to help collect the nails up by hand at the end of the session until one 4-year-old boy suggested I use a magnet. We had explored magnetism a couple of weeks previously, using magnets and paper clips, and he had made the connection – and ever since we have used magnets to collect up nails and screws! Magnetic dishes are also available that can be used for containing nails and screws on the workbench, making them much less likely to end up on the floor.

Rulers and tape measures

It's always good to have rulers and tape measures available to support mathematical thinking. It is surprising how often the children to use them for comparing sizes or seeing how big models are. Provide a selection of measuring equipment: rulers, folding wooden rulers, small retractable tape measures and fabric or cloth tape measures. Avoid larger retractable tape measures that can retract at high speeds and could cause injury. Small 1m retractable tape measures are available that are safe.

Getting started

Set square or carpenter's square

A set square is a right angle and it can be useful to mark a cut perpendicular to the wood. Young children are more than capable of learning to use it.

Spirit level

Children really enjoy exploring the spirit level and can be useful in some of the more extensive extended learning projects (see Chapter 7).

Adjustable wrenches and spanners

Adjustable wrenches and spanners are used with nuts and bolts. This is an interesting addition to the woodworking area as children can drill larger holes and combine pieces of wood together using nuts and bolts and then tighten them with either the adjustable wrench or the spanner. They are also useful for deconstruction projects (such as disassembling a tricycle).

Consumables

Nails

Always keep a large quantity of 25mm bright round flat-headed nails. Nails are either galvanised (zinc coated) or regular steel, which are referred to as 'bright' and are cheaper. A flat head provides a larger hitting surface and enables removal by levering out. They are readily available from all hardware stores. A cost-effective way to buy these is in bulk – a 25kg box will last many months. This size is ideal, being easy to hammer into wood, relatively thin and short, but long enough for the children to be able to grip comfortably. These nails are ideal to combine with the initial 25mm × 25mm balsa wood sections and also perfect for joining various pieces to soft wood. The 25mm nails are an ideal size for gaining confidence with hammering and once they have the skill down, children will be able to hammer away with larger nails.

In addition, have a wide selection of different-sized nails with flat heads available. I would recommend including 40mm/50mm/65mm bright round nails with a narrow diameter (2.65mm is a common width and is suitable). Again, these can be purchased in bulk from any number of suppliers. It is worth remembering that the larger the diameter of the nail the harder it will be to hammer into the wood. Young children often choose the largest nail possible! If they are finding it difficult it may be worth suggesting they try a thinner nail. If they can use the small 25mm nails, so much the better. Avoid very large nails, as they are designed to be used with adult hammers and will require much more strength, and if you provide nails that are too long it is likely the children will want to take a workbench home with them!

Screws

Getting started

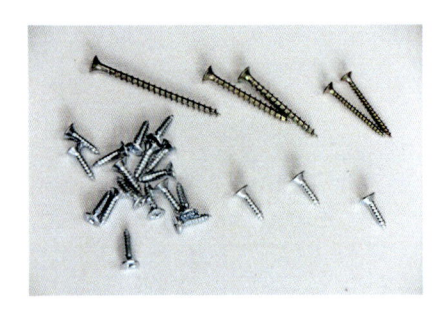

I would recommend starting with a quantity of relatively short Pozidriv screws. Screws are categorised by their length and thickness. The length will be in mm but commonly still in imperial inches. The width will be listed as the diameter or the gauge number. I recommend length: 3/4 inch – 15mm. And size: No. 10 gauge (5mm diameter) or No. 8 gauge (4mm diameter). Being short, they are relatively quick to screw in. This will make the task easier and develop confidence.

Ensure the screws have a Pozidriv cross head and combine with the stubby Pozidriv screwdriver. (A Phillips head screwdriver will still work but can be more prone to slip.) As children's skills develop, have a selection of other screws available of various lengths but keep to a similar width (No. 8 or No. 10).

Sandpaper

It is important to have sandpaper as we need to ensure splinters and rough edges are removed. Sandpaper is a good product to introduce early on. The texture of sandpaper is intriguing to most children and they enjoy seeing its effect on wood. To introduce sandpaper, have the children sand a small block of pine. Children could initially try sanding pencil marks off the surface of the wood. Sanding also releases some of the wood's aroma. It is not necessary to sand balsa wood as it is so soft and splinters are never an issue, but sandpaper can be used very easily to shape pieces of balsa wood. As soon as children start working with softwood such as pine they will need to start sanding edges.

Traditionally, sandpaper is wrapped around a small block and then rubbed over the surface. This proves quite difficult for young children as they find it hard to grip the sandpaper around the block. The most effective way to sand for young children, commonly used in Japan, is to glue a sheet of sandpaper to a board of MDF. Several different grades of sandpaper could be glued to different boards to give different finishes. Using the sandpaper in this way is so much easier for young children. In addition, a few small loose squares of sandpaper would be useful to reach parts that are more difficult to reach with the board. Coarse grade is the most useful for smoothing rough edges. Also provide medium and fine sandpaper to allow children to really be able to get wood smooth.

Another option available is a small block with Velcro that small sandpaper discs can be attached to.

Dust masks

For regular work it is not necessary to wear dust masks. Dust masks should be worn if excessive sanding is undertaken and they are likely to inhale significant amounts of dust. Realistically, children are unlikely to create the volumes of dust that would cause a problem; however, if doing a lot of sanding it may be worth considering, particularly for asthmatic children. Wearing protection gives the message that we need to protect our lungs from dust. Adult dust masks will not fit but there are many child-size facemasks available, often sold for virus or pollen protection.

Drill bits

It is good to have drill bits in reserve. The smaller ones will snap from time to time. The 3mm stubby drill bits can be purchased in packs of ten. Larger drill bits (6–10mm) used with the brace and bit are stronger but will become worn over time and will also need replacing.

Wood glue

I am often asked about combining woodwork with glue. I believe it is better on the whole to avoid using glue when children are combining with nails and screws, as using glue breaks their flow because they have to set their model aside to dry. Of course, children may very well wish to glue items to the models when they have finished the woodworking stage, and on occasion using glue will be the best method to join. PVA glue works well with wood. But allow two hours to dry and 12 hours to be fully hard. PVA is quite slippery so the join may need clamping, or holding firm with a weight, tape, elastic band or tacks. If children are familiar with using a glue gun this can provide a more instant way to combine additional elements.

Nuts and bolts

Have a selection of nuts and bolts and washers for children to use with the adjustable wrench and spanners. The best sizes to use are 6mm, 8mm and 10mm. Avoid going any smaller as they tend to be too fiddly. Wing-nuts are also popular, being easy to tighten by hand.

Getting started

Hooks and eye hooks

These can provide a nice additional resource, especially when combined with other materials such as string, wool or wire. A small hole needs to be made first with at bradawl, gimlet or small drill.

Tool maintenance

Regularly check tools for damage or wear. For example, check hammer heads are not working loose or saw blades becoming dull. It is good to lightly oil metal parts occasionally to prevent the build-up of any tarnishing or rust. Wooden handles can be looked after with an occasional thin coating of linseed oil.

Tool organisation

Tool organisation will very much depend on how the woodwork area is accessed and whether it is always available as part of continuous provision. Issues to think about are arranging tools so they can easily be accessed independently and then returned to their correct place. Safety considerations such as limiting access to certain tools, how tools are carried and ensuring tools remain within the woodworking area will all need addressing.

Suppliers

There are a number of educational suppliers that stock tools for children (see Resources and suppliers). Any tools that are harder to source can easily be found through online suppliers. Many are also available from regular hardware stores, as are consumables such as nails, screws and sandpaper.

> If I did it again I would join the wings after, then, it would be easier to join the lights and the wheels.
>
> Kara, aged 4

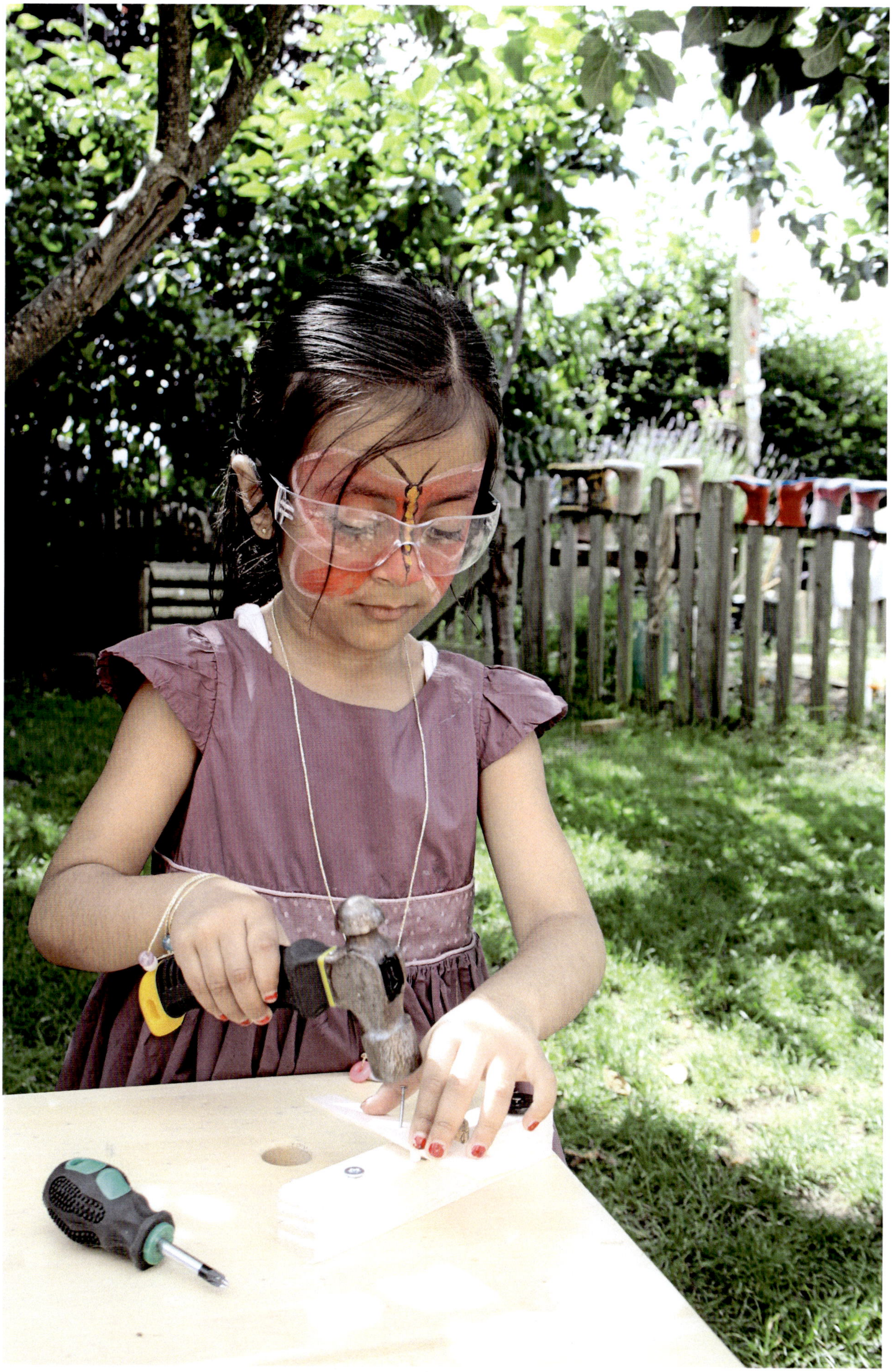

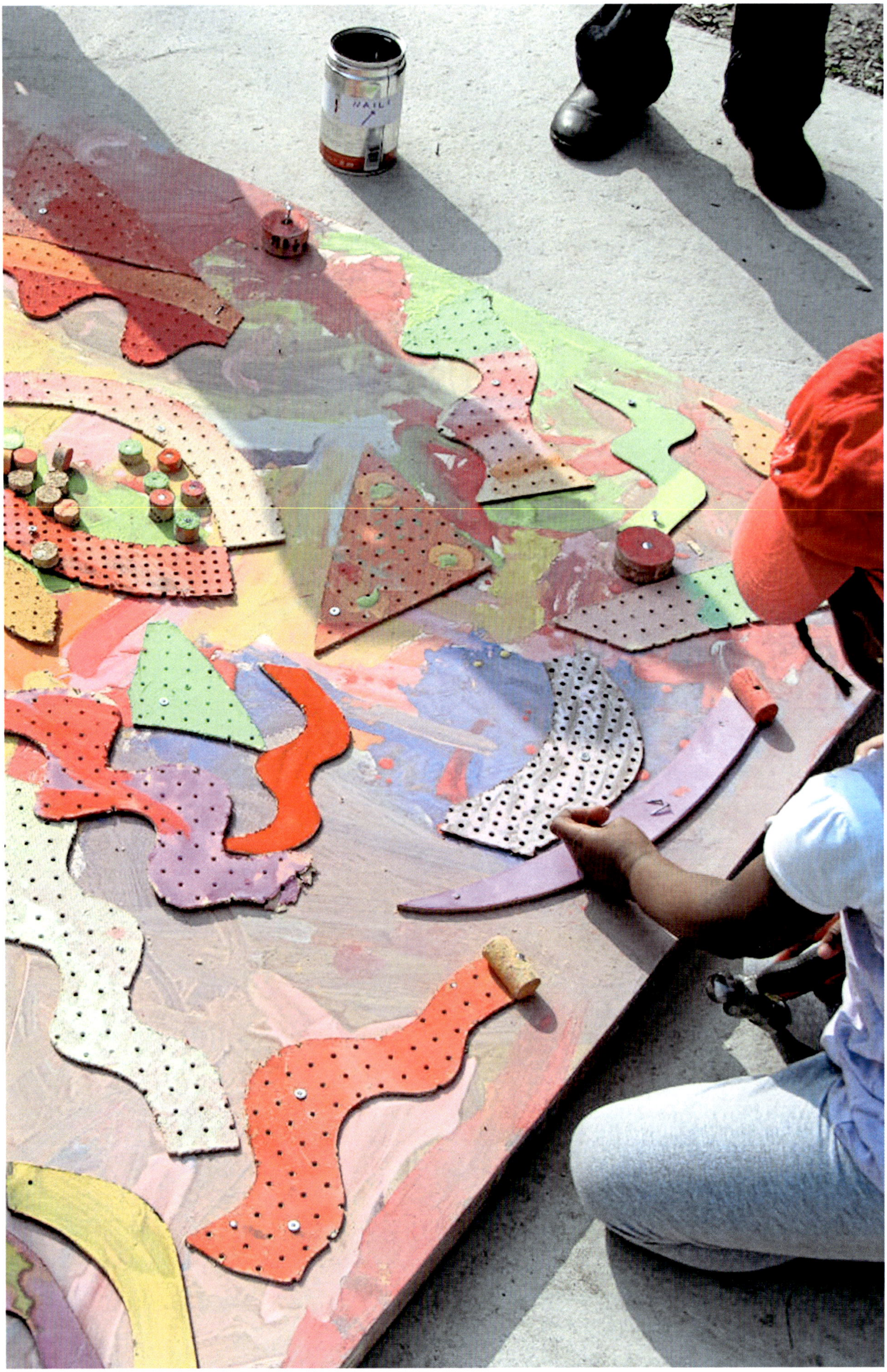

CHAPTER 7

Extended learning projects

Woodwork offers young children so much of what they need to thrive and grow. I am convinced that it should form a key part of rich and rewarding provision in every setting.

Jan White, early years consultant

Chapter overview

This chapter looks at examples of longer-term projects, which often last over several weeks or even months. Initially, I explain what extended learning projects are and the context of project-based learning in bringing together different areas of learning. I then provide examples of specific projects that emerged from children's interests.

Sculpture ▶ 142	
Sound garden ▶ 145	
Wooden frieze ▶ 148	
House ▶ 149	
Deconstruction ▶ 153	
Mud kitchen ▶ 155	

Extended learning projects are a wonderful way to extend learning. They encourage more in-depth investigation, build on developing skills and combine different areas of learning. Children discover real-life applications of various tools and techniques.

Extended projects can last over several sessions, weeks or even months and are collaborative, with a group of children working together. They provide a wonderful opportunity for children to learn from each other. They gain experience of how others think, thus expanding their creative and critical thinking skills. They build on each other's ideas as they refine designs and work out potential solutions to problems together.

Project-based learning (PBL) has had many advocates over the years. The Reggio Emilia approach has embraced project-based learning for many years and Chard and Katz in particular have championed the project approach. Project-based learning is a child-centred pedagogy, through which children acquire a deeper knowledge by active exploration of real-world questions and challenges. Children learn about a subject by working for an extended period of time to investigate and respond to a complex question, challenge, or problem. It is a style of active learning and inquiry-based learning. Projects are cross-curricular in nature.

Ideally, ideas for extended projects will emerge from children's interests, a driving question, a problem to be solved, or from authentic necessity of something that needs repairing or adding to the setting. In one project children decided to make a scarecrow to keep the birds away from seeds planted during a gardening project. This became a project that lasted over many weeks as children developed their ideas, collected materials and created their scarecrows. Another example is children planning and then repairing a broken garden bench.

Other examples have evolved from children being consulted about what additions they would like for their outdoor environment. On one occasion, from these discussions it emerged that the children wanted a playhouse. We then embarked on a long-term project to design and make a playhouse rather than buy one from a catalogue. Obviously, there was a significant amount of adult input, with this being a more involved project, but with sensitive close involvement of children throughout the entire design and making process, they were involved at a high level. Personally, I feel children vote with their feet and we can quickly see if a project is successful by the way children remain passionately engaged and excited and persist with it right through to the end. I have found that it is possible to retain high levels of engagement as we work through these extended projects, and the sense of pride that the children take at the end of the project is a delight to see.

Project learning phases:

1 Initial concept/challenge arising from children's interests.
2 Exploration of concept/challenge.
3 Possible approaches – inquiry phase – building on each others' ideas – co-inspiration.
4 Selecting a course of action.
5 Implementation – Monitoring – Refining.
6 Reflection – Evaluation – Co-critique – Feedback.

Below are some examples of the extended projects we have undertaken.

Sculpture

Creating wooden sculptures is always a very engaging project for children and provides a great way to expand developing woodwork skills. Sculpture, like other art forms, gives children the opportunity to express their ideas in a number of different ways as they represent thoughts, experiences and feelings in physical form.

This project could start by looking at pictures of sculptures to get a deeper understanding, discussing types of sculpture, and then evolve by exploring making sculptures in a variety of different media such as in clay, paper and card.

Extended learning projects

The children could then move on to creating their own wooden sculptures. As soon as children are joining wood they are in effect creating three-dimensional objects. I've found that a great starting point, much as in the same way a piece of paper is a starting point for a drawing, is to provide a piece of wood vertically mounted on a base. I then provide a large selection of all sorts of offcuts, with a wide variety of shapes and sizes.

The children then choose pieces they like and start to construct their sculpture, choosing to join with nails or screws. They use a whole array of skills and there are many opportunities for expressing their imagination, problem-solving and thinking creatively. Making sculptures with wood also develops spatial thinking, and provides many opportunities to use thinking from other areas of learning.

Young children are very powerful visual thinkers and have a clear sense of aesthetics. Vision comes before words and seeing is children's first language. It is always impressive just how thoughtful the children are in their arrangements, seeming to have a natural understanding of shape and form.

Another dimension of a sculpture project could be to work together creating larger collaborative sculptures. Here it would be good to discuss options and follow the children's interest. Various ideas may evolve: a totem pole-like structure, a giant spider web, a giant windmill, and so on. A simple way to make a large collaborative sculpture is to start with a substantial length (2–3m) of 2 by 1 (50mm × 25mm) or 2 by 4 (50mm × 100mm) pine and add various elements to this.

143

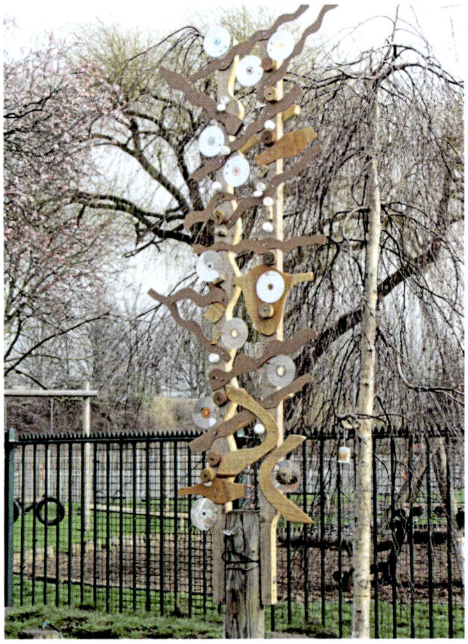

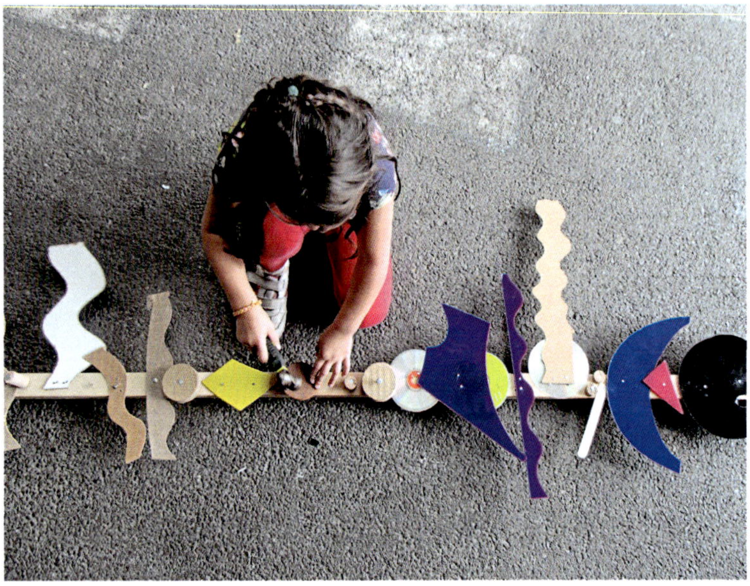

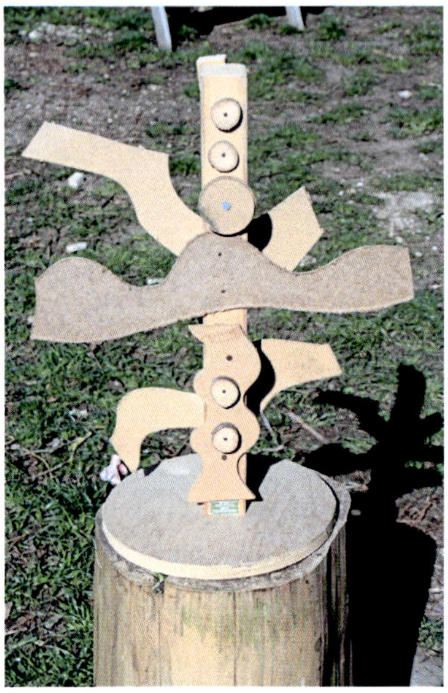

With sculpture projects it can be interesting to combine other materials, adding drilled pieces of coloured plastic, pieces of hose pipe and so on to make a real mixed media sculpture. The sculptures are suitable to remain in the outdoor environment and look great for months. They can provide a strong message that the setting really encourages creativity.

Some settings have taken the opportunity to celebrate their sculptural project by exhibiting the children's sculptures in a commercial gallery space. The children had previously experienced visiting galleries and museums and were delighted to share their work with their extended families and the public through the exhibition of their work. Witnessing the collection of children's work assembled together was quite remarkable and received incredibly positive feedback. The wider community were taken aback by the creativity and skills shown by such young children. Projects that allow children to share their work with the community show that young children have something to contribute and that they should be valued as equal members of society. It is also a good opportunity for the setting to connect with the local community.

Sound garden

This project evolved from ideas to find a solution for existing broken outdoor sound equipment. The children decided they would like to create some new sounds themselves and use their woodwork skills to construct a sound garden. The project started by children and parents bringing in a selection of old kitchen utensils. Children then explored them by experimenting with the different sounds that they could make and then choosing the sounds that they particularly enjoyed making. The sounds metal can make can be investigated thoroughly by hanging up objects and listening to their sounds when tapped or banged together. Metal items could be arranged on the floor to see how they sound as drums. Children could experiment with scraping or rattling sounds and so on. I remember one boy experimenting with a large washer and piece of threaded rod, fascinated by the way the washer slowly spiralled down, making a delightful sound. Needless to say, this was another element that was incorporated in their sound garden.

After the metal and sound exploration the children moved on to think about designing their sound garden, and the final stage was the construction. Children can be fully involved in all the construction, sawing the wooden supporting structure, taking it in turns to get through the really thick sections and bolting it together. They added the sound elements using their woodworking skills: sawing, drilling, some joining by nailing, some screwing and sometimes use of the wrench and coach bolts.

Being designed by the children ensures that the sound garden is engaging and has elements they like. There is rarely a moment when a child is not playing in our sound garden, with its wonderful eclectic mix of different sounds.

Sound and sensory gardens or apparatus can be made to different scales and for very limited budgets. If you are considering buying new equipment for your outdoor area it may well be worth considering how you could involve the children and undertake such a project yourselves.

Case study 7.1 Extended thinking during the sound garden project

Will, Max and Freddie are working on the sound garden. They need a wood beam from which to hang some saucepan lids.

The three boys make a pencil mark on a fence post they wish to cut so it will fit between two uprights. They carry the fence post to be cut to the workbench and tighten it firmly in the vice. They quickly realise it is going to be difficult to cut as the pencil mark is actually inside the vice claws.

Max: 'We're going to cut into the workbench!'
Teacher: 'Ah, what are our options then?'

The boys concentrate, staring intently at the problem, hands in pockets. After considerable time Will makes a suggestion.

Will: 'Why don't we just cut it here?' (indicating as close as possible to the pencil mark but still some distance away.)

Max: 'No, that won't work, it will be too long!'
Teacher: 'Well, let's have a think to see if we can think of any other options.'

Again the boys are quiet for several minutes, just observing and thinking, then some more discussion: perhaps cutting pieces, getting a different workbench. . . then finally a big smile appears on Freddie's face.

Freddie: 'We need to say take it out and move it.'
Will: 'Yes! Let's try that.'

They undo the vice and slide the wood along and then tighten it again.

Will: 'Yes, now the saw can reach the line.'
Teacher: 'That's great – you really thought hard to come up with different ideas and find a solution – well done.'

They then take turns to cut through the thick fence post. Max then unclamps it and together they proudly carry it back across the playground to the sound garden area with a swagger in their step.

Wooden frieze

Extended learning projects

This was a project to create a wall panel for our local hospital where most of the children were born. The local hospital has a tradition of incorporating artwork into the building to promote patient well-being. They approached us to see if we would create an artwork. It was a wonderful opportunity for us to create permanent work for the community, and importantly show that children have something to contribute to society and that they should be valued and respected.

Initially, there were discussions about what we could make for the hospital – children were keen to make a wooden picture and for it to be really bright and colourful to make patients happy. First, we made the panel using pine and plywood, then children joined many pieces of wooden offcuts to create wonderful wooden collage. There was a lot of hammering, drilling, sawing and screwing as children chose different sections of wood to add to the composition. After the panel was completely covered we painted it, thinking carefully about colour, mixing our own shades. Then we painted additional pieces of wood and added them on top.

I then coated the entire work with varnish to protect it in the long term and we hired a minibus to take the panel to the hospital. The children helped install the work. We included an information panel documenting their work on the project and the local press celebrated the event.

The resulting artwork looked striking – colourful and energetic – and was much appreciated by the hospital, with many saying that this vibrant piece was their favourite artwork! The hospital has just been rebuilt and the artwork now takes pride of place in the new entrance lobby. In similar projects we have contributed our artwork to local health centres, libraries and public spaces.

House

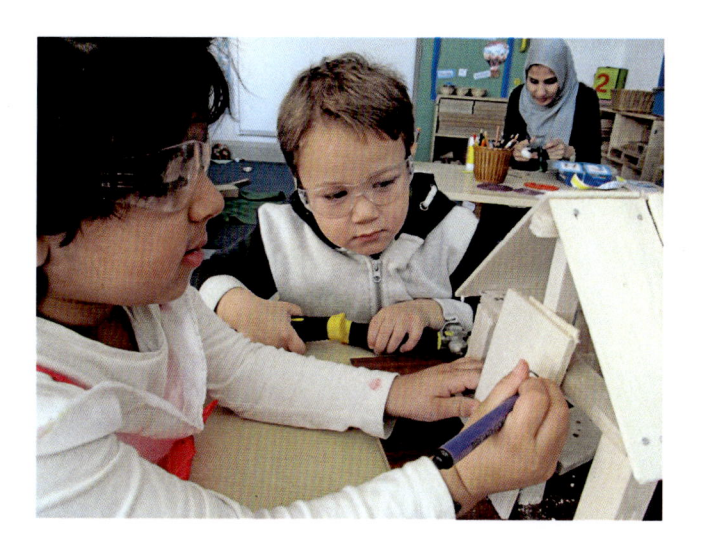

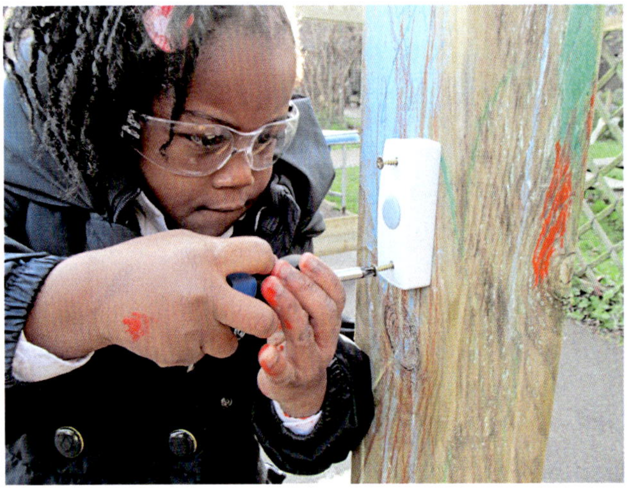

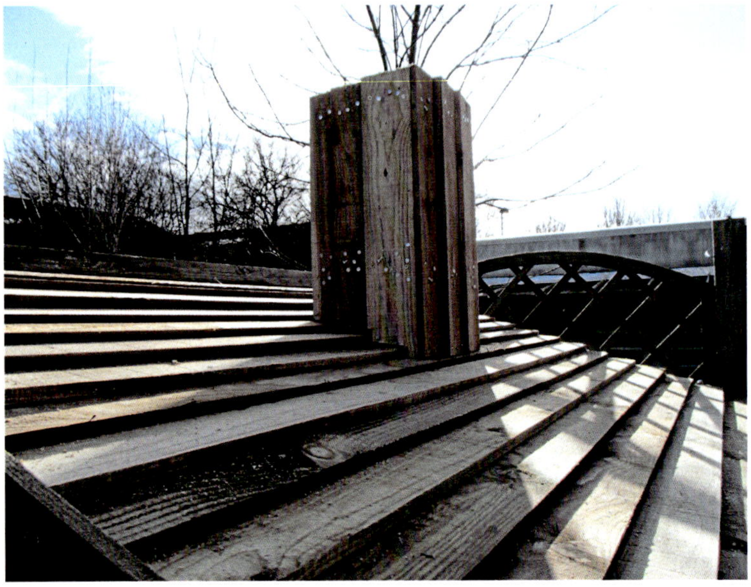

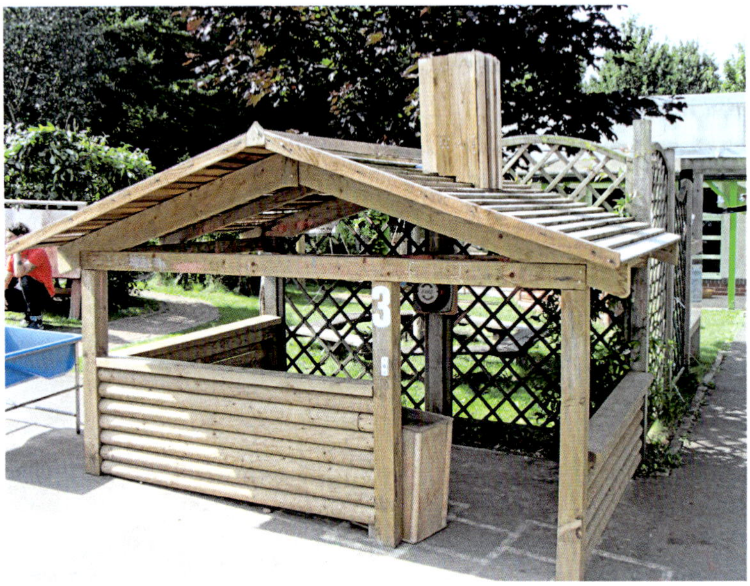

This project evolved from the children's desire to have a playhouse in the outdoor area. Instead of buying one we decided to involve the children as much as possible in designing and making their own playhouse. This was a long-term project lasting over six months. We felt the children were capable of helping design and construct the building and that the entire process could further develop their skills and open up new areas of learning.

After looking at many examples of wooden houses and discussing them, the children became architects, exploring designs in different media. They expressed ideas using mark-making, building with Jenga blocks, building with Lego, making cardboard houses, using lollipop sticks, glue and paper, and building with large wooden blocks. Many ideas evolved from this process, including the need to have a chimney just to make sure Father Christmas would be able to visit. The next stage was to make a small model house in balsa wood, exploring construction ideas and investigating different ways of joining. So many ideas evolved, as well as many problems that needed to be resolved.

This project incorporated many additional avenues of exploration. We spent several sessions investigating pulleys as we used a pulley to lift the roof boards. It was wonderful working as a group to lift up the roof boards and the children were captivated by how easy it was to lift heavy objects.

As part of our exploration we investigated construction, and looked at methods of joining and building, seeing how we could make things robust and strong. This was explored in a number of ways: we made many towers using corks and cardboard, really thinking about how to make strong rigid structures; buildings were made out of blocks; a cardboard house was constructed; bolted wooden constructions were made; and wood was joined in a variety of different ways using nails and screws.

After coming up with a design we liked, and deciding on construction methods, we started building the playhouse, marking out the area and then building a simple frame to which planks were attached to create walls. There were endless opportunities for numeracy and for exploring shape, space and measure, and many opportunities for problem-solving.

The project lasted six months but throughout children remained engaged and focused. As soon as the house was complete it immediately became a cafe, a petrol station, a hospital, a fire station, its use changing and evolving with children's interests.

Case study 7.2 Problem-solving during the house project

After completing the house frame we were ready to start joining the half round fence rails to use to make the walls.

Child: 'Now we need the walls!'
Teacher: 'Do you think these might work for the walls?'
Child: 'Yes! They would be really strong.'

A small group of children pick up the long fence rail and try and manoeuvre it into position

Child: 'It's much too long.'
Teacher: 'I wonder if there is any way we can solve that problem?'
Child: 'Cut it of course with the saw!'
Teacher: 'Couldn't we just make the house bigger?'
Child: 'No, then we'd have to move everything again.'
Teacher: 'Yes, that would create a lot of extra work, so I wonder how we make the wood the right size to fit.'
Child: 'With the tape measure.'

(continued)

(continued)

The children measure the distance and make a mark on the tape measure with a whiteboard marker. They then place the tape measure on the wood and mark the place to cut. They work together carefully to lift the wood and place it in the vice. They take turns with the sawing as it is quite thick wood. Halfway through the saw gets stuck. The supporting bar on the Japanese saw does not allow thick cuts. The children quickly realise they need the bigger saw. As the wood falls the cut splinters a bit.

Teacher: 'I think the sharp bits might be a little bit dangerous, I wonder how we could best remove them.'

Again a lengthy discussion and then children use the saw to trim the edge and then rub the edge with a rasp. They then carry wood together to start the wall. It takes considerable co-ordination and discussion to manipulate the wood to the correct orientation.

Children: 'No, it's the wrong way round.' 'We need the bumpy bit on the outside.' 'We have to have to take it outside the house and come back in again.' 'That's better. . . oh it's still too long . . . it won't fit!'
Teacher: 'I wonder if there's anything we can do to solve this new problem?'
Child: 'We need to cut this little bit off here.'
Teacher: 'That sounds like a good idea. I wonder what we could have done if it was too short?'
Children: 'We could add a bit.' 'We could move the post.' 'We could make it (the post) bigger.' 'We could get a new board.'
Teacher: 'You guys have so many great ideas. There is a saying: "measure twice and cut once."'
Child: 'That's silly.'

Teacher: 'I guess it's saying it's good to measure twice to check because it's easy to make a mistake and it will stop us having to cut twice to correct the mistake. There are lots of sayings that help give advice, like "don't count your chickens before they hatch".'

At this stage we have a lengthy digression talking about eggs and chickens. . . it's a slow process building a house!

Teacher: 'Shall we try measuring again?'

The children proceed to measure and make a mark again.

Teacher: 'So, now let's measure twice.'

They repeat and the line is now in the same place. The children then cut the wood again. They then carry the wood and rotate it until it fits the wall.

Child: 'It fits!' is shouted with delight.
Teacher: 'I wonder what would be the best way to fix it?'
Children: 'Sellotape.' 'Glue-stick.'

More discussion and testing of ideas.

Child: 'No, we need to hammer now and nail to fix it.'
Teacher: 'I wonder which would be the best sized nail to use?'
Child: 'This long one.'

The children proceed to hammer the board on.

As the children continue to construct the wall they build on their previous learning and after adding several sections of wood it is incredible to see just how competent and confident they have become.

Deconstruction

Deconstruction is an exercise in discovery. Children enjoy using their skills with tools to deconstruct items. They are curious to discover what lies inside and are fascinated to investigate how things work. They focus intently on this detective role and learning often expands as they investigate.

Deconstruction deepens children's understanding of how things are made. As they break an appliance down into parts, they can investigate each component and they will discover how they were assembled, building knowledge of how things are manufactured. They will discover how elements interact. They can think about the purpose of each component and the complexity of what is needed to make an appliance function. (See Chapter 3, Understanding the world, for more about deconstruction.)

Start by collecting old apparatus such as an old bike or tricycle, a whisk, a hand drill, some mechanical weighing scales, a mechanical clock or an old slide projector. There are some potential hazards when deconstructing certain appliances and electronic equipment. Some advice is common sense, such as removing plugs, but there are other potential hazards that are less well known. Large capacitors can store charge and should be avoided – these are found in many appliances such as microwaves. Currently there is conflicting advice about potential contact with toxic elements in deconstructing electronic equipment. I avoid deconstructing items that contain printed circuit boards such as TVs, computers, etc., due to any potential hazards of toxic elements

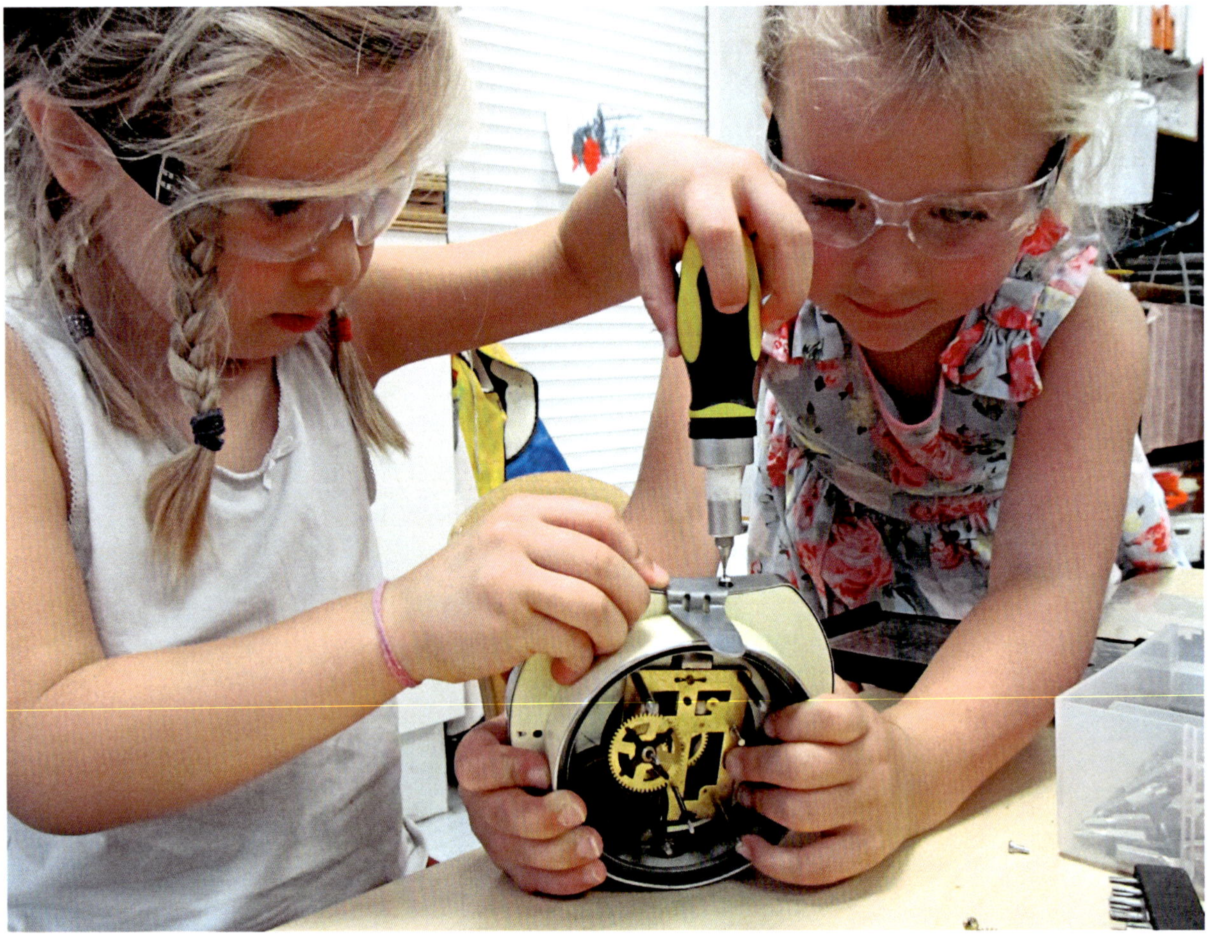

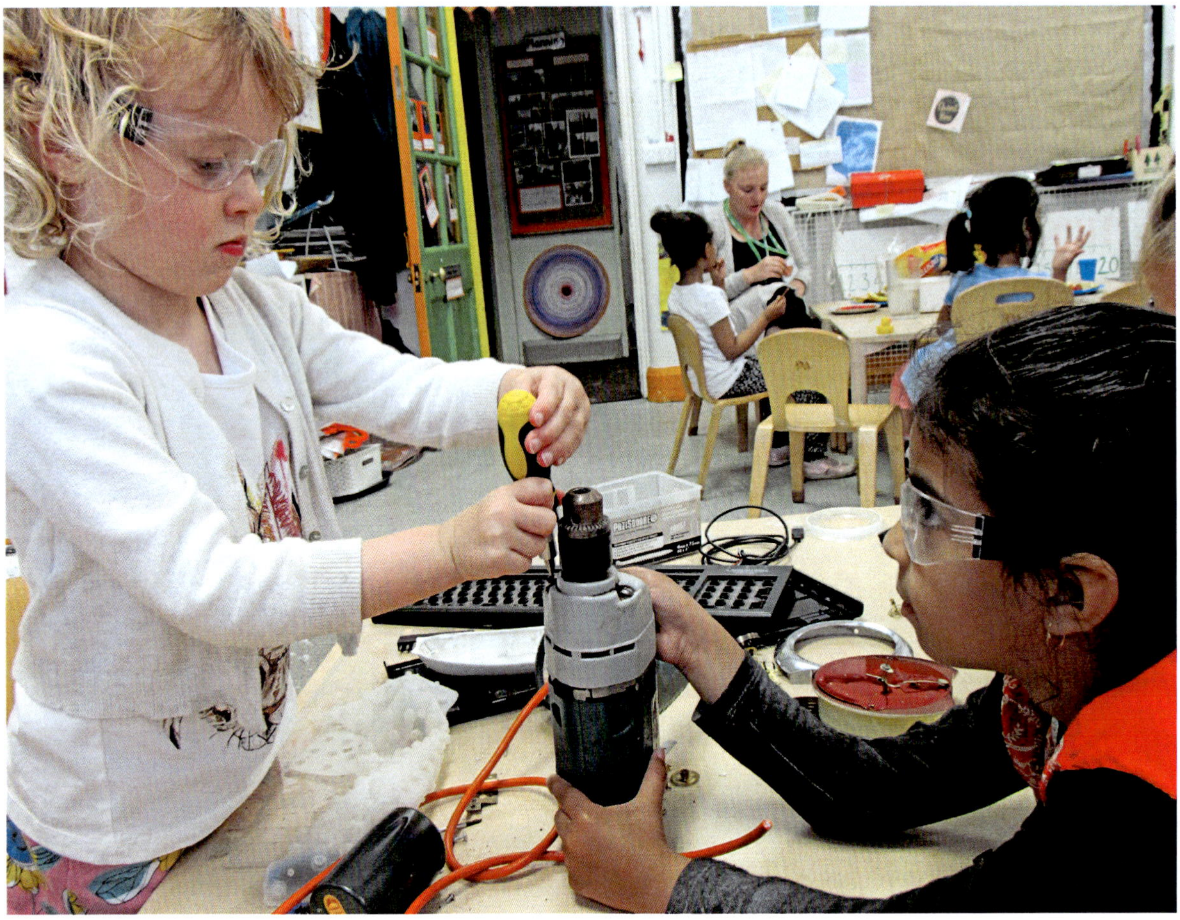

and stick to older more basic electrical equipment or use mechanical equipment, but others advise it is sufficient to wash hands after touching circuit boards.

In the Resources and suppliers section there are links to general safety advice for deconstructing. If in any doubt, it is better to avoid electrical appliances and stick to more mechanical objects.

You may need to purchase an additional set of screwdrivers as many gadgets and appliances incorporate a wide variety of screw types and sizes that require matching screwdrivers. I find a small stubby screwdriver that takes interchangeable bits works very well and you can even get them with a ratchet mechanism which makes them even easier for young children to use.

The children work intently on deconstructing the appliances, captivated by discovering what is inside the cases, and really focus as they dissect and investigate the different parts inside. Learning often branches out in all sorts of directions as the children investigate what interests them. It may be the way objects stick to a magnet, it could be noticing the way that cogs rotate with each other, or the way a wheel turns on an axle.

Investigation through deconstruction always sparks children's curiosity and they are full of questions, such as, 'What are the wires for?' This may lead to creating a simple electric circuit to explore it further. We made a circuit with a small light bulb, which then led on to making a lighthouse . . . which led to making wooden boats . . . which led to creating an ocean . . . which led to a storm and many narratives!

To extend this project further the children can make constructions out of the deconstructed parts. Very post-modern! Sometimes they become robots, sculptures or mobiles. The children like to combine parts with their wooden constructions and as designs develop their imagination really takes off.

Mud kitchen

This project evolved from children's ideas about how they could make improvements to their outdoor area and adding a mud kitchen was one of their choices. This project started by looking at pictures of different mud kitchens as a way of collecting design ideas. We had parents and children contribute kitchen items they no longer needed.

Children can again be fully involved in the design and arrangement and in the majority of the construction, sawing the wooden supporting structure, taking it in turns to get through the really thick sections and bolting it together. They can start to add the metal objects using their woodworking skills: sawing, drilling, some joined by nailing, some by screwing and sometimes using the wrench and coach bolts.

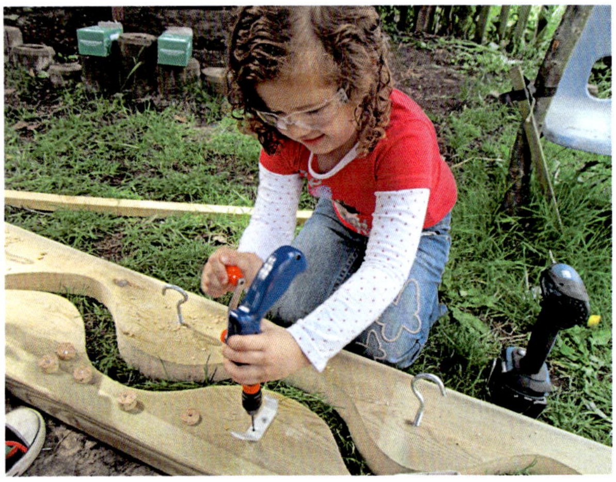

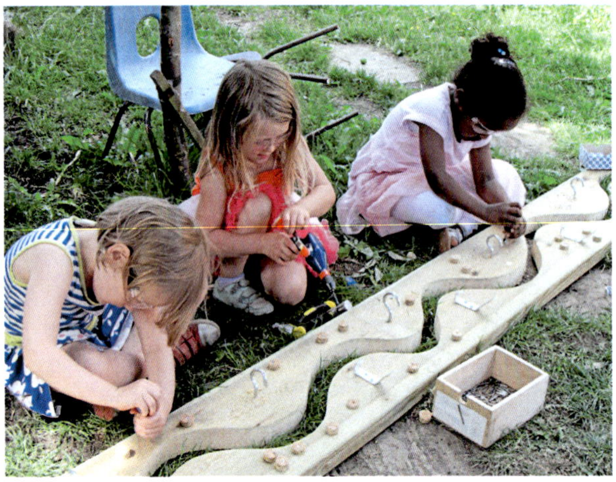

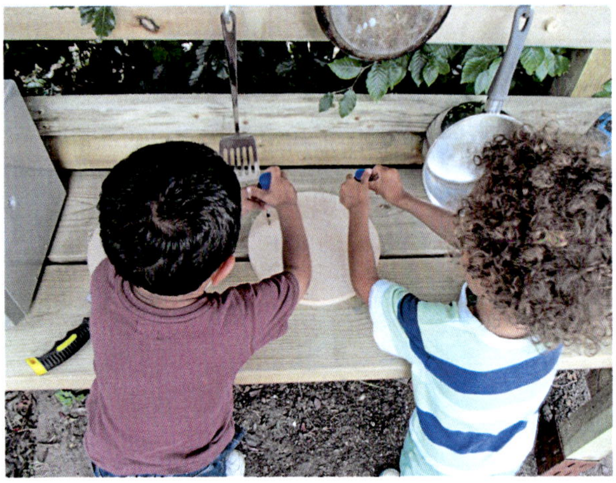

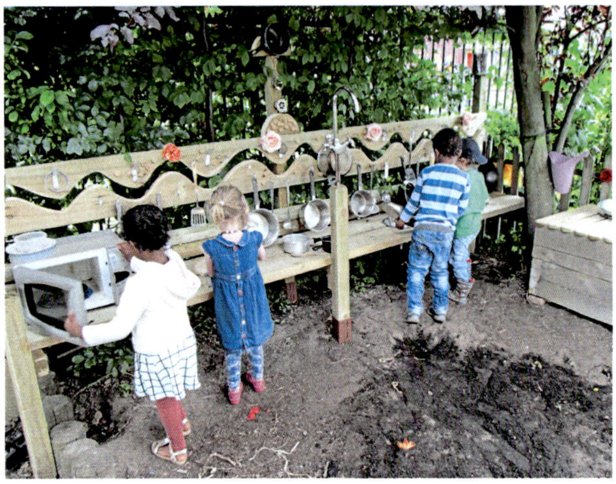

Extended learning projects

Being designed by the children ensures the mud kitchen will be engaging and has elements they like. There is rarely a moment when a child is not playing in our mud kitchen, with a wonderful mixture of pots, pans, sinks and bowls. The children also decided they wanted to add some very basic tables and chairs, which was a nice addition, encouraging role play.

We made the decision to keep the water source at some distance from the mud kitchen so the children could use various methods of transporting the water to the soil – with cups, jugs, etc., or by making a stream with drainpipe sections.

Below are some examples of other longer-term projects we have undertaken that have included making:

- Scarecrows
- Guitars or other stringed instruments
- Robots
- Instruments: drums, rattles, etc.
- Boats
- Petrol station
- Windmill
- Essential oil scented wood pieces
- Go-kart
- Bolted sculptures using nuts and bolts
- A friendship bench
- A story throne
- Bug hotel
- Bird feeders
- Wheels: topic exploring transport and how things move
- Making stilts
- Making kites
- Making drums and drum sticks
- Making traffic signs
- Geo boards (nail boards) with rubber bands
- Creating patterns with nails
- Rockets
- Bridges
- Postboxes
- Waterwheels
- Flags
- Weather station
- Making props for dramatic play such as a crib.

Anything that needs repairing within the setting could become an interesting authentic project as children use their woodworking skills and apply their problem-solving skills to find solutions and make repairs.

> The wood was so big we had to take turns cutting it but we did it all the way through. Then we fixed it by making a hole with the drill and using really big nails.
>
> Hassan, age 4

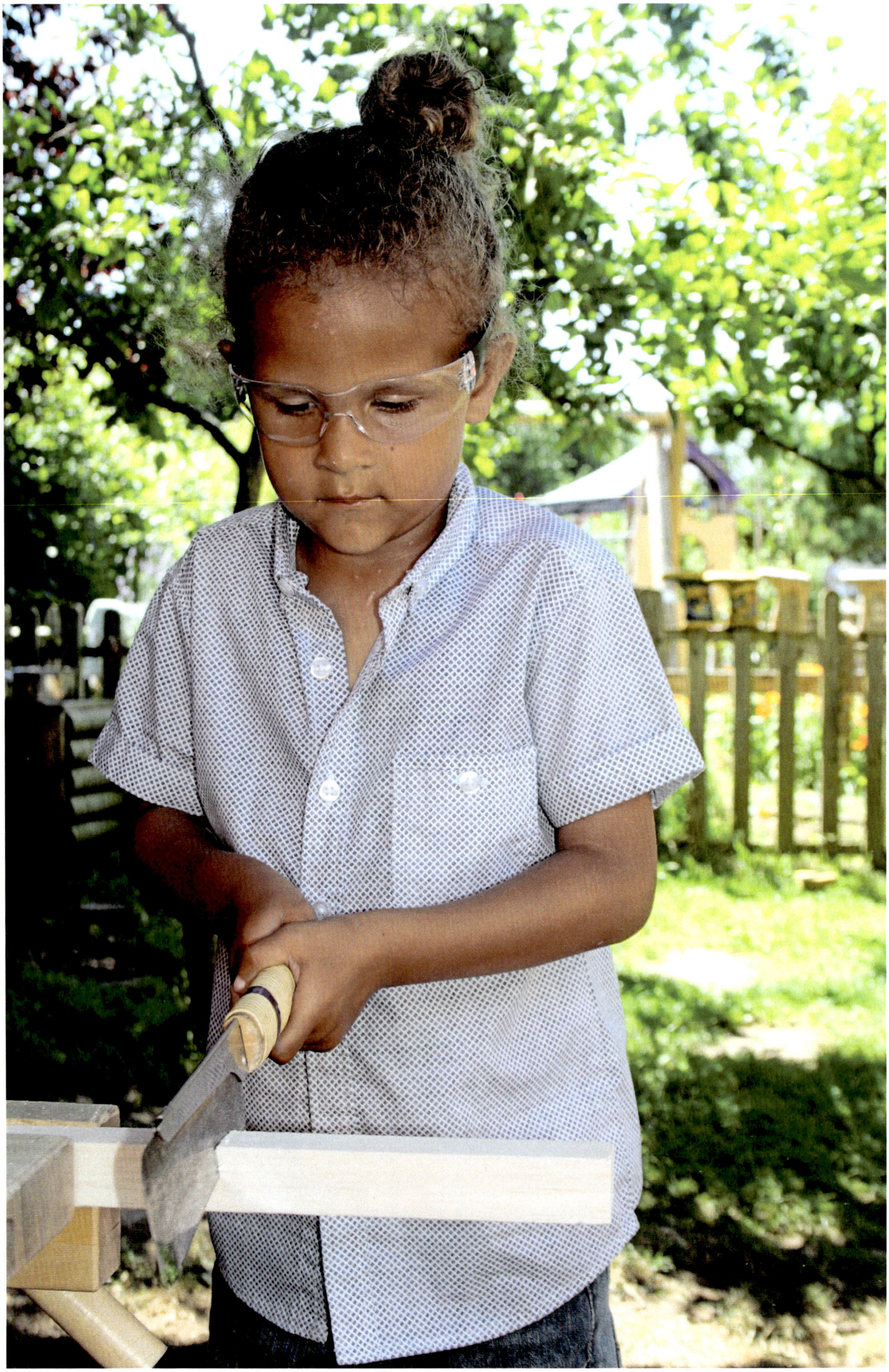

CHAPTER 8

Health and safety

> Risk is a normal part of life, and it is our responsibility at this stage in their development to support risk-taking in a controlled environment.
>
> Liz Jenkins, head teacher, St Werburgh's Park Nursery School, Ofsted inspector

Chapter overview

This chapter looks at what we need to do in order to keep children safe whilst woodworking. I start by looking at risk and the importance of young children learning to manage risk themselves within a controlled environment. I explain the importance of completing a risk assessment and provide a checklist of all the health and safety measures that need to be in place in order to ensure woodwork is a safe and low-risk activity. The chapter concludes by highlighting the importance of having teacher training to ensure all staff supervising the woodwork area are confident with the tools, understand how to support and encourage children and know how to ensure safety measures are always in place.

Understanding risk ▶ 160
Risk assessment ▶ 164
Health and safety checklist ▶ 168
First aid ▶ 170
Staff training ▶ 171

Health and safety

Understanding risk

> If you are going to keep children safe . . . you must provide places in which they can get the thrills they need; there must be trees they can climb and ways in which they can safely get the experience of adventure and the sense of challenge that they crave.
>
> (Susan Isaacs, 1937)

Woodwork and risk

Concern is often raised about the potential risk of injury whilst woodworking. Many adults perceive that woodworking is a high-risk activity and that there is a high probability of serious injury. This is far from the reality. Woodwork is a low-risk activity if introduced and supervised correctly. Of course there will be small injuries from time to time such as a banged finger, a small cut or a splinter, but certainly nothing more than what is usually sustained in the playground. In my experience of using saws regularly over a 15-year period we have had two children get small surface cuts requiring just a plaster. To avoid doing woodwork because of this low risk of injury defies common sense. Children naturally want to protect themselves and know some actions will hurt them. It is also an innate subliminal response to keep our fingers away from potential impact. Children really respond to being trusted and given the responsibility to use real tools. They feel empowered and valued and rise to the occasion.

Managing risk

Woodwork provides children with valuable opportunities to learn about making judgements, avoiding hazards and managing risk in a controlled environment, which is a crucial part of their development. We can't eliminate risk completely, nor would we want to, as risk is part and parcel of living. Life is full of risks and challenges and we need to prepare children to meet these by allowing them to take risks within a safe environment. If we don't allow children to be exposed to risk they are prevented from learning how to risk assess themselves, and in turn become more likely to succumb to accidents. Children are naturally drawn to activities that challenge them and that contain risk and these are often the very activities children seem to enjoy the most, and learn the most from. Challenge is integral to development. Woodwork also offers a way to teach children respect for things that can be harmful and highlights the need for care in certain situations.

Woodworking will develop co-ordination, motor skills, agility and dexterity, which, combined with a growing understanding of cause and effect, will lead to greater self-control, lessening the likelihood of injury.

Litigation and legislation

In the UK many school activities were affected by overzealous health and safety policies in the 1980s and 1990s. At the time the feeling was that health and safety should be paramount, but this was at the expense of opportunity and irrespective of the benefits of experiencing risk. This climate of risk aversion was heavily influenced by the increasing litigation and compensation culture.

But health and safety laws were essentially designed around preventing death, serious injury and illness. It became abundantly clear that many interpretations were misguided and as a result children were losing out on valuable experiences needlessly.

Health and safety

Fortunately, the climate is now changing. Initially this was pioneered by Lord Young's Review of Health and Safety spanning industry and schools. The recommendations of the review, 'Common Sense, Common Safety', were immediately accepted by the Government in October 2010. The emphasis of the report in relation to educational settings was to encourage them to embrace risk in a positive sense and not to limit valuable opportunities available to children.

> This disproportionate approach (to health and safety) has had a negative impact on education in this country and has decreased the number of opportunities available to children to experience risk in a controlled environment.
>
> (Common Sense, Common Safety 2010)

Lord Young stated: 'I believe that with regard to children's play we should shift from a system of risk assessment to a system of risk-benefit assessment, where potential positive impacts are weighed against potential risk.' The report highlighted the importance of children being able to experience risk as it is vital for children's development and should not be sacrificed because of overzealous health and safety and disproportionate risk assessments.

In 2012 the Health and Safety Executive published a report with similar recommendations and this was followed in 2013 by the Department of Education report (updated in 2014).

The key points of the Department of Education's Health and Safety advice to schools (February 2014) were:

- Children should be able to experience a wide range of activities. Health and safety measures should help them to do this safely, not stop them.
- It is important that children learn to understand and manage the risks that are a normal part of life.
- Common sense should be used in assessing and managing the risks of any activity. Health and safety procedures should always be proportionate to the risks of an activity.
- Staff should be given the training they need so they can keep themselves and children safe and manage risks effectively.

The Health and Safety Executive (HSE) provides the following guidance:

1. Health and safety laws and regulations are sometimes presented as a reason why certain play and leisure activities undertaken by children and young people should be discouraged. The reasons for this misunderstanding are many and varied. They include fears of litigation or criminal prosecution because even the most trivial risk has not been removed. There can be frustration with the amounts of paperwork involved, and misunderstanding about what needs to be done to control significant risks.
2. The purpose of this statement is to give clear messages which tackle these misunderstandings. In this statement, HSE makes clear that, as a regulator, it recognises the benefits of allowing children and young people of all ages and abilities to have challenging play opportunities.
3. HSE fully supports the provision of play for all children in a variety of environments. HSE understands and accepts that this means children will often be exposed to play environments which, whilst well-managed, carry a degree of risk and sometimes potential danger.
4. HSE wants to make sure that mistaken health and safety concerns do not create sterile play environments that lack challenge and so prevent children from expanding their learning and stretching their abilities.

The Health and Safety Executive's key message is:

> Play is great for children's well-being and development. When planning and providing play opportunities, the goal is not to eliminate risk, but to weigh up the risks and benefits. No child will learn about risk if they are wrapped in cotton wool.
>
> (HSE 2012)

Developing understanding of risk in children

It is important that children have some understanding of the context and meaning behind the rules and boundaries imposed. Thus it will raise their awareness of taking both individual and collective responsibility to keep safe. Teaching children about the concept of risk will help them to make their own decisions about risk so that they can recognise hazards and make judgements in a range of contexts.

The HSE and the Qualifications and Curriculum Authority (QCA) collaborated to provide guidance as to how risk should be discussed with children undertaking Design and Technology in primary and secondary schools. Clearly the guidance needs adapting for children in their early years but the same fundamental principle applies – that it our duty to dedicate time to discussing risk and health and safety rules.

The HSE/QCA statutory statement relevant for those teaching design and technology in primary and secondary schools says:

> When working with tools, equipment and materials, in practical activities and in different environments, including those that are unfamiliar, pupils should be taught:
>
> ▶ about hazards, risks and risk control;
> ▶ to recognise hazards, assess consequent risk and take steps to control the risks to themselves and others;
> ▶ to use information to assess the immediate and cumulative risks;
> ▶ to manage their environment to ensure the health and safety of themselves and others;
> ▶ to explain the steps they take to control risks.

They go on to emphasise the benefits of learning about risk:

> Teaching about the concept of risk will help pupils make their own decisions about risk so that they can:
>
> ▶ recognise the existence of hazards, risks and uncertainty in a range of contexts;
> ▶ assess their own ability, and the ability of others, to deal with different situations;
> ▶ assess the consequences when dealing with hazards presented to themselves and to others (for example, within school, the environment, the home);
> ▶ seek advice from appropriate sources to minimise and manage risk;
> ▶ understand that rules and regulations follow from risk assessment and help define individual and collective responsibility.
>
> (HSE 2012)

Safety measures to reduce risk are addressed in the health and safety and risk assessment sections below and also in detail in the section on tools and equipment (p. 116).

Reducing risk in woodwork

Although it is beneficial to expose children to opportunities that embrace an element of risk it is important that we take steps to reduce risk levels as far as possible to ensure woodwork is low risk and that it is a safe activity for children. Risk is reduced by following the health and safety guidelines and by completing a risk assessment, and then implementing the control measures that reduce the likelihood of injury. Risk is also reduced by knowledgeable teachers. It is advisable that staff undergo basic woodwork training so teachers are familiar with working with tools and understand how to introduce woodwork safely (see p. 171).

Parents' concerns

Parents can be anxious about the risk of children working with tools and have little understanding of the many benefits. Talking about woodwork at a parents' evening or through a newsletter highlighting the safety measures that are put in place can be helpful to inform and reassure them that woodwork is safe. It also provides an opportunity for parents to get a better understanding of the associated benefits of learning and development.

Aggressive behaviour

Teachers occasionally voice concerns over potential aggressive behaviour with tools. Of course this is possible, just as it is with any implement such as a block, trowel, fork, stapler or pencil. In my experience children's behaviour has been exceptional in the woodwork area. I think this is largely due to the fact that children are deeply engaged, feeling competent and empowered. When children feel competent and happy they rarely argue with each other. We must of course remain vigilant, and any untoward behaviour must not be tolerated. If necessary, children should be removed from the woodworking area until they can manage their behaviour appropriately. It is of course important to know your children, and children with unpredictable behaviour will require closer supervision or even a 1:1 supervision ratio.

Further reading

For further reading around the subject of risk, Tim Gill's book *No Fear* is illuminating. Gill has been a pioneer in championing children's adventurous play and his book provides a wonderful insight into these issues of risk and opportunity. Play England also produced a useful resource: 'Managing Risk in Play Provision'.

Risk assessment

By risk, we mean the likelihood of coming to harm or injury by a potential hazard. Risk assessment is the process of assessing the likelihood of risk, the potential level of injury and looking at what control measures can be taken to reduce the risk.

Key terms:

- **Hazard** means anything that can cause harm.
- **Risk** is the chance, high or low, that somebody will be harmed by the hazard.
- **Risk control** involves taking steps to reduce the chance, and/or mitigate the consequences, of the hazard causing harm.
- **Risk assessment** evaluates the risks and decides whether precautions are adequate or more should be done.

It is essential to undertake a risk assessment of your woodwork provision tailored specifically for your particular setting and children. This is often a requirement of local authorities.

A risk assessment evaluates all the potential risks. It scores the likelihood of their occurrence and level of potential injury. Control measures are then listed, stating what precautions are undertaken to reduce the likelihood of injury. The risk level is then scored again reflecting the impact of the control measures.

Risk assessments are sometimes referred to as risk-benefit assessments to highlight that the potential risks are outweighed by the benefits. With woodwork the opportunities clearly vastly outweigh the risks involved. The benefits from the learning and development discussed in Chapter 3 can be combined with a risk assessment to create a risk–benefit document, but it will become quite lengthy! I believe a risk assessment suffices.

An example risk assessment is shown below but it's is important that you create your own risk assessment, responding to your setting. The risk assessment must be read by all adults involved and reviewed regularly, not just filed away. Attaching it to the wall in the woodwork area is recommended.

Risk assessments should contain the following features:

- What risk is being assessed?
- What is the potential hazard?
- What is the rating of the potential injury: low/medium/high?
- What precautions are put in place to eliminate/reduce likelihood of risk?
- What is the likelihood of occurrence: low/medium/high?
- Overall risk rating: low/medium/high?

Elements that you need to think about risk assessing:

- woodwork area
- workbench
- clamps, vices
- misuse of tools
- children with challenging behaviours
- eye protection
- toxic materials
- wood
- hammering
- sawing
- carrying tools
- nails and screws
- sawdust
- misc. tools
- heavy items
- splinters.

An example risk assessment form is given on pp. 166–67

School: Adapt this assessment to respond to *your* setting

Date of Assessment: xx/xx/2017 Assessed by:

What is being assessed?	What hazards may be present?	What degree of injury could be reasonably expected?	What precautions have been put in place to reduce the risk of injury?	What likelihood is there of risk still occurring?	What is the risk rating?
Woodwork area	Impact with tools Tripping	Medium	Monitored at all times by staff member (either in vicinity or close proximity). Locate woodwork area in a position that reduces flow/ traffic. Locate away from distractions. Ensure that the floor is clear of obstacles that could cause tripping. Limit number of children working if small area.	Low	Low
Splinters	Infection	Low/high	Avoid working with very splintery wood. Adults to sand very rough edges, if necessary, first before children use wood. Children to initially sand any rough edges, and sand after sawing if rough. Splinter to be removed immediately if reasonably possible by first aider, if not inform parents to seek medical attention and monitor site for possible infection.	Low	Low
Eye protection	Injury to eye from nail rebound, debris in eye	High	Safety glasses *always* to be worn. Children that already wear glasses will suffice. Goggles to be worn if excessive dust.	Low	Low
Woodwork clothing	General injury	Low	Ensure children wearing suitable clothing to move freely; for example, remove gloves and scarves to facilitate coordination. Shoes to be worn.	Low	Low
Treated wood	Toxicity	Low	Avoid using painted or chemically treated wood. If in doubt the wood should not be used.	Low	Low
Tools general	Impact	Low	Walk when transporting tools and hold by side. Instruction on how to use tools safely (introductory1:3 ratio, saw, nail puller 1:1). Ensure regularly checked, e.g. hammer head not loose. All equipment to remain in woodwork area. Misuse of tools will not to be tolerated. Keep checklist of who has been taught which tool.	Low	Low
Hammer	Impact to fingers/ hand	Medium	Instruction on how to use hammer safely. Dangers clearly explained. Fingers moved away when hammering hard. Initial adult supervision 1:3. Eliminate distractions.	Low	Low

Saw	Cuts Impact injury to another child	Medium	Instruction on how to use saw and supervised 1:1 at all times. Sawing – ensure no children are watching from in front of the sawing area – practitioner to stand in this area to prevent children getting close to saw. Child sawing with Japanese saw or pull saw to hold the saw with two hands or with Western saw – with one hand and other hand holding bench well away from wood being cut. After being used – saw to immediately be put out of reach. Wood always clamped in vice when being sawn. Practitioner to check held firm in vice before sawing commences.	Low
Hand drill/ brace and bit	Injury to body	Low	Ensure work is clamped (G clamp or vice) before drilling.	Low
Dust	Dust – inhaled and eyes	Low	Any significant amounts of cutting/sanding to be done outdoors. Eye protection – goggles if a lot of dust. Dust mask to be worn if high levels of dust Children not to cut MDF.	Low
Nails/screws	Pierce skin Swallow	Low	Any protruding nails to be made safe (hammered over) or removed. All nails/screws to be collected off floor after session (magnet). Do not hold nails/ screws in mouth. Many builders do this. Do not model this habit!	Low
Misc. tools – wrench, spanners, screwdrivers, hand drills, nail puller	Impact injuries Cuts, bruises, etc.	Medium	Children to be given clear instruction for safe use of any new tool. Emphasise tools are not toys. Children initially to be supervised 1:3. Nail puller to be used as a lever and only used closely monitored 1:1.	Low
Plywood	Splinters	Medium	Care with plywood. It is hard for young children to work with and plywood splinters badly.	Low
Hard wood	Injury	Medium	Avoid – as hard and very difficult for children to work. More chance of nail rebounding. Also, children would have to hammer extremely hard, increasing risk.	Low
MDF	Dust	Medium	Caution with MDF. Do not cut MDF in school due to excessive levels of irritating dust. MDF is hard so should be drilled first when joining.	Low
Battery screwdriver	Injury to fingers	Low	Clear instructions for safe use and then only used with close adult supervision. Eliminate distractions. Material being drilled to be clamped.	Low
Children with SEN	General injury	Medium	Higher supervision ratio. 1:1 if necessary.	Low
First aid response	Delayed treatment	Low	Know location of first aid kit and appointed first aider.	Low

Health and safety

Health and safety checklist

Ensure this is read by all staff monitoring the woodwork area:

Personal protection

- ▶ Safety glasses: wear safety glasses at all times to protect eyes. Having children learn about safety culture and looking after themselves is an important lesson. Children are much more comfortable in safety glasses rather than chunky goggles. Adults to also wear safety glasses.
- ▶ Children and adults watching in close proximity also to wear safety glasses.
- ▶ Shoes to be worn when working in the woodwork area.
- ▶ Dust masks to be worn if excessive sanding is undertaken.

Supervision

- ▶ Ensure all children are given proper instruction on the correct use of all tools. Remind children that tools are for a purpose and are not toys. Draw attention to sharp edges/points of tools. Keep a checklist of who has learnt to use which tool.
- ▶ Initial ratio for safely introducing tools: 1:3.
- ▶ Children must be supervised at all times, initially with very close supervision. When children are confident using tools, ratios can be relaxed with the exception of sawing monitored with a 1:1 ratio. A staff member should always remain in the proximity to monitor the woodworking area.
- ▶ Be aware of children with additional needs – some children will need additional support, perhaps having a 1:1 ratio at all times.
- ▶ Avoid nearby distractions. Remind children of the need to keep looking at their work whilst using tools.

Area

- ▶ Keep floor area clear – most accidents in design and technology are from trips and falls.
- ▶ Limit the number of children at the workbench so they are not working in too close a proximity. Allow enough space so not to endanger others.
- ▶ Locate the workbench in a protected space to minimise traffic and other distractions.

Tools

Saw

- ▶ Ensure no children are watching from in front of the sawing area – practitioner to stand in this area to prevent children getting close to saw.
- ▶ Child sawing with Japanese saw or pull saw to hold the saw with two hands or with European cross-cut saw with one hand – hand not holding the saw to be well away from the saw and holding the bench.
- ▶ After use, immediately place saw out of reach.
- ▶ Wood always to be clamped in a vice when being sawn. Staff to ensure vice clamped tight.

Hammer

- ▶ When hammering into harder wood, children will be using considerably more force. After the gentle taps to get the nail started, hold the work well away from the nail before hammering hard.

Other tools

- ▶ Ensure when children are carrying tools that they are held by their side and to walk. Never run with tools.
- ▶ Caution when children are using vices, clamps and pliers that fingers do not get pinched. Ensure fingers kept away from clamping area. Close vices when not in use.
- ▶ Caution with Japanese nail puller – useful for levering out nails but closely monitor use 1:1 so children do not 'yank' upwards toward themselves. Ensure it is only used as a lever.
- ▶ Inspect tools periodically to ensure tools are in good repair or replaced when worn. For example, remove a hammer with a loose head or a dull drill bit or saw.
- ▶ Keep tools tidy – return to original locations. Tools must not be removed from the woodwork area.
- ▶ Power drills should be avoided with young children due to the high speeds and high torque. Children could easily lose grip and clothing or hair could also become caught.

Caution

- ▶ Remove or make safe protruding nails from work before children take work home.
- ▶ Do not blow sawdust – as highly likely to end up in eyes.
- ▶ Area to be kept as dust-free as possible. Sweep up sawdust as necessary. Asthmatic children to wear dust mask if high levels of dust.
- ▶ Do not carry nails or screws in mouth.

Wood

- ▶ Avoid hardwoods. They are too difficult for young children to work with and there is a possibility that nails could rebound. Plywood also splinters badly.
- ▶ Avoid wood treated with preservatives.
- ▶ Caution with plywood. The way it is made creates significant splinters. It is also relatively hard to work.
- ▶ Caution with MDF. Do not cut MDF in school due to excessive levels of irritating dust. MDF is also relatively hard.
- ▶ Check wood for splinters. Avoid very rough splintery wood. Rough wood can initially be sanded. Sand edges after sawing if rough. Remove splinters if reasonably possible. Caution: splinters can be a source of blood poisoning.
- ▶ Do not store or provide wood with any nails sticking out.

First aid

- ▶ Ensure first aid kit available and know location. Know who is first aid qualified.

This is a comprehensive health and safety list designed for staff guidance. We want to avoid overloading children with too many rules and just focus on the most essential for them. Supporting adults can ensure that the other health and safety measures are in place.

For details of safe tool use and safety glasses see the Tools section above.

Health and safety

First aid

Disclaimer: first aid practices vary so it is important that you are familiar with your local policies and current best practice.

Working with tools there will be occasional small injuries. The most likely injuries with woodwork are:

Bruising

Place under cold water and supply ice pack to the bruised area.

Splinter

First aider to carefully remove splinter (if exposed and reasonably possible and if your guidance allows it) with sterilised tweezers. Clean area. Apply antiseptic. Apply plaster. If it is not possible to remove inform parents and advise that splinter is monitored or seek medical attention. Advise parents that even if the splinter is removed the splinter site should be monitored for possible infection.

Blood blister

Allow to dry up naturally. Do not burst.

Cut

First aider to wash wound area. Keep cut raised. Apply pressure to stop bleeding. Apply antiseptic. Apply plaster. In the unlikely event of a deeper cut seek medical advice.

General

First aid treatment should be undertaken by a trained paediatric first-aider. Methods of treatment can vary so ensure you are familiar with current practice in your locality.

Health and safety

In all cases parents should be notified of accidents in writing. Alert parents that they should monitor cuts and splinter sites to ensure there are no signs of infection. This is particularly important with splinters, which can be a source of blood poisoning.

Staff training

It is certainly not necessary to have a specialist come in to do woodworking sessions with children. All staff can become more than capable and confident to introduce woodwork and monitor sessions. Many teachers have little personal experience of tools so can feel unconfident about introducing young children to working with tools. This can be easily remedied with basic staff training.

Woodwork teacher training should cover:

▶ Learning and development aspects of woodwork relating to the curriculum.
▶ Gaining an understanding about risk and safety issues.
▶ Explanations of the most suitable tools and instruction on how best to use them.
▶ Looking at the most suitable woods.
▶ Explanations on how to set up a woodworking area.
▶ Suggestions for activities, open-ended explorations and longer-term projects.
▶ Practical sessions for practitioners to explore the tools, gain confidence and share the experience of making creations in wood.

The practical sessions are particularly useful giving teachers the opportunity to become really familiar using all the tools and their safe use. Staff get experience being creative with wood and seeing the rich potential for first-hand problem-solving, which gives an insight into what the experience is like for children.

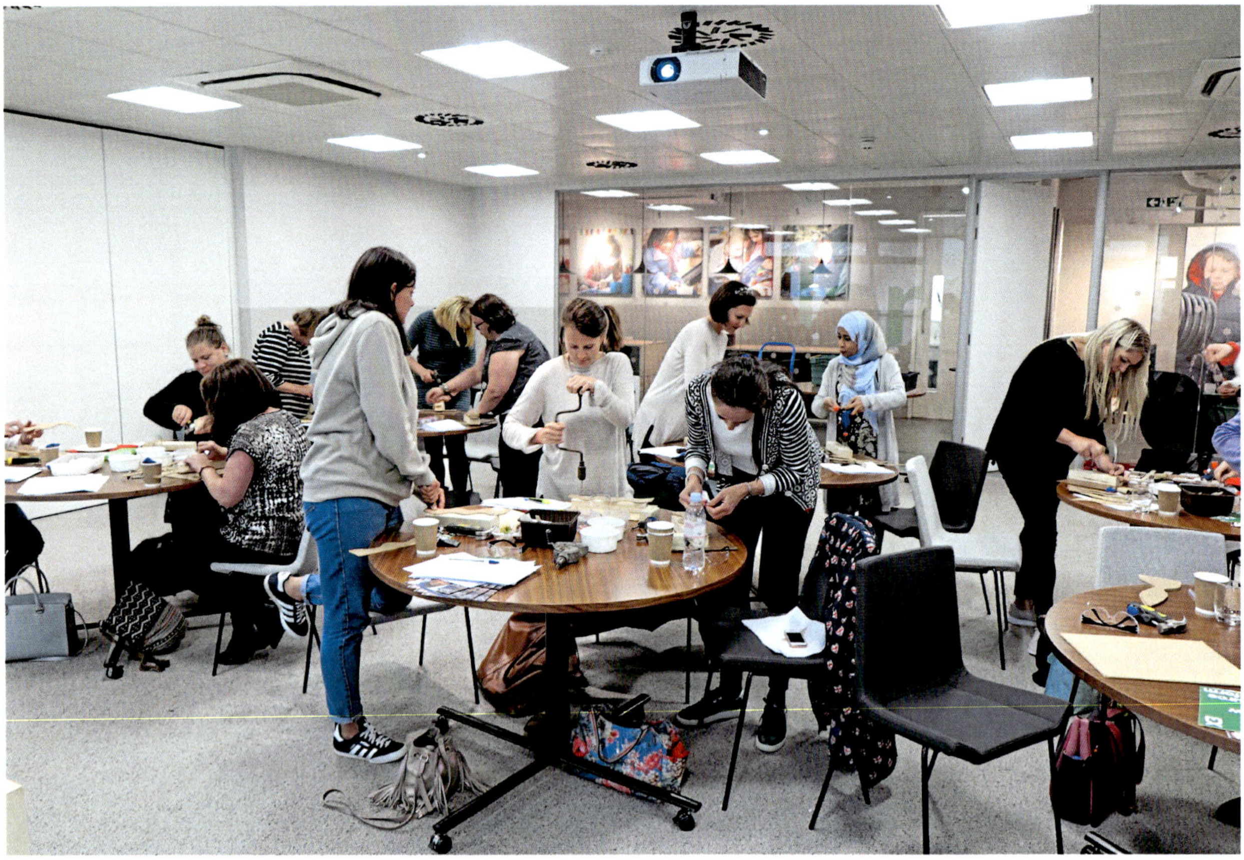

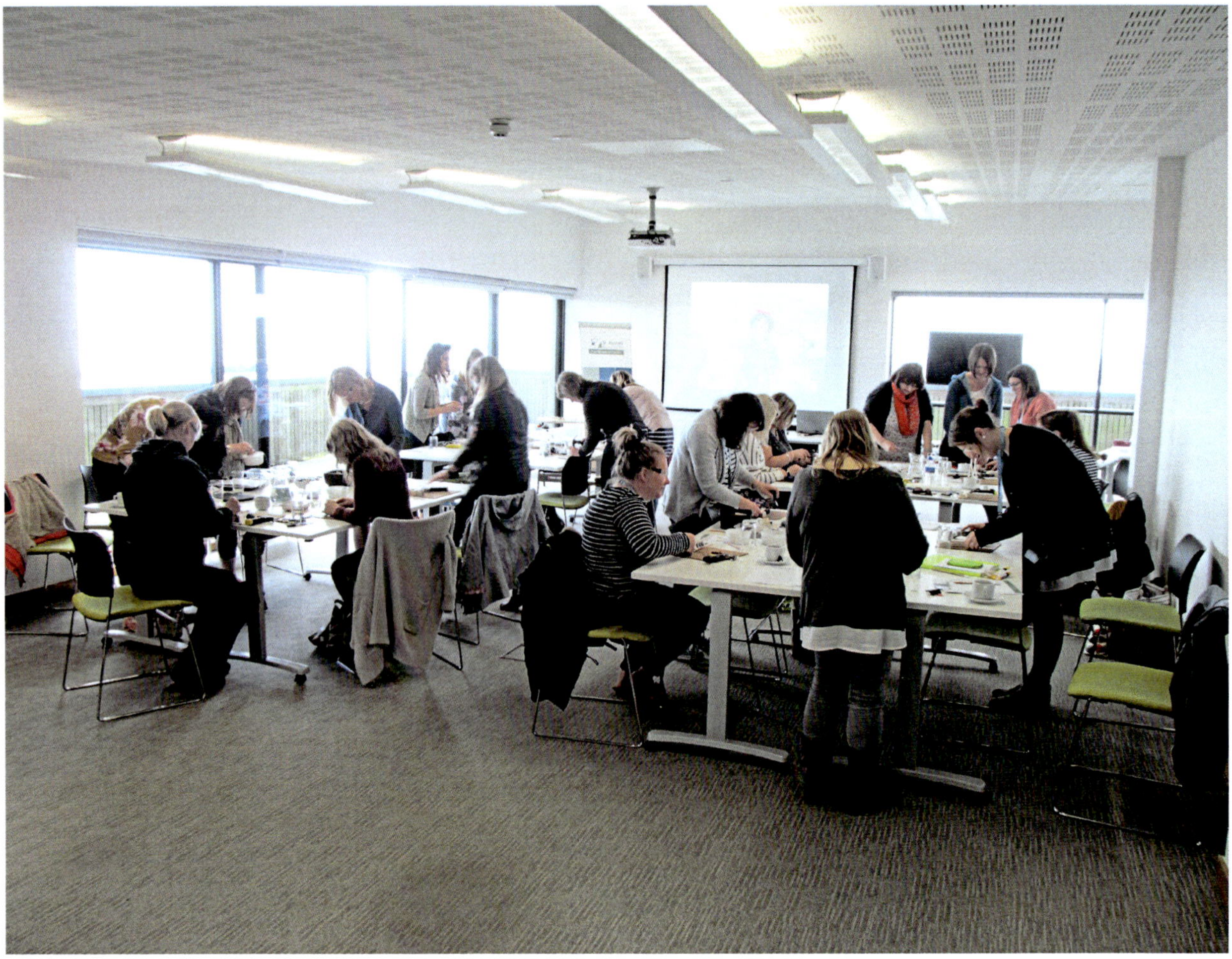

Health and safety

To successfully embrace woodwork in the setting it is much better for all staff to have a level of competency and confidence than to rely on only one or two teachers, so having training for the whole staff team is very much recommended. It is also good to visit a setting that is already doing woodwork. Seeing children engaged in their woodwork is both inspiring and reassuring.

One issue can be sustaining the commitment to woodwork. Occasionally settings have started doing woodwork but for a variety of reasons it has fallen off the agenda and the woodwork bench gathers dust.

To embed practice and ensure positive outcomes from CPD training it is beneficial to have some continuing support and a follow-up session from the trainer. There is a huge amount of information to take in in one session for an inexperienced teacher and it is inevitable that staff will have questions and need some additional support. Here is an example of a more thorough programme:

1. Training session 1: 'Woodwork in Early Years' training – theory and practice.
2. Email exchange between trainer and settings to offer continued support/advice.
3. Trainer to visit settings during a woodwork session.
4. Training session 2: Sharing of case studies. Evaluation of children's experience. Reviewing setup/area/provision. Respond to needs/questions of the group.

Health and safety

The wheel would not go round . . . it was stuck so I had to pull it out a bit. I used a screwdriver. Look, now it turns!

Raffi, age 4

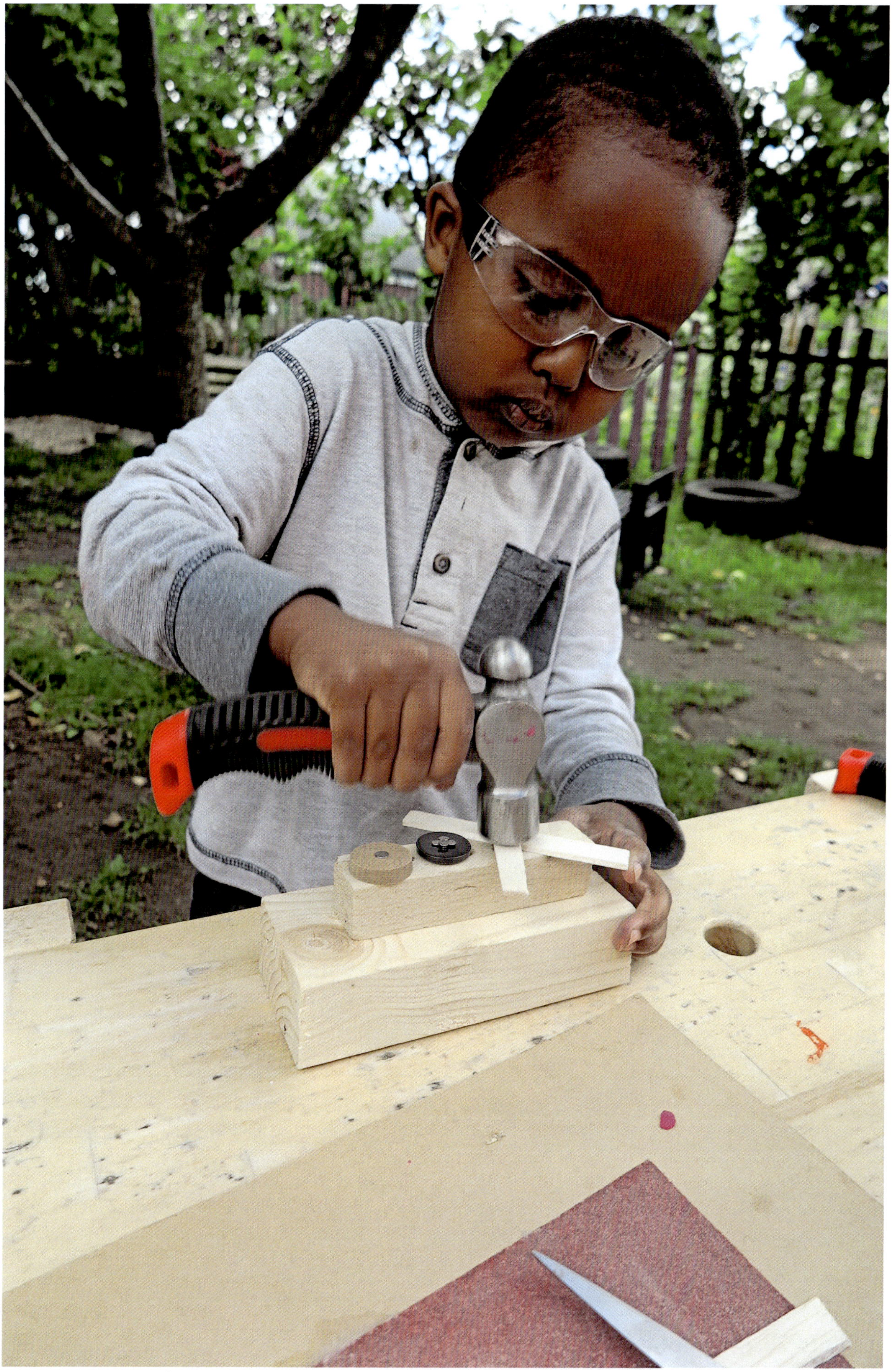

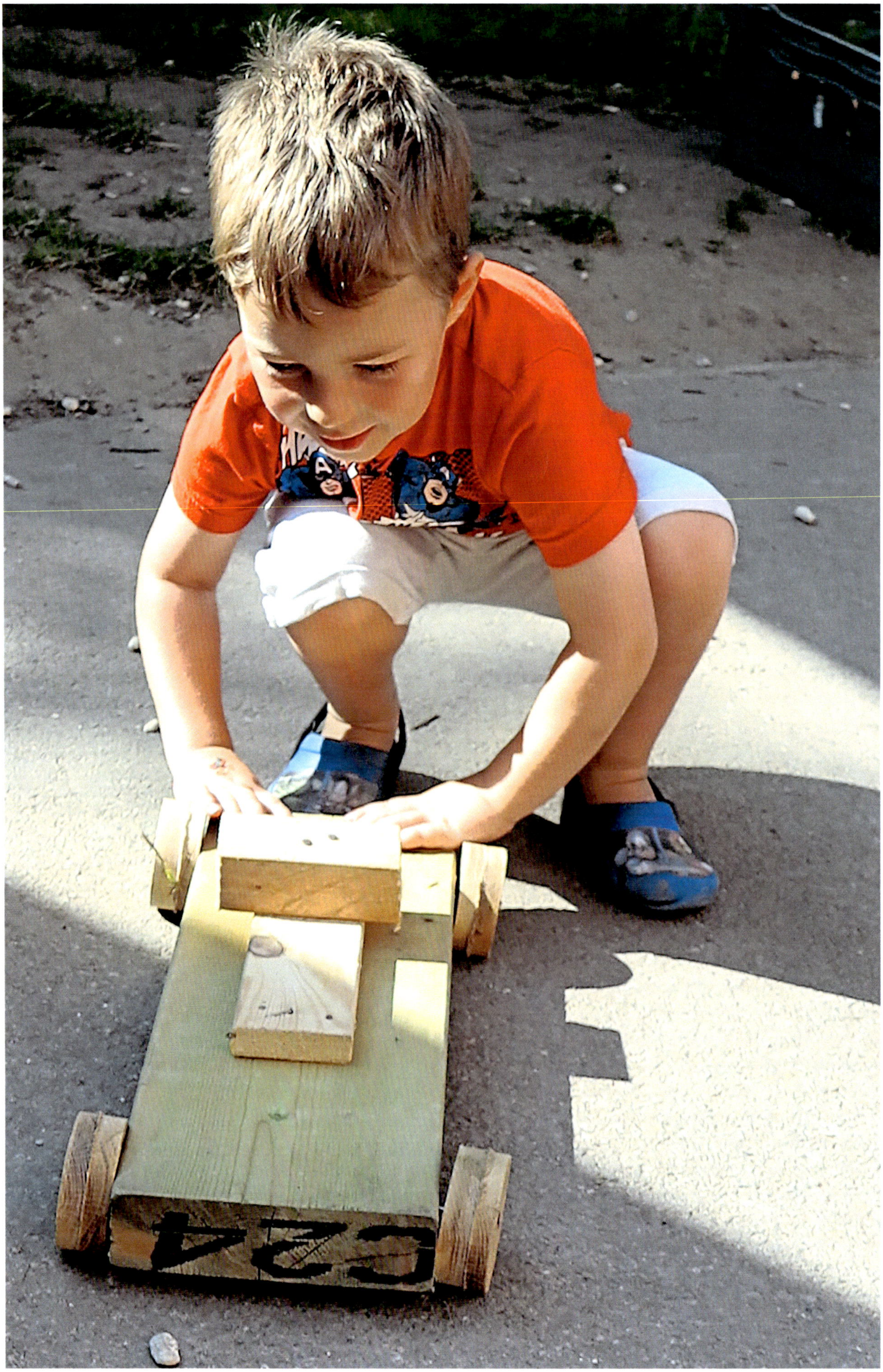

CHAPTER 9

Final words

> I have few very clear memories from my own nursery school days, but my absolute favourite is joyfully hammering nails into little odd-sized pieces of wood. What I was making is now lost in the mists of time, but it hardly matters. What is important is that the experience has stuck in my mind for more than three decades, the sheer, unfettered excitement of being allowed to use real tools to create something.
>
> Sally Ashworth, (2016), Educational writer and teacher[1]

We have seen how working with real tools offers children many new experiences and encompasses so much learning and development.

Woodwork allows children to become makers, sculptors, tinkerers, engineers and architects. The early years may very well be their only chance to experience woodwork in their entire education. But being a kinaesthetic experience it embeds a deep memory. Once having learnt how to use tools, the experience becomes a part of children's DNA.

It does take some effort get started with woodwork – sourcing the tools and wood, ensuring staff feel confident and that you have sufficient ratios to introduce and monitor it properly – but it is very much worth the investment. Once everything is in place you won't look back and you'll be amazed by the levels of engagement and depth of children's explorations.

It would be wonderful if every child could have these experiences. As a practitioner, it is a joy to see children so deeply focused on an activity, witnessing their growing confidence, their persistence with challenge and their resilience in the face of failures. It is a delight to watch their creativity, observe their problem-solving and see their pride in their achievements – it always leaves me feeling uplifted.

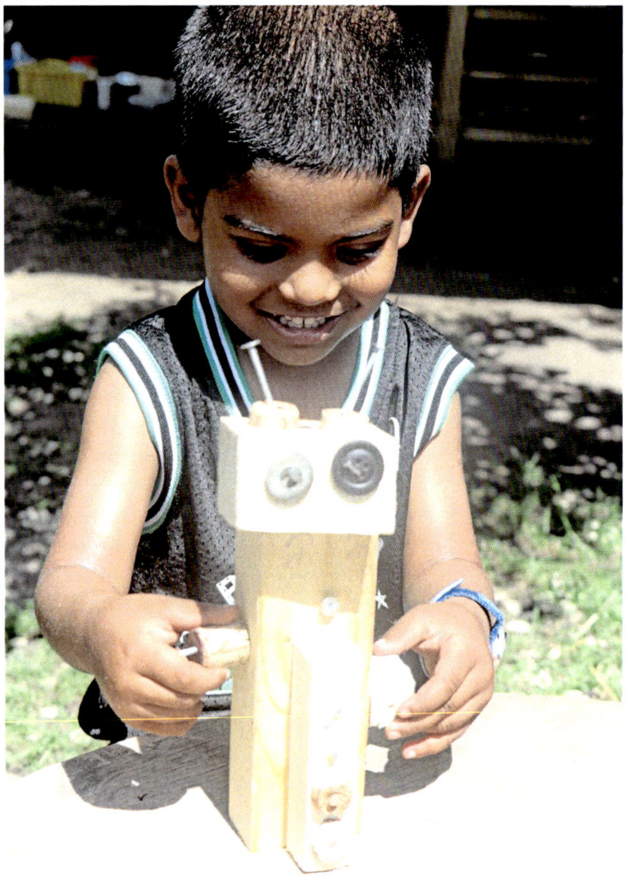

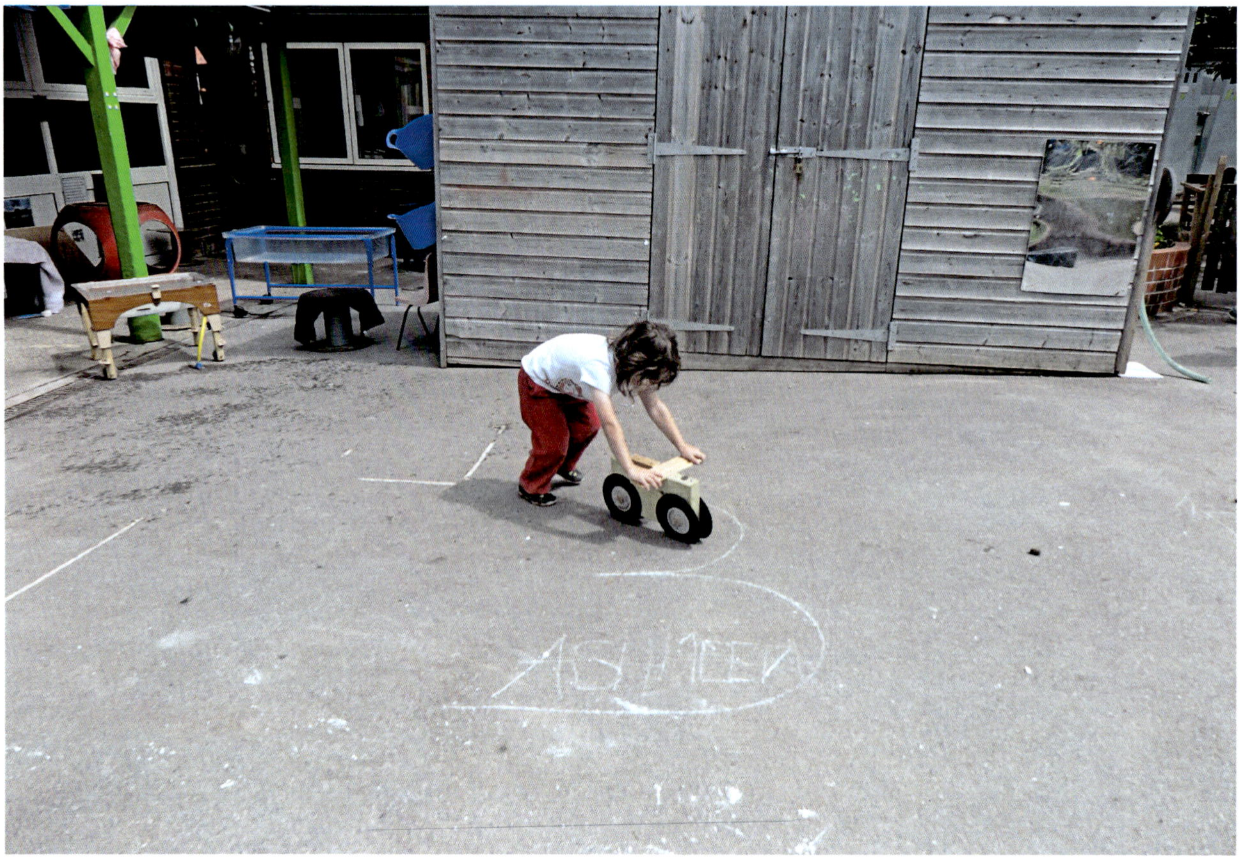

Final words

As children make with wood they are learning skills that will empower them to shape their world.

Let's provide all children with this valuable opportunity.

I can be contacted through my website irresistible-learning.co.uk. If you would like any further advice or clarification I will do my best to help out where I can. Likewise, if you have any contributions that you feel would be useful for other teachers please do let me know.

Note

1 Ashworth, S. (2014) 'Wonderful Woodwork', in Early Years Educator VI 16(5), September, pp.v–vii. Available online: http://dx.doi.org/10.12968/eyed.2014.16.5.v (accessed 27 July 2017).

Bibliography

Anderson, Chris (2012) *Makers: The New Industrial Revolution*, New York: Crown Business.

Arieti, Silvano (1976) *Creativity: The Magic Synthesis*, New York: Basic Books.

Barter, S. (1892) *Manual Instruction: Woodwork (The English Sloyd)*, London: Whittaker.

Brehony, Kevin J. (2000) The kindergarten in England 1851–1918, in Roberta Wollons (ed.) *Kindergartens and Cultures: The Global Diffusion of an Idea* (pp. 59–86), New Haven, CT: Yale University Press.

Bruce, Tina (2001) *Learning Through Play*, London: Hodder Education.

Bruce, Tina (2004) *Developing Learning in Early Childhood*, London: SAGE Publications.

Bruner, Jerome (1960) *The Process of Education*, 2nd edn, Cambridge, MA: Harvard University Press.

Carson, Rachel (2017) *The Sense of Wonder*, New York: Harper and Row.

Clapp, Edward P., Jessica Ross, Jennifer O. Ryan, and Shari Tishman (2016) *Maker-centered Learning: Empowering Young People to Shape Their Worlds*, San Francisco, CA: Jossey-Bass.

Csikszentmihalyi, Mihaly (1990) *Flow: The Psychology of Optimal Experience*, New York: Harper Perennial.

Csikszentmihalyi, Mihaly (1996) *Creativity: Flow and the Psychology of Discovery and Invention*, New York: Harper Perennial.

Dweck, Carol (2006) *Mindset: The New Psychology of Success*, New York: Random House.

Dweck, Carol (2012) *Mindset: How You Can Fulfil Your Potential*, London: Constable & Robinson Limited.

Early Education (2012) *Development Matters in the Early Years Foundation Stage (EYFS)*, London: Early Education.

Fisher, Julie (2016) *Interacting or Interfering? Improving Interactions in the Early Years*, Maidenhead: McGraw Hill Publishing.

Fröbel, Friedrich (1826) *Die Menschenerziehung* [On the education of man], Keilhau, Leipzig: Wienbrack.

Fröbel, Friedrich (1885) *The Education of Man*, New York: A. Lovell & Company. Translated by Josephine Jarvis.

Fröbel, Friedrich (1887) *The Education of Man*, New York, London: D. Appleton Century. Translated by W.N. Hailmann.

Gandini, Lella, Lynn Hill, Louise Cadwell and Charles Schwall (eds) (2015) *In the Spirit of the Studio: Learning from the* Atelier *of Reggio Emilia*, 2nd edn, New York: Teachers College Press.

Gill, Tim (2007) *No Fear: Growing up in a Risk Averse Society*, London: Calouste Gulbenkian Foundation.

Bibliography

Harms, Thelma and Richard M. Clifford (2004) *Early Childhood Environment Rating Scale (ECERS)*, New York: Teachers College Press.

Heerwart, E. (1884) The kindergarten in relation to the various industrial products, in *The Health Exhibition Literature* (Vol. XIII, pp. 96–105), London: William Clowes.

Houk, Pamela, Lella Gandini and Loris Malaguzzi (1998) *The Hundred Languages of Children: The Reggio Emilia Approach – Advanced Reflections*, Westport, CT: Ablex Publishing.

Hughes, Fergus P. (1991) *Children, Play, and Development*, Thousand Oaks, CA: Sage.

Isaacs, Susan (1937) *The Educational Value of the Nursery School*, London: Nursery School Association.

Judd, Joseph Henry (1906) *'Learn by doing': A Scheme of Simple Woodwork Designed on Froebelian Principles*, Manchester: Clarkson & Griffiths.

Kalb, Gustav (2009 [1895]) *The First Lessons in Hand and Eye Training; Or Manual Work for Boys and Girls*, Chicago, IL: W.M. Welch. Translated by W.G. Field.

Kuroyanagi, Tetsuko (1996). *Totto-Chan : The Little Girl At The Window*. Tokyo: Kodansha International. Translated by Dorothy Britton.

Lawrence, Evelyn (2011) *Friedrich Froebel and English Education*, Abingdon: Routledge.

Louis, Stella (2013) *Schemas and the Characteristics of Effective Learning*, London: British Association for Early Childhood Education.

Louv, Richard (2010) *Last Child in the Woods: Saving Our Children from Nature-Deficit Disorder*, London: Atlantic Books.

McLellan, Todd (2013) *Things Come Apart*, London: Thames and Hudson.

McMillan, Margaret (1919) *The Nursery School*, London: Dent.

Marenholtz-Bülow, Bertha von (1883) *Hand-Work and Head-Work: Their Relation to One Another, and the Reform of Education, According to the Principles of Froebel*, London: Swan Sonnenschein. Translated by A.M. Christie.

May, Pamela (2006) *Sound Beginnings: Learning and Development in the Early Years*, London: David Fulton Publishers.

Moorhouse, Pete (2015) *Woodwork in The Early Years*, East Sussex: Community Playthings.

Piaget, Jean (1970) Piaget's theory. In P. Mussen (ed.), *Carmichael's Manual of Child Psychology* (Vol. 1, pp. 703–772). New York: John Wiley & Sons.

Piaget, Jean (1973) *To Understand is to Invent: The Future of Education*, New York: Grossman Publishers.

Salomon, Otto (2010 [1891]) *The Theory of Educational Sloyd 1891*, New York: Nabu Press.

Salomon, Otto (2013 [1892]) *The Teacher's Hand-Book of Slöjd*, Wilmington: Toolemera Press.

Solly, Kathryn (2014) *Risk, Challenge and Adventure in the Early Years*, Abingdon: Routledge.

Thomas, AnnMarie (2014) *Making Makers: Kids, Tools, and the Future of Innovation*, Sebastopol, CA: Maker Media.

Tovey, Helen (2016) *Bringing the Froebel Approach to your Early Years Practice*, 2nd edn, Abingdon: Routledge.

Vygotsky, Lev (1978 [1930]) *Mind in Society: The Development of Higher Psychological Processes*, Cambridge, MA: Harvard University Press.

White, Jan (2013) *Playing and Learning Outdoors*, 2nd edn, Abingdon: Routledge.

Digital content

Chard, Sylvia and Lilian Katz, The project approach, http://projectapproach.org/ (accessed on 13 July 2017).

Common sense, common safety (2010), www.gov.uk/government/publications/common-sense-common-safety-a-report-by-lord-young-of-graffham (accessed 13 July 2017).

Department of Education (2014) Health and safety advice to schools: health and safety: advice on legal duties and powers. For local authorities, school leaders, school staff and governing bodies, www.gov.uk/government/publications/health-and-safety-advice-for-schools (accessed 13 July 2017).

Eco-schools, www.eco-schools.org.uk and www.eco-schools.org.uk/resources/ljmu-early-years-resource-packs (accessed 13 July 2017).

Education for Sustainable Development (ESD), https://en.wikipedia.org/wiki/Education_for_sustainable_development (accessed 13 July 2017).

Gill, Tim (2007) No fear, Calouste Gulbenkian Foundation, https://gulbenkian.pt/uk-branch/publication/no-fear (accessed 13 July 2017).

Gleave, Josie (2008) Risk and play – a literature review, www.playday.org.uk/wp-content/uploads/2015/11/risk_and_play___a_literature_review___summary.pdf (accessed 13 July 2017).

Gopnik, Alison (2010) How babies think, www.alisongopnik.com/papers_alison/sciam-gopnik.pdf (accessed 13 July 2017).

Health and Safety Executive (HSE) (2012), Health and Safety Executive children's play and leisure – promoting a balanced approach, www.hse.gov.uk/entertainment/childrens-play-july-2012.pdf (accessed 13 July 2017).

Health and Safety Executive and QCA (n.d.) General teaching requirement for health and safety, www.hse.gov.uk/education/qca.htm (accessed 13 July 2017).

Laevers, Ferre (2005) Leuven scales – Developed by the Research Centre for Experiential Education at Leuven University, Belgium, www.kindengezin.be/img/sics-ziko-manual.pdf (accessed on 13 July 2017).

Makerspace (2013) Makerspace playbook: School edition, www.makered.org/wp-content/uploads/2014/09/Makerspace-Playbook-Feb-2013.pdf (accessed 13 July 2017). (first published 2012).

Play England (2012) Managing risk in play provision, www.playengland.org.uk/media/172644/managing-risk-in-play-provision.pdf (accessed 13 July 2017).

Project Zero, Making by design, Harvard University, www.pz.harvard.edu/projects/agency-by-design (accessed on 13 July 2017).

Sloyd at Nääs (n.d.) http://uk.naas.se/crafts/teacher-training-at-the-school-of-crafts-1875-1966 (accessed on 13 July 2017).

Youth Makerspace Playbook 2015 (PDF) Maker Education Initiative, http://makered.org/makerspaces/ (accessed 13 July 2017).

Reports and journal articles

Ashworth, Sally (2014) Wonderful woodwork, *Early Years Educator*, 16(5) (September): v–vii.

Brehony, Kevin (1998) Even far distant Japan is showing interest in the English Froebel movement's turn to sloyd, *History of Education*, 27(3): 279–295.

Chapman, Evelyn. (1887) Slöjd, *Journal of Education*, IX(Feb.): 71–74.

Moorhouse, Pete (2012) Wonderful woodwork, *Early Years Educator*, 13(11) (March): viii–ix.

Moorhouse, Pete (2012) Introducing young children to working with wood, *Early Years Update*, 97(April): 7–8.

Moorhouse, Pete (2012) All about woodwork, *Nursery World*, 14–27 (May): 17–22.

Moorhouse, Pete (2015) Woodwork in the early years, *Small Talk*, Wales PPA, 10: 13–17.

Struthers, J. (1895) Sloyd and kindergarten occupations in the elementary school. Great Britain: Scottish Education Department, HMSO.

Turner, Camilla (2017) Information from Association of School and College Leaders (ASCL) and Design and Technology Association, *Telegraph Education*, March 2017.

Virta, Kalle, Mika Metsärinne and Manne Kallio (2013) Supporting craft sense in early education, *Techne Series: Research in Sloyd Education and Craft Science*, 20(3): 1893–1774.

Ward, M. (1888) Slöjd at Nääs, *Journal of Education*, X(Dec): 562–563.

Ward, W. (1896) A short account of the early history of sloyd in this country, *Hand and Eye*, IV(40): 178–181.

Wienstein, Nicole (2016) Touch wood! *Nursery World*, 19 September–2 October 2016: 26–28.

Resources and suppliers

(All links correct as of 13 July 2017.)

Early Years Woodwork Association

www.stwerburghs.com/early-years-woodwork-association

Early years woodwork training: CPD and INSET

www.irresistible-learning.co.uk

www.early-education.org.uk

www.stwerburghs.com

Risk assessment form and health and safety checklist

www.irresistible-learning.co.uk/resources

Deconstruction: general safety advice

www.ifixit.com/Info/Device_Safety

www.makered.org/wp-content/uploads/2015/09/Youth-Makerspace-Playbook_FINAL.pdf (pp. 68–69)

Tools

A comprehensive list of all tools with suppliers can be accessed online:
www.irresistible-learning.co.uk/resources

Demonstration videos of tool use:
www.irresistible-learning.co.uk/resources

Suppliers

Workbench

www.communityplaythings.co.uk

www.cosydirect.com

www.creativecascade.co.uk

www.earlyexcellence.com

Tools

www.cosydirect.com

www.muddyfaces.co.uk

Balsa wood

www.balsacabin.co.uk

www.fredaldous.co.uk

www.educationsupplies.co.uk

www.cosydirect.com

Books for children

Fiction

Klinting, Lars (2005) *Harvey the Carpenter*, US: Kingfisher Books.

Portis, Antoinette (2009) *Not a Stick*, London: HarperCollins.

Non-fiction

Edwards, Nicola and Jane Harris (2003) *Wood: Exploring the Science of Everyday Materials*, London: A&C Black.

Hughes, Monica (2004) *What is a Forest?*, US: Heinemann Library.

Langley, Andrew (2008) *Wood*, London: Crabtree Publishing Company.

Llewellyn, Claire (2004) *Wood*, Mankato, MN: Franklin Watts.

Nelson, Robin (2012) *What Does a Saw Do?*, Minneapolis, MN: Lerner Publications.

Nelson, Robin (2012) *What Does a Hammer Do?*, Minneapolis, MN: Lerner Publications.

Nelson, Robin (2012) *What Does a Screwdriver Do?*, Minneapolis, MN: Lerner Classroom.

Oxlade, Chris (2005) *Wood*, Oxford: Heinemann-Raintree.

Pluckrose, Henry (2003) *Find Out About: Wood*, London: Franklin Watts Ltd.

Children's books challenging stereotypes

Beaty, Andrea (2013) *Rosie Revere, Engineer*, New York: Abrams Books for Young Readers.

Kügler, Tina and Carson Kügler (2015) *In Mary's Garden*, Boston, MA: Houghton Mifflin.

Schwartz, Coren Rosen and Rebecca J. Gomez (2015) *What About Moose?*, United States: Atheneum Books for Young Readers.

Spires, Ashley (2017) *The Most Magnificent Thing*, Toronto: Kids Can Press.

Underwood, Deborah (2015) *Interstella Cinderella*, San Francisco, CA: Chronicle Books.

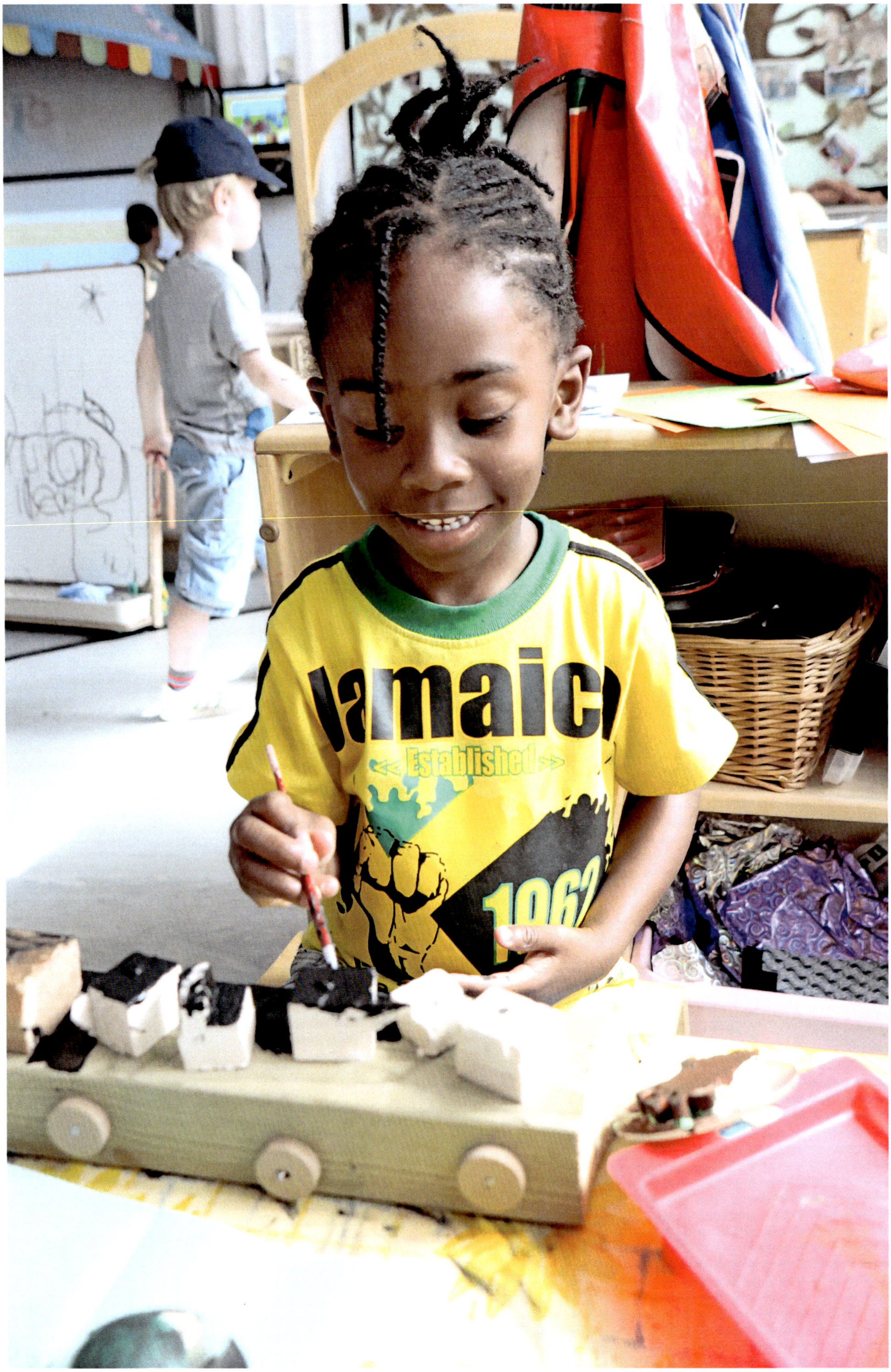
Established

Songs

(A quick search will lead to the full text.)

Construction workers song:

This is the way we pound nails . . .

Johnny works with one hammer . . .

If I had a hammer, I'd hammer in the morning . . .

Hammer, hammer, and hammer . . .

Index

abstract work 53
active learning 12, 16, 20, 22–24, 28, 142
active listening 43
adult support 70, 75–84
aesthetics 4, 58–59, 143
age to start woodwork 88–89
agency 3, 23, 29, 32
aggressive behaviour 164
agility 39, 161
Arieti, Silvano 25
artwork 148–149
Ashworth, Sally 177
assessment 63
attention 14
attention deficit hyperactivity disorder (ADHD) 71
attention to detail 33
augers 115, 126
autonomy 29
awls 115, 122

balance 39
ball-pein hammers 115, 117–119
balsa wood 30, 104–107, 113, 122; case study 70–71; environmental concerns 61; nails 135; sandpaper 136; sawing 131; suppliers 185
battery screwdrivers 122, 167
beauty 4, 14, 58–59, 61
block planes 115, 133
blood blisters 170
blood poisoning 169, 170
boys 69–70
brace and bit 115, 124–125, 167
bradawls 113, 115, 122
brain development 27
branches 110–111
Bruce, Tina 112
Bruner, Jerome 4, 16, 23

'can-do' attitude 3, 17, 31, 32
carpenter's squares 134
cause and effect 51, 161
cedar 107, 108, 109
challenge 5, 78
chemically treated wood 110, 166, 169
child development 16
clamps 113, 115, 126; health and safety checklist 169; risk assessment 165, 167; scientific understanding 51; workbenches 101–103, 104
claw hammers 41, 50, 115, 119
clothing 166
cognitive development 13, 27
collaboration 29, 35–36, 58; collaborative extended learning projects 93, 94; sculptures 143
Comenius, John Amos 12
communication 3–4, 13, 43–44, 67
complexity 5, 14, 94

concentration 2, 13, 33–34, 64; active learning 20, 22, 23; difficulties with 71; disadvantaged children 68; 'flow' 25; personal development 29
confidence 3, 8, 17, 75; disadvantaged children 68; personal development 28, 29, 30, 31, 38; pride in achievements 36; risk taking 33; staff 78, 171; Steiner Waldorf education 15
construction 56, 92–93, 94, 151
consumables 115, 116, 135–138; *see also* nails; screws
continuous provision 77
cork 110, 151
counting 45–47, 48
craft sense 59
creative expression 53
creativity 1, 4, 9, 19, 24–27, 90, 177; adult support 81; disadvantaged children 68; effective learning 21; extended learning projects 142; involvement 23; language 42; observation and assessment 63; sculptures 143, 145–146; tinkering 91–92; valuing of 17
critical thinking 4, 19, 24–27, 64, 90; adult support 81; disadvantaged children 68; effective learning 21; extended learning projects 142; language 42; observation and assessment 63; sustainability 61; valuing of 17
cross-cut saws 115, 127, 130–131, 168
Csikszentmihalyi, Mihaly 25
curiosity 1, 21, 27; ADHD 71; creative and critical thinking 24; deconstruction 155; disadvantaged children 68; experiential learning 5; exploration 22; independence 31; investigating wood 96; Malting House School 15; motivation 30; new experiences 30; nurturing 17, 93; tinkering 92
curriculum 6, 14, 16, 20
Curriculum for Excellence (Scotland) 20
Curtis, Lesley 67
cuts 170
Cygnaeus, Uno 13

decision-making 80–81, 163
deconstruction 52–53, 134, 153–155, 185
design 56, 60
Design and Technology (D&T) 16, 163
Dewey, John 16, 58, 79
dexterity 14, 39, 90, 161
dialogue 42–43, 59, 61, 72, 81, 82
didactic approach 79
disabilities 70–72
disadvantaged children 68
displays 94
documentation 63, 82; skills checklist 64, 115
dowel 108
dozuki pull saws 127, 128–129; *see also* Japanese pull saws
driftwood 111
drill bits 50, 51, 115, 123–124, 137

Index

drills 115, 122–126; introducing to children 113; left-handed children 73; physical development 41; risk assessment 167; scientific understanding 50, 51; skills checklist 64
dust masks 109, 116, 137, 167, 168, 169
Dweck, Carol 23

Early Childhood Environment Rating Scale (ECERS) 17
Early Years Foundation Stage (EYFS) 20
Early Years Woodwork Association 184
Eco-schools 61
Education for Sustainable Development (ESD) 61
elder 111
emotional development *see* personal, social and emotional development
empathy 29, 36, 68
empowerment 3, 17, 29, 31, 32
engagement 2, 5, 27, 33–34, 64; active learning 22–23; collaborative work 58; deep 75; personal development 29
engineering 16, 51–52
English as an Additional Language (EAL) 72
enjoyment 2, 5, 27
entrepreneurialism 17
environmental understanding 61
envisioning 59, 61
Ephgrave, Anna 71, 75
equal opportunities 67–73
equipment 15, 48, 115–116; *see also* tools; workbenches
estimation 47
excitement 36, 71, 177
expectations 78
experiential learning 5, 16, 28, 79
experimentation 13
exploration 20, 22; child-led 57; investigating wood 96–97; open-ended 8–9, 27, 94, 171; technology 50
expressive arts and design 53–59
extended learning projects 93, 94, 141–157
extended thinking 27, 48, 78, 82
eye hooks 116, 138
eye protection 36, 115, 116–117, 165, 166, 167, 168

files 39, 115, 132
fir 108
first aid 167, 169–171
fixed mindset 23
flat nail-pullers 115, 120
Fletcher-Gardiner, Liberty 64
'flow' 25, 43
Forest School 17, 110, 111
Freeman, Lucy 17
friezes 148–149
Froebel, Friedrich 6, 11, 12–13, 14, 22, 58

G-clamps 103, 104, 113, 115, 126, 167
Gandini, Lella 80
gender 69–70
'gifts' 13
Gill, Tim 164
gimlets 115, 126
girls 69–70
glue 93, 116, 137
Gopnik, Alison 27
Gould, Terry 27, 87
green wood 110–111, 131
growth mindset 23–24

'hack spaces' 5
hacksaws 131
hammers 115, 117–119; case study 72; health and safety checklist 168; house project 153; introducing to children 90, 113; maintenance 138; physical development 41; risk assessment 165, 166; skills checklist 64; younger children 89
hand drills 64, 113, 115, 122–124, 167
hand–eye coordination 39, 41, 89
hardboard 109
hardwood 108–109, 116, 118, 167, 169
hazards 163, 164–165, 166–167
hazel 111
health and safety 8, 80, 159–174; checklist 168–169; decline in woodwork due to fears 6, 12, 16; first aid 169–171; risk assessment 164–167; staff training 171–173; understanding risk 160–164; Young Review 17, 162; *see also* safety
Health and Safety Executive (HSE) 162, 163
heuristic play 50, 89
hooks 116, 138
Houk, Pamela 80
house project 149–153
Hughes, Fergus 92

imagination 4, 9, 25–27; collaborative work 58; creative and critical thinking 24–25; creative expression 53; Froebel 13; open-ended enquiry 57; sculptures 143
inclusion 70
independence 14, 17, 28, 31, 64, 77
induction 90
injuries 160, 164, 166–167, 169–170
inquiry-based learning 27, 142
integrity 33
interaction 80–81, 82–83
interests 11, 13, 27, 57, 93, 142
International Baccalaureate 20
involvement 23, 25, 75
Isaacs, Susan 15, 160

Japanese nail-pullers 41, 50, 115, 120, 169
Japanese pull saws 113, 115, 127, 128–129, 152, 167, 168
Jenkins, Liz 19, 159
jigsaws 111
jobs 16, 60
Judd, Joseph 13, 14

Kalb, Gustav 13
Kilpatrick, William H. 16
kinaesthesia 27, 39, 42, 70
knowledge transfer 59
Kuroyanagi, Tetsuko 59

Laevers, Ferre 23
language 3–4, 42–43, 67, 72, 89
larch 108
learning 3, 19–65; active 12, 16, 20, 22–24, 28, 142; adult role in supporting 78–82; characteristics of effective 20–21; communication and language 42–44; creative and critical thinking 24–27; curiosity 21; disadvantaged children 68; experiential 5, 16, 28, 79; expressive arts and design 53–59; extended learning projects 93, 94, 141–157; life-long 17, 21, 24; literacy 59; mathematical thinking 44–48; observation and assessment 62–64; parental involvement 83–84; personal, social and emotional development 27–38; physical development 38–42; play and exploration 22; skills for life 60; sustainability 60–61; understanding the world 49–53; visible 82
learning diaries 82
learning stories 63
leaves 49, 96
left-handed children 72–73
legislation 161–162
life-long learning 17, 21, 24
lime 107, 108

189

Index

listening, active 43
literacy 59
litigation culture 6, 16, 161, 162

magnets 99, 115, 133
Maker Movement 5
Makerspace Playbook 36
making 5, 17; agency 32; collaboration 36; craft sense 59; curiosity 21
Malaguzzi, Loris 80
Malting House School 15
manipulative skills 39, 59
mark-making 59, 92–93
mastery 2, 3
materials: additional 57, 111–112; experience of making 5; properties of 49; tinkering 92; *see also* wood
mathematics 3, 44–48, 51–52, 133
Mathieson, Kay 71–72
McMillan, Margaret 15
MDF 104, 109, 112, 116, 118, 136, 167, 169
measure 47–48, 133, 151–153
memory 8, 24, 42, 60, 177
meta-cognition 28, 29, 38, 59
metals 145
mindfulness 29, 34
mindsets 23–24
mistakes, learning from 33, 34
models 93
monitoring progress 63
Montessori, Maria 58
Mori, Mari 61
motivation 27, 28, 30, 34
motor skills 39, 59, 89, 161
mud kitchen project 155–157
muscular strength 39, 41, 107

Nääs School 13–14
nail-pullers 41, 50, 115, 120, 167, 169
nails 107, 115, 135; case study 72; health and safety checklist 169; house project 153; introducing to children 113; mathematical thinking 45, 48; picking up 99, 133; resourcing 80; risk assessment 165, 167; scientific understanding 50, 51; sculptures 143; using a ball-pein hammer 117–119; using a claw hammer 119; workbenches 100
narratives 93
natural wood 110–111
new experiences 28, 29–30
New Zealand 12, 20
noise 98
non-verbal communication 44
numeracy 45–47, 48, 151
nuts and bolts 41, 116, 134, 137

observation 52, 63, 78
'occupations' 13
offcuts 61, 108, 111, 143
open-ended enquiry 57
open-ended exploration 8–9, 27, 94, 171
outdoor woodworking areas 64, 97

paint 57, 93
palm drills 115, 125–126
parents 72, 83–84, 164, 170
patience 14, 33
pedagogy 78, 79–80, 83, 142
perseverance 14, 32–33, 41, 75
persistence 15, 23, 29, 32–33, 34, 38, 177
personal, social and emotional development 3–4, 27–38, 67
perspective 29, 36
Pestalozzi, Johann Heinrich 12

Phillips head screwdrivers 120–121, 136
photography 27, 43–44, 48, 59
physical development 3–4, 14, 38–42, 67
physical support 80
Piaget, Jean 15, 16, 28, 79
pilot holes 118
pincers 115, 120
pine 104, 107, 108, 113, 136
planes 115, 133
play 20, 22, 43; health and safety 162; heuristic 50, 89; independence 31; 'play spiral' 16, 23; tinkering 92
Play England 164
playhouse project 149–153
pliers 115, 118, 133, 169
plywood 109, 167, 169
poplar 107, 108
positional language 39, 41
posture 41
power drills 169
Pozidrive screwdrivers 115, 120–121, 136
praise 81
precision 14, 39, 41
preformed wood 109
pride 3, 28, 29, 30, 36, 93, 177
Primary Years Program (PYP) 20
problem-solving 4, 9, 75, 177; adult support 81; agency 32; creative and critical thinking 24, 25; house project 151; mathematical 45, 47, 48; sculptures 143; skills for life 60; sloyd movement 13
progress monitoring 63
progressive education 79
project learning 35, 93, 94, 141–157
Project Zero 28
proprioception 39, 70
pull saws 113, 115, 127, 128–130, 167, 168
pulleys 151
Pupil Premium 21, 65n1

Qualifications and Curriculum Authority (QCA) 163

rasps 115, 132, 152
reasoning skills 25
redwood 108
reflection 25, 59, 61, 142
Reggio Emilia approach 142
repair 5, 60, 157
resilience 29, 33, 34, 68, 177
resources 48, 77, 80, 111
responsibility 29, 36, 160, 163
risk 16, 17; definition of 165; risk assessment 80, 162, 163, 164–167, 184; risk-benefit assessment 162, 165; risk control 163, 165; sawing 128; staff training 171; taking risks 29, 33, 36, 72, 159; understanding risk 93, 160–164
role modelling 69
role play 89, 93, 116, 157
Rousseau, Jean-Jacques 12
rulers 48, 116, 133
rules 36, 163

safety 76, 80, 93, 159–174; checklist 168–169; deconstruction 53, 155, 185; first aid 169–171; induction 90; introducing tools 113; physical development 39, 41; risk assessment 164–167; self-regulation 36; staff training 171–173; tool organisation 138; understanding risk 160–164; *see also* health and safety
safety glasses 36, 115, 116–117, 166, 168
Salomon, Otto 13–14, 28, 79
sandpaper 41, 51, 115, 132, 136–137
satisfaction 36
sawdust 57, 91, 98, 137; health and safety checklist 169; investigating wood 49, 94, 96; risk assessment 165, 167

Index

saws 115, 126–132; adult supervision 76, 77, 128; case study 71–72; fine motor skills 39; health and safety checklist 168; house project 152; introducing to children 76, 90, 113; left-handed children 73; low risk of injury 160; maintenance 138; risk assessment 165, 167; skills checklist 64; workbench height 103
scaffolding 23, 79, 80
Scandinavia 12, 13–14
schemas 63
science, technology, engineering and maths (STEM) 51–52
scientific investigation 3, 49–53
scissors 72–73
Scotland 20
screwdrivers 30, 115, 120–122, 155; introducing to children 90, 113; left-handed children 73; physical development 41; risk assessment 167; skills checklist 64
screws 91, 107, 115, 121–122, 135–136; introducing to children 113; mathematical thinking 48; picking up 99, 133; resourcing 80; risk assessment 165, 167; scientific understanding 50, 51; sculptures 143; workbenches 100
sculptures 17, 53, 59, 142–146, 155
self-care 29, 36
self-esteem 3, 17; disadvantaged children 68; feeling valued 29; personal development 28, 30, 38; pride in achievements 36; risk taking 33; Steiner Waldorf education 15
self-regulation 28, 29, 36, 59
senses 39, 41
sessions 76–77
set squares 48, 116, 134
shape 47, 151
sharing 35, 38, 42–43, 44
skills 9, 90, 179; age to start woodwork 88; balsa wood 107; checklists 64, 115; complex 94; creative and critical thinking 24–25, 27; equal opportunities 68; gaining new 28, 30; for life 8, 60; mathematical thinking 48; motor 39, 59, 89, 161; passing on 31; practical 16; progression 93; reasoning 25; sharing 38; sloyd movement 14; social 29, 35
sloyd movement 6, 13–14, 59, 79
social development see personal, social and emotional development
social skills 29, 35
softwood 104, 107–108, 113, 122, 131, 135
Solly, Kathryn 1
sound gardens 145–147
space 47, 151
spanners 115, 134, 137, 167
spatial awareness 39, 41, 59, 143
special educational needs and disabilities (SEND) 70–72, 167
spirit levels 116, 134
splinters 89, 132, 136, 160; first aid 170; plywood 109, 167, 169; risk assessment 165, 166
spruce 108
staff training 78, 162, 163, 171–173, 184
Steiner Waldorf education 15
STEM (science, technology, engineering and maths) 51–52
stereotypes 69
sticks 110–111
supervision 76, 77, 128, 168
suppliers 138, 184
support 70, 75–84
surforms 115, 132

sustainability 60–61
sustained shared thinking 81

tables 104
tape measures 48, 116, 133, 151–152
tasks 57
Te Whāriki 12, 20
technology 3, 8, 50–51
therapeutic benefits 29, 34
thinking skills 17; see also critical thinking
tinkering 8–9, 21, 52, 57, 91–92, 94
tools 2, 4, 5; basic toolkit 115; cause and effect 51; concentration 23; confidence to work with 8; Forest School 17; health and safety checklist 168–169; introducing 76–78, 90–91, 112–115; knowledge of 93; lack of opportunities to work with 16; left-handed children 72–73; maintenance 138; memories of using 8, 177; nurturing curiosity 17; organisation of 99, 138; physical development 38–41; risk assessment 165, 166, 167; risk taking 33; self-care 36; skills checklist 64, 115; skills for life 8, 60; sloyd movement 14; staff training 171; suppliers 138, 184; technology 50–51; using 116–135; younger children 89; see also consumables
toxic materials 110, 165, 166
training 78, 162, 163, 171–173, 184
transfer 59
trees 49, 61, 94–96
trial and error 4, 25, 92
'Triton' 103
turn taking 35, 43, 44, 78

understanding the world 49–53
uniqueness of children 93

valued, feeling 29
vices 115, 127–128; adult supervision 77; health and safety checklist 168, 169; left-handed children 73; physical development 41; risk assessment 165, 167; scientific understanding 51; workbenches 99, 100–101, 103
visual language 59, 143
vocabulary 42–43, 89
Vygotsky, Lev 4, 23

well-being 28, 33, 58, 162
wheels 110, 112
White, Jan 141
Wilson, Jamie 11
wire cutters 115, 133
wood: aesthetics 4, 58; case study 72; context and properties of 90, 93; environmental understanding 61; health and safety checklist 169; investigating 49–50, 94–97; preparing 111; risk assessment 165; staff training 171; varieties of 104–111; younger children 89; see also balsa wood
wood glue 116, 137
woodworking areas 64, 97–100; health and safety checklist 168; risk assessment 165, 166; staff training 171
workbenches 100–104, 115, 127; case studies 64, 71; continuous provision 77; health and safety checklist 168; left-handed children 73; risk assessment 165; woodworking area 99
'Workmate' 103
wrenches 41, 115, 134–135, 137, 155, 167
writing skills 59

Young, Lord 17, 162

zone of proximal development 23

Taylor & Francis eBooks

Helping you to choose the right eBooks for your Library

Add Routledge titles to your library's digital collection today. Taylor and Francis ebooks contains over 50,000 titles in the Humanities, Social Sciences, Behavioural Sciences, Built Environment and Law.

Choose from a range of subject packages or create your own!

Benefits for you
- Free MARC records
- COUNTER-compliant usage statistics
- Flexible purchase and pricing options
- All titles DRM-free.

REQUEST YOUR FREE INSTITUTIONAL TRIAL TODAY

Free Trials Available
We offer free trials to qualifying academic, corporate and government customers.

Benefits for your user
- Off-site, anytime access via Athens or referring URL
- Print or copy pages or chapters
- Full content search
- Bookmark, highlight and annotate text
- Access to thousands of pages of quality research at the click of a button.

eCollections – Choose from over 30 subject eCollections, including:

Archaeology	Language Learning
Architecture	Law
Asian Studies	Literature
Business & Management	Media & Communication
Classical Studies	Middle East Studies
Construction	Music
Creative & Media Arts	Philosophy
Criminology & Criminal Justice	Planning
Economics	Politics
Education	Psychology & Mental Health
Energy	Religion
Engineering	Security
English Language & Linguistics	Social Work
Environment & Sustainability	Sociology
Geography	Sport
Health Studies	Theatre & Performance
History	Tourism, Hospitality & Events

For more information, pricing enquiries or to order a free trial, please contact your local sales team: www.tandfebooks.com/page/sales

Routledge Taylor & Francis Group | The home of Routledge books | www.tandfebooks.com